C000215694

IT'S ALL IN THE MIND

IT'S ALL IN THE MIND

THE LIFE AND LEGACY OF

LARRY STEPHENS

JULIE WARREN

unbound

First published in 2020

Unbound
6th Floor Mutual House, 70 Conduit Street, London W1S 2GF
www.unbound.com
All rights reserved

© Julie Warren, 2020

The right of Julie Warren to be identified as the author of this work has been asserted in accordance with Section 77 of the Copyright, Designs and Patents Act, 1988. No part of this publication may be copied, reproduced, stored in a retrieval system, or transmitted, in any form or by any means without the prior permission of the publisher, nor be otherwise circulated in any form of binding or cover other than that in which it is published and without a similar condition being imposed on the subsequent purchaser.

Photographs reproduced in this book are from the author's personal collection except where otherwise credited.

While every effort has been made to trace the owners of copyright material reproduced herein, the publisher would like to apologise for any omissions and will be pleased to incorporate missing acknowledgements in any further editions.

Text Design by PDQ Digital Media Solutions Ltd

A CIP record for this book is available from the British Library

ISBN 978-1-78352-862-2 (hardback)
ISBN 978-1-78352-863-9 (ebook)

Printed in Great Britain by CPI

1 3 5 7 9 8 6 4 2

In memory of Mike Brown

Dedicated to
Arthur Baseley (5 Commando)
Svend Aage Lindhardt Boll (Danish Commando)
James Brown, MM (5 Commando)
Mick Collins (5 Commando)
Ronald Davies (5 Commando)
Robert Donnison (5 Commando)
Arthur Raymond Green (3 Commando)
G. F. Harris, 'Geordie Lad' (4 Commando)
John 'Chips' Heron, MC (5 Commando)
Ken Humphries (5 Commando)
Ken McAllister (2 Commando)
Joe Rogers, MM (2 Commando)
and all their Second World War commando comrades

'United We Conquer'

Contents

Author's Note

My grandmother used to talk to me about all sorts of things: about sleeping with her hair tied in rags so she would wake up with curls; about Cromwell tethering his horse at the local church (Thomas or Oliver? I can no longer remember); and about her nephew, Larry Stephens. Had I known that thirty-plus years later, Larry would become such an important part of my life, not only would I have paid more attention to my grandmother but I would have made copious notes too.

When I started trying to find out more about Larry in 2010, all the people who had known him when he was a child were dead and very few of those who served with him during the war were still around. I often had to rely on archives and anecdotes, photos and handed-down family memories.

Much of Larry's personal archive was thrown away a few years after his death and at certain times he didn't leave much of a mark on the records – just a bit of a smudge – so although it is possible to make assumptions about some things, there are a few gaps in his life. As time passes and more archives are opened up and digitised, it may be possible to fill in some of these gaps but we may never find out the full story of Larry's life, work and influence.

What follows is everything we do know about the dramatic life of this remarkable man.

London, January 1959

Larry's head hit the table in a clatter of plates and cutlery. The cigarette slipped from between his fingers onto the floor and the red wine from his toppled glass bloomed across the tablecloth. The knives and forks of the other diners paused above their meals as they glanced over in disapproval at the noise.

'Larry Stephens died conveniently; it was very nice of him.'[1]

Part One
GLARNIES

QUINTON AND HINTON

1

The Histories of Silas the Elder

They built the west wing of their ancestral home in
1883, the east wing was completed the following year
and the year after that... it flew away.[1]

Conversation between Larry Stephens and Tony Hancock

Family legend tells that Larry Stephens' great-great-grandfather was
somewhat partial to sampling the finished product from his brewery,
and by the time he died the barrels and coffers were both dry. It is said
that all he had left to bequeath was a drinking glass for each of his
seven daughters and a killer financial hangover for his five sons. Had
the great-great been teetotal, Larry might well have been remembered
today as a member of an illustrious brewing family with a name as
familiar as that of Guinness or Boddington.

The great-great-grandfather, Silas Stokes, was born in Wednesbury,
Staffordshire in 1812 and was full of entrepreneurial spirit as well as
alcoholic spirits. He settled in the Lyng area of West Bromwich and
owned land and property in Paradise and Pleasant Streets. He was listed
in various business directories as a coach smith and a railway carriage iron-
work manufacturer but he soon found another way of making money.

The Beerhouse Act had made it possible for anyone to buy a licence to brew and sell beer and Silas created a public house called the Smiths' Arms in his property in Pleasant Street. The Smiths' Arms was a mere hop's throw away from Spon Lane, a thoroughfare renowned for the number of pubs along its length. In the second half of the nineteenth century, there were at least twenty-seven[2] of them in operation in the lane at the same time and Hitchmough's *Black Country Pubs* lists more than thirty of these former watering-holes, none of which remain.

Silas seems to have broken the terms of his beer licence on a regular basis – generally by 'keeping his house open during illegal hours'[3] – and popped up in newspaper court reports from time to time, paying the associated fines.

Silas died in 1873 at the age of sixty-one, leaving more money than family legend would have you believe. His estate was valued at somewhere between £50 and £100 – equivalent to as much as £50,000 in 2017 – and most of it went to his widow, Phebe, with the exception of his horse and cart, which he instructed should be passed to his youngest son as soon as he reached the age of twenty-one, and the seven drinking glasses for seven daughters, which continue to be passed down through the female line and sit quietly on the shelves of each successive generation.

Larry's grandfather, John Stephens, was born the year Silas died, one of nine children produced by Silas's daughter, Phoebe, and her husband, Hezekiah Stephens. The entrepreneurial spirit began to be smelted and polished away. Hezekiah and his sons worked in foundries or spring-making firms while his five daughters went into service. Silas's business interests became transformed through family lore. The horse and cart was now a chaise and four, the pub in Pleasant Street a vast brewing empire in London. Despite their inaccuracy, John must have found these tales of past glories inspirational as within two years of moving into 46 Florence Road, West Bromwich, with his new bride, the gentle Honor, John had abandoned his job as a spring-maker and converted the dwelling house into a grocer's store with living quarters. Larry's father, Albert, was the couple's first child and he was followed by Doris, Ivy, Frank, Edna and Dennis.

John Stephens was a Wesleyan Methodist, intensely religious and strictly teetotal. Hymns were sung in the Stephens household every evening to the accompaniment of a huge reed organ which took up the whole of one wall in the parlour. The children had to take it in turns to pump the organ's bellows and also to read Bible passages aloud. There were two visits to the Wesleyan Chapel Sunday School in Beeches Road each week and from 1901 John began teaching there.

As they grew older, the children were given a halfpenny a week each as pocket money but only on condition that they spent it in their father's shop. Doris, the eldest daughter, supplemented their supplies by crawling along the shop floor behind the counter, out of sight of their father, so that she could steal liquorice to be shared among the siblings.

At the time of the 1911 census, Larry's father, Albert, now aged sixteen, was working in the chemical industry as an office clerk but in his spare time he taught himself shorthand and went to night school to further his education. But the outbreak of the First World War put a stop to Albert's personal development programme. He served in France with the Royal Army Ordnance Corps, initially on attachment to the South Staffordshire Regiment as a Lance Corporal and later on a temporary commission as a Second Lieutenant with the East Surrey Regiment.

While Albert was away, his family became extremely influential at the Sunday School and by 1921 his father, John, was the superintendent, his brother, Frank, the assistant secretary and his sisters, teachers. Albert's time was spent on less spiritual matters though; he had fallen in love and become engaged to a girl who lived around the corner in

Mary Road and he was now working as a solicitor's cashier, saving as much of his income as he could before embarking on married life.

On Boxing Day 1921, Albert Stephens and Annie Hughes – known to all as Bert and Nancy – were married at the Beeches Road Chapel. They set up home in a brand new council house at 33 Beaconsfield Street on the recently built Tantany estate to the north of West Bromwich town centre and on 16 July 1923 there was a new arrival in the small terraced house when their son, Lawrence Geoffrey 'Larry' Stephens was born.

Albert Stephens and Annie Hughes' wedding day.

2

Black Country Childhood

When Larry was two years old, Bert and Nancy moved five miles south of West Bromwich to Quinton, an area that was considered to be more upmarket. Known to locals as Little Russia, Quinton is the highest settlement in the Birmingham area and sits on a ridge 730 feet above sea level. It is supposedly brushed by winds blowing across Europe from the Urals, hence its nickname.

The Stephens family's new home at 28 Perry Hill Road was a three-bedroomed semi-detached house with a small lawn at the front and a large garden at the rear. The village was surrounded by green fields and tree-swathed hills when the family first arrived, but within a few years the development of new housing estates would begin. There was a thriving community with a tennis club, a horticultural society, amateur dramatics and a band. There were also regular whist drives and other social events throughout the year.

In 1927, Albert Stephens secured a new job as assistant to the commercial manager at the Shropshire, Worcestershire and Staffordshire Electric Power Company in Smethwick. With more money to spend, they took Larry along to G. Robson's photographic studio in nearby Blackheath, where he had some portraits taken. Dressed in a hand-knitted jumper, shorts, knee-high socks and lace-up shoes, the smiling little fair-haired boy was posed sitting on a desk alongside a book entitled *All About Trains*. In another photo he was sitting on a corner chair with one leg tucked up underneath him and his hands neatly clasped in his lap, looking pensive. The *Trains* photo was turned into a Christmas card and sent to family and friends, 'with the season's greetings from Larry, Nance and Bert'.

Larry Stephens in 1927.

In September 1928, at the age of five, Larry started at the Quinton Church School, which was a fifteen-minute walk away from Perry Hill Road. The children from Quinton village and the surrounding area were taught here through their infant and junior years until they were old enough to leave for senior school. The Victorian red-brick building was bordered by the cemetery and the churchyard and had a large playground, paved with Staffordshire blue bricks, which had latrine blocks along one side; another small brick building contained coat pegs and washbasins. A furnace generated heat for the schoolrooms and the lighting was via gas pendants and mantles. There was a piano in both the infant and the junior sections of the school.

One of Larry's school friends, who lived in one of the adjacent streets to Perry Hill Road, remembered that he showed signs of leadership from an early age. Larry would put himself in charge of organising all their games and sport. During snowy weather they would go tobogganing and when the weather was fine there would be rounders, cricket, hide-and-seek and marbles. Glass marbles – known locally as glarnies – had only started to become available in the previous few years and were considered something special in comparison to the more common balls of clay. The glarnies were prized possessions that could be bartered for toads, newts and the other wildlife specimens that prove irresistible to small boys.

On 12 April 1929, a sibling for Larry was born and two months later Margaret Mary Stephens was baptised back in West Bromwich at the Beeches Road Wesleyan Chapel. Photographs were taken of five-year-old Larry and his new baby sister in the back yard of their grandfather's house, something the young Larry doesn't look overly happy about. He is dressed in a collar and tie with a handkerchief in the top pocket of his jacket – quite the little gentleman – but looks most aggrieved at having been forced to hold the baby. Another photo of Grandfather John with his new granddaughter in his arms shows Larry standing behind him, scowling. By the time some more formal studio photographs were taken with his sister and mother a few months later, Larry's expression had developed into one of resignation and boredom.

Despite the move to Quinton, the family still paid regular visits to their relations in West Bromwich and spending time at grandfather John Stephens' house in Florence Road was an essential part of each trip. A map of Larry's childhood and ancestral West Bromwich contains several place names that would be included in a *Goon Show* dictionary; as well as Lyng and Spon Lanes there was also Thynne Street (but without the Grytpype), which ran adjacent to Florence Road.

References to a landholder called William atte Sponne have resulted in suggestions that there has been an area known as Spon in West

Bromwich since at least 1344. The word 'spon' first appeared in the seventh series of the *Goon Show* in an episode entitled 'The Nasty Affair at the Burami Oasis'. Wallace 'Bill' Greenslade announced that to fill the time while two men carried a battleship to the water, Ray Ellington would spon. (What actually happened was that the Ray Ellington Quartet performed a number called 'Stranded in the Jungle'!)

From that point on there was a veritable explosion of spons in the *Goon Show*. It was a multi-purpose word assigned to characters (Major Spon, Captain Spon, Lord Spon); places (Fort Spon); diseases (Spon Plague); episode titles ('Spon' – series 8, episode 1); and curses (Great Spons!).

Larry's Aunt Edna was an eternal presence at his grandfather's house. She would keep him and her other nephews and nieces quiet by force-feeding them with vast wedges of caraway-seed cake and mugs of cocoa and would terrify them with laser-beam looks of disapproval if they dared to drop a crumb. Larry's maiden aunt appeared on a list of comedy character names (see Appendix Four) as 'Mrs Edna Cocoa' when Larry began writing scripts in the 1950s. His cousin Alan was less kind in his memories and described Aunt Edna as being 'returned unopened' when she died in 1981.

Larry was much happier when he went to visit his Aunt Doris and he spent a lot of time at her house, playing with his cousins. Doris had married a Scotsman, Donald McKechnie, and had two sons close to Larry's age – Alan and Donald junior. Larry was completely in awe of his Uncle Donald, who told tall tales of his war service with the Argyll and Sutherland Highlanders. Donald was also a talented pianist who provided entertainment in pubs all over the West Midlands and encouraged Larry in the musical promise he was showing. Several members of the Stephens family were accomplished in playing the piano and Larry was sent for lessons with the Beeches Road Chapel organist. He also had plenty of opportunity for practice whenever he visited his grandfather's house – providing someone was willing to pump the bellows for him of course.

In April 1934, Margaret joined her brother at the Quinton Church School but they were only together for a few months as now that he was eleven, the time had come for Larry to start at secondary school.

3
Work, War and All That Jazz

Larry had passed the entrance exam for the Central Secondary School in Birmingham and started there in September 1934. His new school shared a building in Suffolk Street with the Central Technical College and overlooked the noisy goods yard of Birmingham New Street railway station. The building had eight floors and the secondary school, an establishment for approximately 400 boys, was located on the fourth floor.

This shared building had no playground, which led to school life being somewhat free and easy. Larry and his fellow pupils were permitted to wander the streets of Birmingham during their lunch breaks and could spend time watching the trains arriving and departing from New Street station, expanding their minds in the Museum and Art Gallery or expanding their waistlines in Woolworths or Lewis's. There was no uniform, just an optional school tie and cap in maroon, adorned with the golden-yellow school motif of an arm protruding from a crown, clutching a hammer.

There were lessons in Mathematics, English, History, Geography, French, German, Latin, Physics, Chemistry, Biology, Art and Handicrafts. Physical Education involved rugby and cricket and took place at Elmdon Road playing fields, three miles away. This necessitated two half-days each week, with Tuesdays being given over to sports for the seniors and Thursdays for the juniors, but all had to attend school on Saturday mornings in lieu of this.

Despite the Tech building having lots of windows, the corridors were long, gloomy and crowded with lockers; daylight struggled to find its way past the obstacles and into many of the classrooms, but at least the lighting in the school was all electric. Quinton Church School didn't begin to install electricity until 1937 and John Stephens' house in Florence Road remained totally gas-lit until after his death in 1961.

Central Secondary School boys would dare each other into the naughty thrill of climbing the Tech building's stairs, adorned with grotesque stone gargoyles, and exploring the other floors given over to the College. The School of Bakery had a display of marzipan fruits and sugar flowers exhibited in a glass case for schoolboy noses to be pressed against, pharmacists could be spied mixing magical potions and other concoctions and some corridors were barred by elaborate iron gates, giving rise to wild imaginings as to what went on behind the doors beyond. By standing on a chair and peering out of one of the windows on the seventh floor, a spectacular and colourful view across the city could be had: 'variegated posters in Hill Street, the Post Office red of His Majesty's motors in Swallow Street, high green roofs in New Street, the white coat of a policeman on point duty in Navigation Street'.[1]

In 1935, Larry's father Bert was promoted, becoming the personal assistant to the Shropshire, Worcestershire and Staffordshire Electric Power Company's general manager. The company had moved to new premises in 1930 and was now housed at Belle Vue, a grand Georgian mansion at Mucklow Hill, close to the family's Quinton home. Bert's new position and salary meant that there was no problem in finding the money for Larry to attend his first school summer camp.

* * *

Summer camp was a long-standing Central School tradition that took place at Bryntail in Wales every Easter and summer, and Larry's first experience of it was when he joined the summer 1935 expedition. The camp was located three and a half miles from Llanidloes, 1,000 feet up in the hills, and comprised two cottages and three steel 'tents' where the boys spent the night. The floors of the tents were boarded and straw-filled palliasses were provided for sleeping on.

There was always a packed schedule of activities with bathing, sports, walks and treasure hunts when the weather was fine and indoor games and songs if it rained. Each day began at half past seven and finished with prayers and lights out at half past nine in the evening. The party of schoolboys was often joined by fathers and former pupils for a few days.

As there weren't any shops in the vicinity, the camp also had a tuck shop which opened twice daily, selling confectionery and fruit, in case the boys were still hungry after the breakfast, dinner, tea and supper that were provided.

A camp log was always kept but unfortunately the one for summer 1935 was lost and so the report in the school magazine, *The Hammer*, was written from memory by one of the attendees.

Larry and the other boys caught the train from Birmingham to Llanidloes and arrived at Bryntail on 25 July. An advance party had arrived a day earlier to give the camp a general check-over and a spruce-up, and to air the palliasse cases and fill them with fresh straw. The weather was blazing hot and it only rained once, and that was overnight, during their whole week's stay.

One of the boys had brought a lilo with him, which proved to be something of a novelty, as these inflatable mattresses had only recently been developed. It apparently greatly increased their enjoyment of bathing – which was already one of the more popular activities – and great care was taken to protect it from the prickly gorse bushes that lined the footpath from the camp to the river.

When they weren't bathing, Larry and his school friends spent their time playing rugger touch, going on paperchases and taking on the Old Boys at baseball. A whole day was given over to a fourteen-mile walk to Pennant Rocks, resulting in an abundance of blisters. They also watched in fascinated pleasure as two of the adults climbed onto the roof of one of the cottages to clear the chimney of a blockage, which turned out to be a nest containing a decomposed owl. On the final evening before their return to Birmingham there was a banquet and concert.

Larry loved spending time out of doors. One of the few photographs that survive from his childhood gives a snapshot of a family picnic in the park with his grandparents, his Aunt Mabel (née Hughes) and Uncle William – Bert and Nancy's bridesmaid and best man, who had married in 1929. A bare-chested Larry with a broad smile on his face and his hair flopping over his forehead is giving his sister, Margaret, a piggyback and looks as though he has just come running in from somewhere. Photographs that show him smiling – at any age – are exceedingly rare.

The picture must have been taken not long before the Stephens family was hit with a double dose of grief. Grandmother Honor, loved by all for her kind and gentle ways, died in 1937, as did Larry's cousin, Donald McKechnie, at the age of just sixteen, to the shock of everyone.

Bad news was also creeping across the wider world as a war in Europe was becoming increasingly more likely. In 1938, the Air Raid Precautions (ARP) organisation began to regularly hire rooms at Quinton Church School and preparations were made. For the time being, Larry was largely protected from this and continued to live within his schoolboy bubble. He was mentioned in the 'honours list' for the 1937/8 school year after obtaining his School Certificate. The usual age for sitting the School Certificate examination was sixteen or seventeen, and Larry was not quite fifteen when he took it. It meant an exemption from the preliminary examinations in Accountancy, Banking, Law, Medicine and Music and was recognised as being evidence of a good all-round education.

Larry's final year at the school, now renamed Central Grammar School, was 1938/9. He was kept busy and given lots of new responsibilities. He edited the school magazine, was made a librarian and took part in a production of *Le Bourgeois Gentilhomme*, which received a short review in the magazine:

> The school play, 'Le Bourgeois Gentilhomme' was by way of a histrionic success for C. P. Hall, who delighted the audience throughout the play except when he sang. But highlights were provided by other capable actors – the seductive ogling of Bishop, the inspired gymnastics of Thorneycroft, the stony silence of Stephens, and that laugh of Hooley's.[2]

This is the final mention of Larry in school archives. He didn't stay on into the sixth form and the school itself was moved from Suffolk Street to the west wing of King Edward VI Aston School for the start of the 1939/40 school year, a location which was deemed to be safer. Larry's entry in the national register, taken at the outbreak of the war, shows that he had begun working as an estate agent's assistant and by 1942, when he signed up for war service, he had risen to the position of estate agent's clerk.

Although documentary evidence is scant, Larry's life is not a complete blank between 1939 and 1942. He had started to date a young lady called Margery Williams, who had arrived in Quinton to live with her grandmother and aunt, and they spent a lot of time together at the Beech Tree pub in the village and in musical pursuits. Larry's talent as a musician had blossomed over the years, and as well as writing music he had begun playing the piano with Dennis R. Hinton and his Band, a six-piece dance outfit whose members included a trumpeter, saxophonist, clarinettist, double bassist and drummer. The band practised in one of the function rooms at the Uplands pub in Handsworth and played in venues across the region.

In 1942, Dennis R. Hinton and his Band qualified to participate in the *Melody Maker*'s All-Staffordshire Dance Band Championship. The *Melody Maker* magazine had begun organising contests in 1926 and held a series of regional heats with finalists going forward to a national competition. The Staffordshire leg of the 1942 championships took place on Tuesday 16 June at Wolverhampton's Civic Hall, and as well as the competing bands entertainment was provided by the established Jack Andrews and his Band. The evening promised continuous dancing from seven o'clock until midnight in one of the country's top venues.

The Civic Hall had opened in 1938 at a cost of £150,000 and boasted two halls, both with sprung floors, which could accommodate up to 2,500 people. Wartime ARP limits meant that only 1,000 people were permitted to attend in 1942, but even so this was probably the biggest audience Larry had ever played to. There was an array of prizes, cups and trophies on offer, the high value of which seemed to surprise even the *Melody Maker*'s reporter.

The judges included ex-West End bandleader Barney Gilbraith, who was described as one of the greatest swing accordion players, and a well-known vocalist, Billie Campbell, who happened to be in the area at the time and was drafted in at the last minute.

Dennis R. Hinton and his Band, with Larry on the piano, were placed fourth but they were awarded the cup for being the best small band in the contest. Further success was gained by one of their band members who was picked out as the best individual trumpet-player of the evening. The winners of the Staffordshire heat, Billy Monks' New Rhythm Band, went on to win the 'All-Britain' championship so competition had clearly been stiff.

Dennis R. Hinton and his Band were photographed in their practice room at the Uplands pub a few days later by H. A. Mason, a 'camera artist' from Monument Road, Edgbaston. They are all sitting at or holding their instruments as if pausing for applause in the middle of a performance and are dressed in suits with black bow ties. The front row of three musicians sit behind music stands in the art deco style that bear their initials – DT, DH and BG – and standing delightedly at the back are Dennis Hinton's father and uncle. Larry is the only member of the group who isn't smiling. Their silver cups are proudly displayed and a sign placed in front of them reads: 'Dennis R. Hinton and his Band, winners of the All Staffs Best Small Band Trophy 1942 and other cups at the All Staffs Dance Band Championship, Wolverhampton'.

Larry's blossoming music career came to an abrupt end though, when he had to swap piano for pistol and begin his war service.

Dennis R. Hinton and his Band (Larry Stephens Estate collection).

Part Two
GREEN BERETS

TICKS AND MORTARS

4
Military Life

Larry was called up, enlisted in the army and was posted to number 58 Primary Training Wing of the General Service Corps on 1 October 1942 for his basic training, aged nineteen.

First of all he was weighed (137½ lbs); measured (5 feet 9⅝ inches tall, 36½-inch chest); scrutinised (scar on right elbow, mole on back of neck) and had his fitness graded (medical grade – one, army medical category – A1). He was then assigned the army number 14301485 and spent the next six weeks becoming familiar with Blanco and boot polish while being drilled, inspected and shouted at.

When these initial weeks of hell were over, he was transferred to the Argyll and Sutherland Highlanders and told to report to number 8 Infantry Training Centre at Queen's Barracks in Perth, Scotland.

Nicknamed the 'Fair City', Perth was a picturesque and interesting place to be based. If you were to look at its layout on a piece of paper, you would see parkland in its header and footer – known as the North and South Inches – the shimmering River Tay running along its right-hand margin and elegant Georgian buildings and cobbled streets surrounding the historic St John's Kirk contained within the main body of the city. Entertainment and eating possibilities were plentiful with cinemas, a dance hall, canteens and an Italian café which served hot Bovril for a penny a mug.

It may seem odd that a young man from the Black Country would be sent to a Scottish regiment but battalions that had suffered heavy losses and needed to be brought back up to strength would receive new recruits from all over the British Isles. Or perhaps Larry had made the choice himself after being enthralled during childhood by the tales of his Uncle Donald McKechnie, who had served with the Argyll and Sutherland Highlanders during the First World War. Either way, it meant a train journey of at least fourteen hours from his native Birmingham to arrive in the middle of November in a place not exactly known for its high temperatures and mild winters.

Larry would probably have been very aware of the cold as his new uniform set included a kilt, something his frail English knees were not prepared for:

'I wish I'd never joined a Highland Regiment. Harm can come to a young lad wearing a kilt on a night like this.'

The Goon Show, 'The Policy'[1]

Despite his knocking knees, Larry knuckled down and began to learn how to operate the wide variety of weapons in use in an infantry platoon. There were machine guns in a choice of light, heavy or sub; bolt-action rifles; semi-automatic rifles and pistols; mortars and grenades. He took part in exercises and saw his shooting skills begin to improve on the firing range. The leadership qualities Larry had displayed when organising games for his childhood friends very quickly became evident to his superiors and so just two months after his arrival in Perth, he was promoted to the rank of Acting Lance Corporal.

The War Office had announced in 1940 that men would have to wait until they were at least 19¾ years old before they could begin training for a commission, and so the highly ambitious Larry counted down the days until he was old enough to apply. A month later, he headed off to face the War Office Selection Board (WOSB) at Oswald Road in Edinburgh and took his first step towards becoming an officer.

His WOSB interview began on 21 February 1943 and took place over three days. He was questioned and examined by a psychiatrist, a psychologist and a military testing officer, all of whom were overseen by a high-ranking president. As well as undergoing intelligence tests, group exercises and individual tasks, Larry's general behaviour was also closely observed. One of the first things he experienced after he arrived at the WOSB was a formal dinner with the other candidates and the members of the selection board. Although the chance to apply for a commission had been opened up to non-public-school candidates, the board still wanted to be sure that these potential officers had table manners that would be acceptable in an Officers' Mess.

After Larry had been interviewed, sat various written examinations, scrambled over obstacles, taken part in discussions and delivered lectures, the selection board members pooled the results. Larry was given an overall grade of 'B' and deemed suitable infantry officer material. A couple of weeks later he was sent to a pre-Officer Cadet Training Unit (pre-OCTU) at the 148 Training Brigade at Wrotham in Kent.

Hidden away in the woods around Wrotham, at the foot of the North Downs, the camp was the world's largest pre-OCTU at the time and could accommodate up to 10,000 men. The length of time spent there varied from cadet to cadet and would range from just a few days up to eight weeks, depending on the soldier's previous experience.

On arrival at the local railway station, Larry and the other cadets were met by private soldiers from the camp and driven to a reception centre where they immediately had to remove any rank insignia. So

Larry had to say goodbye to his Lance Corporal's stripe barely two months after he had earned it. In the place of his stripe, he had to attach white tapes to his epaulettes and a white band around his cap to distinguish him from the camp's permanent staff. He was then issued with a report card to carry around with him which would be used to record the training he had undertaken and the progress he had made. After the preliminary paperwork was out of the way, Larry was housed in a holding centre overnight.

The purpose of attending the pre-OCTU was twofold: it would weed out the weaker candidates and see them RTU-ed – returned to the unit from whence they had come – and would bring the successful cadets up to the required level of knowledge for onward posting to their OCTU. So after his night's rest in the holding centre, Larry was put through a series of practical exercises to assess how much time he would need to spend at Wrotham. As he had already picked up some of the necessary skills and experience during his five months in the army, he only needed to be trained for six of the potential eight weeks of the curriculum.

There were three wings at the camp for basic infantry instruction, each one run by a different battalion, and Larry was placed on permanent attachment to the 4th Battalion, Royal Berkshire Regiment for his training programme.

An article about Wrotham which appeared in the *Illustrated* magazine edition of 5 June 1943 lists some of the equipment he would have to become familiar with and the vehicles he would have to learn to drive, which included: wireless sets; mortars and mortar bombs; anti-personnel mines; Very light pistols; Thompson sub-machine guns; Short Lee-Enfield .303 rifles; fifteen-hundredweight trucks; motorcycles and bicycles.

The *Illustrated* magazine article and accompanying photographs give the impression that although the chaps had to work jolly hard during the day, their leisure time at Wrotham would be spent in veritable luxury. They could relax in tastefully furnished Nissen huts, wallow in civilian-style baths or avail themselves of the library or music room. The cadets who were actually resident at the camp remember it less fondly though, describing it as an incredibly uncomfortable and generally ghastly place with mud everywhere, bowls of tepid greasy water in which to wash their cutlery and mugs, overflowing latrine buckets and a cramped ablution room, a quarter of a mile away from their sleeping quarters, where they jostled for elbow room at the washbasins every morning.

Improvements were slowly being made while Larry was there, including the building of a Central Hall seating an audience of 1,500 where Entertainments National Service Association (ENSA) shows would be staged. This was something Larry didn't get to see as the first concert in the new hall was held on 24 April 1943 – two days after he had left.

The training itself was varied and covered physical, practical and mental activities. Larry's day began at seven o'clock each morning with a roll call and kit inspection. While he and the other cadets stood to attention by their beds, a sergeant would scrutinise every piece of their equipment and would peer down the barrel of each rifle to ensure it had been cleaned properly. Larry's rifle became his almost constant companion. He took it apart; he put it back together again; he cleaned it; he cared for it; he carried it around with him; he recited the names of each of its constituent parts:

This is the safety-catch, which is always released
With an easy flick of the thumb. And please do not let me
See anyone using his finger. You can do it quite easy
If you have any strength in your thumb.
                                        'Naming of Parts' by Henry Reed[2]

A high level of fitness was expected and the cadets had to go everywhere 'at the double' even if they were on their own or on the way to get something to eat. Anyone spotted dawdling would suddenly hear a bellowed order of, 'CADET! DOUBLE!' The camp's assault course was at the bottom of a steep chalk escarpment and although it was fairly easy to double down it, getting back up at the double immediately after climbing ropes, jumping over walls and crawling under barbed wire was much tougher.

The final part of the training was the most enjoyable for the majority of the cadets when they were transferred to the driving and maintenance wing for two weeks, as at the time very few young men had had the opportunity to learn to drive. There were only two million cars on the road at the start of the war (compared to 30.9 million by the end of 2016) and the driving test had been suspended since September 1939, so it was the first time behind the wheel for most of the cadets, including Larry.

The first week was spent learning to drive and maintain fifteen-hundredweight and three-ton trucks, which were cumbersome and difficult to handle and required double-declutching to change gear. Around four cadets and an instructor would be allocated to each of the trucks and, in convoy with the other vehicles, they would take it in turns to drive. Brigadier John Gray remembers that 'there was a particular crossroads in Maidstone which had a policeman standing on a box in the middle of the two roads directing traffic. The moment he saw our line of trucks bearing down towards him, with eager faces pressed to the windscreens and large "L" signs on the bonnets, he would get off his box, carry it to the pavement and the traffic could go to hell until after we had all passed – he had clearly been knocked off his box so many times that he was taking no chances.'[3]

After mastering the trucks, Larry spent the second week on two wheels, learning to ride a motorbike. For the first couple of days he lumbered around a cinder track at the camp but then he and the other cadets were let loose out on the roads, in convoys again. The culmination of the motorbike course was a ride through a simulated battlefield with craters and rough ground to negotiate while firecrackers exploded overhead.

Larry's time at Wrotham was soon over and he was ready to embark on the next part of his journey towards becoming an officer. He was despatched to Douglas in the Isle of Man for a further seventeen weeks' training, this time attached to 166 OCTU. Although not yet an officer, he had reached the level where he would now be referred to as 'Mr' Stephens.

It was a mixed bunch of cadets, mostly from Scottish regiments, who sailed across the Irish Sea: young inexperienced boys, barely out of school, alongside war-hardened soldiers who had already seen plenty of action. As the land grew nearer, the men could begin to make out a row of grand hotels looking like elaborate white-iced wedding cakes packed side by side along Douglas seafront. The hotels had all been requisitioned by the armed services and it was in the largest of these that Larry was billeted.

The Villiers Hotel was a substantial Victorian stuccoed building which swept around the corner of Victoria Street and into Loch Promenade. It boasted 200 bedrooms, a lift to all floors and a magnificent view of the bay and headlands. It was only a two-minute walk from Victoria Pier where Larry and the other cadets disembarked.

The men gathered in the hotel foyer and waited while their names were called from an alphabetical list and they were allocated to the room that was to be their home for the next few months. Large rooms that had previously been the restaurant and grillroom, with delicious aromas wafting their way towards the noses of the well-to-do pre-war holidaymakers, now housed twenty soldiers who filled the rooms with smells of a less pleasant kind. The tiny rooms at the top of the building took only two men each, men who were initially thankful for a bit of privacy but soon came to detest the number of stairs they had to climb to bed when they realised the lifts never seemed to work.

Isle of Man residents had already got used to seeing and hearing the cadets' training exercises in the years before Larry's turn came. Field training was carried out in the sandpit at Pulrose and on the rough at the golf course. Any discarded unfired rounds became the prized possessions of local boys, who would gather them up, prise them open, empty them of the yellowish vermicelli-like cordite and then set fire to it to create a satisfyingly loud fizz and bang. Other coveted items were any of the parachuted flares which had failed to ignite during night-time exercises and which offered the boys further opportunities for dangerously exciting experiments.

Larry was kept very busy during these four months and there was little time to relax, but he had an occasional free period at the weekend when he was able to spend an evening at the Palais de Danse in nearby Strand Street or explore the unspoilt beauty of the island. The Manx scenery must have been captivating for someone from the landlocked Midlands: palm trees rustling in the breeze along the coastal roads; caves gouged out of the cliffs and ancient stone circles peppering the hills. Through military eyes the beauty of the natural features ceased to exist though, and instead they simply became things to take cover in, scramble up or prop a gun against.

Another source of fascination was the camps further along the promenade from the Villiers Hotel, which housed Italian and German internees. They were caged behind barbed-wire fences, watched closely by their armed guards, and only the musical chatter of the Italians managed to escape past the barriers.

Larry and the other would-be officers continued with the physically and mentally arduous training before facing their final endurance tests: they swam in full kit in a large tank of seawater, pounded the pink asphalt of the promenade within set time limits and took turns to be the company commander. Larry relished these tests of strength and stamina and, keen to take the ultimate test, he volunteered to join the commandos, a recently formed group of elite soldiers.

5

Duties of a Hazardous Nature

The commandos had been formed in 1940, in the 'clouded and urgent days',[1] as the Queen Mother would later describe them, following the colossal military disaster of Dunkirk when Britain's morale was plummeting. In June 1940, Prime Minister Winston Churchill had written to the Chiefs of Staff proposing the raising of a special force to enable Britain to regain the upper hand. 'Enterprises must be prepared with specially trained troops of the hunter class, who can develop a reign of terror first of all on the "butcher and bolt" policy,' he wrote.[2]

This new force began to receive worldwide media coverage from late 1941 when details of the ferocious training programme were released by the War Office. The *Daily Express* described how the commando soldier was able to sneak up behind the enemy and use close-combat techniques such as ju-jitsu when a shot would reveal his presence. The *Daily Mirror* called them simply 'tough guys' and an article in the *Toronto Daily Star* explained how the soldiers were encouraged to become independent units: they were each given an allowance of six shillings and eightpence a day, with officers receiving double, with which they had to find and pay for their own accommodation and rations, rather than relying on the army to do it for them. All of this must have seemed incredibly glamorous in comparison to the regimented life of regular units.

On 21 August 1943, after successfully completing his OCTU training, Larry was commissioned into the Royal Warwickshire Regiment, allocated a new number – 289715 – and posted to the Commando Depot, the force's basic training centre in Achnacarry, fourteen miles from Fort William in Scotland. But first he was granted home leave until 27 August and was eager to see Margery again and to spend time at the Beech Tree pub.

As a new Second Lieutenant he was now pocketing eleven shillings a day in pay and was allocated a generous 221 clothing coupons. Under rationing restrictions, civilians were only entitled to thirty-eight clothing coupons per year. With his 221 coupons, Larry had to buy service dress, a greatcoat, at least two shirts and four collars, two pairs of shoes, ties, socks, underwear and two serviceable battledresses. Once he was fully kitted out, he had a professional photograph taken, wearing his new uniform and with his hair freshly cut. His proud mother sent the image to family and friends as her 1943 Christmas card.

Larry Stephens in 1943.

Once his short period of home leave was over, Larry once again said goodbye to his friends and family in Quinton and West Bromwich and began the journey up to Spean Bridge, the closest railway station to the Commando Depot at Achnacarry.

Although he was facing another long train journey into Scotland – he would need to travel to Glasgow first and then change to the service towards Mallaig for the five-hour journey to Spean Bridge – this would be much more comfortable than the trip he had made to Perth nine months previously; now that he was an officer he would be travelling first class, and the late summer weather would hopefully be more clement when he arrived.

The train chugged and chuffed its way northwards and Larry watched as the view from the window morphed gently from the smoke-scarred red brick of Birmingham into craggy granite hills, criss-crossed with tumbling, spilling streams. Sheep and deer, startled by the train, scrambled over the rocks with a look of panic on their faces. The skeletons of isolated, roofless grey stone cottages gazed blankly through their empty windows.

Eventually the train halted at Spean Bridge, and as Larry stepped onto the platform the station became a mass of khaki as soldiers burst out of every other carriage of the train. Kit bags were loaded onto a waiting lorry but anyone who expected to jump on after them was going to be disappointed. They were ordered to form up in threes as they would be speed-marching the rest of the way – seven miles.

Led by a kilted pipe-band for the first part of the march, the tramp, tramp of boots left Spean Bridge station towards 'Castle Commando'. The 'tramp, tramp' would often be more of a 'splash, splash', as if it wasn't already raining, it soon would be; it always seemed to be raining. They crossed Thomas Telford's bridge spanning the River Spean and then began the march up the steep hill leading away from the village, past battalions of pine trees standing to attention. Once over the

Caledonian Canal at Gairlochy, they followed a narrow road which meandered upwards from the bottom edges of Loch Lochy until the sight of an imposing granite structure in the distance began to wink at them through gaps in the trees.

The commando training base was located in the house and grounds of the twenty-fourth chief of Clan Cameron, Donald Cameron of Lochiel. Achnacarry House had been built in 1802 in the 'Scottish Baronial' style on the site of a ruined seventeenth-century castle. The view of the turreted grey building with its lancet windows and vast entranceway topped with the red and gold coat of arms was somewhat spoiled by the addition of a Nissen hut on either side of the door but at least this was in keeping with the symmetry of the house. The tree-lined River Arkaig curled around the back of the house and the surrounding landscape rose to a series of contrasting peaks: barren mountains and gentler forested slopes which were daubed with mustard yellows, terracottas and greens, changing from pastel shades to almost black as the cloud shadows brushed over them.

If Larry thought his OCTU training was tough, he soon realised it was nothing compared to the two weeks of training he was about to endure in these rugged surroundings. One of the first things he saw as he followed the pipers, who had rejoined them for the final procession through the gates and into the grounds, was a row of graves: each earthy mound was encircled by white stones and had a wooden cross planted at one end. Every cross bore an epitaph which detailed various dangerous actions:

This man fired a 2-inch mortar under a tree

This man failed to splay the pin of his grenade

This man advanced over the top of cover

Larry and the other trainee commandos were unsure whether these mocked-up graves were real or not, but they certainly served as a chilling warning to them as the inscriptions detailed ways in which men really had been killed and injured.

Any hopes Larry may have had of special treatment now that he was an officer were quickly dispelled when he learned that not only would he undergo exactly the same training as the men but he might well have to endure additional instruction in the evening. We don't know the details of his sleeping arrangements, but if he was lucky he would have shared a room in the castle with other officers. However, if there were large numbers to be accommodated, as a junior officer he may well have ended up sleeping in a Nissen hut or under canvas. He would be washing in cold water and he wouldn't be enjoying the services of a batman. There were a couple of minor concessions to his officer status though. The first, as the Reverend Joe Nicholl discovered during his time at Achnacarry, was that, 'when drilling on the square, the officers were expected to assist the guards sergeants by remaining aloof and decorative, but not interfering in any way'.[3] The second was that he wouldn't have to dress for dinner in the Officers' Mess... unless the Commandant, Lieutenant Colonel Charles E. Vaughan, specifically requested it of course.

Entering an Officers' Mess for the first time must have been quite a daunting experience for Larry and the other officers who had been newly commissioned from the ranks. To help them, a guide book called 'Customs of the Service' had been published in 1939 with many pages of dos and don'ts. The advice included only drinking one short or sherry before a meal so as not to appear ill-educated; how to avoid becoming an 'intolerable bore'; occasions when it was acceptable to wear a lounge suit rather than a dinner jacket; the importance of paying meticulous care in the selection of 'mufti'; and the etiquette around mentioning ladies at the Mess table.

Achnacarry's Mess with its leather armchairs and high ceilings embellished with elaborate cornices had received a recent makeover. Lance Corporal Brian Mullen had drawn commando soldiers on the walls to look as though they were scaling the window frames and parachuting from the ceiling, and above the bar at one end of the room he had painted a large Combined Operations Command emblem flanked by ships and tanks and a formation of planes flying overhead.

Away from the Officers' Mess, Larry's time was spent in lectures and training films, tactical and endurance exercises, forced marches and fieldcraft lessons, all of which were designed to produce a strong team spirit, a superior knowledge of survival techniques, a confidence to be able to take on anything and a level of fitness close to that of a professional athlete.

Larry and his fellow trainees took part in a series of speed marches, the ultimate goal of which was to be able to cover a distance of seven miles in an hour. The gradual build-up to this began in the opening couple of days of the course and followed a route around Achnacarry Castle which was to be completed in around fifty minutes. It took in a narrow road known in Gaelic as the Mìle Dorcha (Dark Mile). This route, which came to be called the 'Commando Dark Mile', was actually five miles long and wound around the castle through avenues of beech trees that had been planted so closely together that little light could penetrate. The second level was a seven-mile march, immediately followed by the digging of a trench, all of which had to be accomplished within an hour and ten minutes. Next came an hour and thirty minutes spent marching for nine miles and then shooting at moving targets; then a twelve-mile march followed by drill to be completed within two hours and ten minutes; and finally fifteen miles of marching, an assault course and more shooting, for which two hours and fifty minutes were allocated. And all of this in full equipment while carrying a rifle and ammunition.

These marches took place across a terrain that could be described as 'undulating' and the frequent heavy rain made the going muddy and slippery. For some of the trainees the effort was just too much and they would collapse exhausted at the side of the road. For them it would be the ultimate humiliation: RTU – returned to their unit as unsuitable.

The physical training Larry underwent while at Achnacarry was wide-ranging and as well as rock climbing, boating, scaling Ben Nevis and learning unarmed combat, he and the other trainees were able to practise their best Johnny Weissmuller moves on a Tarzan course and a treetop range with swings and bridges connecting tree to tree, using British ropes rather than jungle vines.

Among the more well-known features of the commando assault course was the 'death ride', which received a lot of publicity at the time and later appeared in a modified form as part of the physical ability test on *The Krypton Factor* in the 1970s, 1980s and 1990s. A thick rope was attached to the top of a tall tree and then the other end was secured to the base of a tree on the other side of the fast-flowing River Arkaig. The aim was for the men to slide from the top to the bottom of this thick rope by clinging onto a looped toggle rope slung over it. And just to add a bit of extra spice, live ammunition exploded in the river beneath them during the descent (the inclusion of this aspect would certainly have made *The Krypton Factor* more interesting!). Larry discovered that if he lubricated the toggle with a generous serving of spit before setting off, it helped to give him enough momentum to slide safely to the bottom, rather than grinding to a halt halfway down and having to plunge into the cold, churning waters below.

The use of live ammunition during training was not without dangers and this, combined with the hazards posed by the rugged Scottish environment, led to some of the 25,000 men from all over the world who passed through the gates of Castle Commando losing their lives. Many others were injured: a member of 44 Royal Marine (RM)

Commando had his hand blown off by a grenade and an American Ranger suffered a bullet in the buttock after failing to obey orders to sit in the bottom of a boat rather than on the side of it.

There was also great emphasis placed on 'spit and polish'. A special correspondent with *The Times*, who spent a long weekend with the commando trainees at Achnacarry in 1943, was impressed to see that they were impeccably turned out and their surroundings were spotless, despite the challenging conditions. The reporter praised boots and mess tins that were so shiny you could use them as mirrors, faultless equipment and immaculate huts. Lieutenant Colonel Vaughan insisted that during training Larry and the other officers cleaned their equipment and uniforms to this high standard themselves so that in the future they would be aware of how long such tasks should take their men.

As well as improving Larry's physical strength, the instructors were also increasing his knowledge. He was taught how to operate enemy weapons so that in a combat situation he would be able to turn them and use them against their previous owners; he also sat through a series of lectures and training films, and he learned how to memorise a route and how to live off the land.

The survival training, taught by Sergeant Major Moon, was one of the most memorable aspects of the instruction for many of the commando recruits. As well as demonstrating how to construct shelters suitable for different weather conditions, Moon showed the trainees how to build fires and ovens from a range of materials and taught them that they need never go hungry: they learned how to lay traps, how to skin deer and which wild vegetation they could safely pick and eat. The grand finale of the instruction was when Sergeant Major Moon produced a lump of baked clay from the embers of one of his demonstration fires and cracked it open to release a tantalising smell. With its fur sticking to the clay crust, a perfectly cooked, clean and juicy small animal revealed itself as the 'prize' in the centre. Moon would slice the meat up and invite his hungry students to taste it and guess what it was, but no one ever got the right answer – it was Achnacarry rat.

When Larry's two weeks of training came to a successful end and he had earned the right to wear the prized green beret, he was surprised to receive an order to report to Lieutenant Colonel Vaughan's office.

6

Castle Commando

It must have been with some trepidation that Larry knocked on the Camp Commandant's door and awaited the bellowed command to enter. He needn't have worried though; he must have excelled in the training, as Charlie Vaughan asked him to stay on for a while longer as an instructor.

The weeks from September to December of 1943 were set to be very busy at Castle Commando as six units from the Royal Marines, comprising 180 officers and 3,300 other ranks, were due to undergo their training. There was a shortage of instructors available to handle such a large intake and so Lieutenant Colonel Vaughan was recruiting from the best of those who had recently passed the course. One of Vaughan's guiding principles was that every instructor had to have an exceptional level of ability, to enable them to perform each task more quickly and more accurately than the men who would be training under them. There was also a strong focus on leadership and so the instructors had to be natural leaders too.

Larry therefore spent a further two months at Achnacarry, living in the castle. He was put in charge of No. 2 Section of E Troop, supported by TSM (Troop Sergeant Major) Jessop, and worked in close conjunction with No. 1 Section under the command of Lieutenant Maidment and Sergeant Greenaway.

The first would-be commandos to come under his instruction were members of 44 RM (Royal Marines) who arrived at Spean Bridge station on 7 September. Larry joined the other instructors in meeting the train and putting the men through their paces from the moment of their arrival: they were ordered to disembark, not onto the platform, but to drop down onto the railway line and then clamber up onto the platform on the opposite side before beginning the seven-mile speed march to Achnacarry.

For the next three weeks, Larry guided and encouraged his charges through the training. There was no let-up for the instructors, who had to lead by example and share in each danger and difficulty. Larry urged his men on by passing on the wisdom he had inherited from Lieutenant Colonel Vaughan and his staff: 'it's all in the mind...' a phrase that would later appear in the *Goon Show*.

Larry's E Troop trainees went through one of the most dramatic elements of the course on 30 September. The night-time opposed landing was a realistic representation of an amphibious assault, carried out in the darkness and using live ammunition. Groups of eight each boarded a canvas-sided Goatley boat at Bunarkaig boathouse and then paddled it the quarter of a mile across Loch Lochy to the opposite shore. Before setting off, the marines' weapons were stacked into the bottoms of the boats and they were warned to keep their heads down and to make sure that only their arms were visible over the sides, since almost from the moment of setting off, bursts of machine-gun fire would be aimed in their direction by Larry and his fellow instructors on the bank.

Tracer ammunition lit up the sky like Fireworks Night but the crack of bullets inches away from the boats was real and potentially lethal. On the final approach to the shore, hand grenades were lobbed towards them, sending plumes of water high into the air, and visibility was suddenly reduced as Larry and the other instructors ignited smoke grenades and a cloud began to creep across the loch. The men leapt into the icy shallow water and waded ashore before scrambling into position as quickly as they could. Machine-gunners rushed the Brens forward and began firing at metal targets on the opposite hill while the assaulting troops ran squelching through the mud and got into position.

As soon as the gunners had scored enough hits, the instructors yelled the command to assault. The marines clawed and squelched and slipped their way up the bank until the land flattened out and they were faced with another line of metal targets. They threw themselves onto the sodden ground, took aim and fired. Panting for breath, they scrambled to their feet and ran towards a battalion of straw-filled sacks. They speared them with bayonets, teeth gritted.

A white Very flare was fired, signalling that the time had come to skid and slide back down towards the boats and begin the journey back across the loch. As they began to paddle away, the instructors bombarded them with grenades and machine-gun fire again, and although Larry and the other instructors were skilled in shooting to miss, the marines could feel the bullets whistling past them and occasionally thumping into the paddles and smacking them out of their hands.

The men of 44 RM completed their training on 2 October, and a couple of days later 42 RM arrived at Spean Bridge, giving Larry a new set of officers and men to train. Bill Stoneman of 42 RM related his experiences of Achnacarry in his memoirs:

We found the Camp well organised and the instructors, who were Army personnel, very efficient. They had a keen sense of rather excitable rivalry and made every effort to urge the unit they were training to complete the fastest speed march of 7 miles, 12 miles and 30 miles and cat crawling across a fast flowing river on a rope where, if you lost your hold, you crashed down to the fearsome rocks below. When this happened the team instructor would offer odds on how many times the poor sod would bounce on his way down.[1]

By the end of October, 42 RM had also been awarded their green berets and after a short period of leave, on 6 November 1943 Second Lieutenant Larry Stephens, Lieutenants Housden, Dashwood and Pammenter were released from the Commando Depot and posted to No. 5 Commando in Bognor Regis.

No. 5 Commando had taken up residence on the Greenways School site, formerly a private preparatory boarding school for boys which had been evacuated in 1940. Preparations were under way for a move to a tropical climate. A week later they travelled north and on a damp and grey day they embarked on HMT *Reina Del Pacifico* at Liverpool Docks, bound for an unknown destination.

7

Destination Unknown

On board the *Reina Del Pacifico* with Larry and the other twenty-six officers and 430 men of No. 5 was another Commando unit, 44 RM, that Larry had already got to know quite well. In the months ahead they were to become close friends and allies, but when it came to sport, bitter rivals. The other passengers on board the vessel included soldiers, sailors, airmen, nurses, Wrens and even a handful of civilians, but it was the two Commando units who would have priority for training spaces and they would take it in turns to use the upper deck for this purpose.

Rumour was rife within No. 5 about their intended destination and even though they had been issued with tropical kit and bush hats (surely just a ploy to fool the enemy) they passed the time speculating on the different possibilities:

'Italy for sure. Just look at Salerno. Bags of room for another Commando there – probably more than one.'

'Look at Burma. No commandos there yet. Just our bloody luck: leeches and cannibals.'

'Look at Australia. Sydney...'

'Coo, I know a girl from there too. Real smasher.'[1]

After two days docked at Liverpool, the ship sailed north to Gourock on the Clyde. With a backdrop of the snow-capped Greenock hills they joined the other ships that were to form their convoy, including the *Ranchi*, carrying No. 1 and 42 RM Commandos, who together with No. 5 and 44 RM formed 3 Commando Brigade. The convoy also included HMT *Rohna*, which was soon to be wiped from the records for several decades.

In the frosty dawn light of 15 November, the *Reina Del Pacifico* eased herself down the Forth until she reached open sea and then began the long journey to carry her charges to active service overseas.

Conditions on board the ship were fairly grim for the men; their quarters were cramped and claustrophobic and reeked of sweat and seasickness. In some areas the bunks were stacked eight high in the gangways. Larry had much more favourable sleeping arrangements and was allocated to one of the cabins, which slept a maximum of three officers. He also had access to what had been the first-class areas of the former passenger liner with their Moorish-influenced wood panelling, elaborately carved with cornucopias, schools of fantastical sea creatures, grape-laden vines and frolicking plump cherubs. The *Reina del Pacifico* was scrapped in 1958 and some of this wooden panelling from the ship's interior now decorates the Cornmarket pub in Liverpool.

The first week of the voyage was a fairly uneventful round of lectures and lessons, weapon, semaphore and first-aid training, although boxing and tug-of-war competitions were arranged to help keep everyone fit and entertained. No. 5 Commando's RSM (Regimental Sergeant Major) Des Crowden remembered that one day, 'two Japanese turned up on deck. We couldn't believe it because obviously they were the people we were going to fight. They turned out to be two former Japanese who were now naturalised Americans and they were there to teach us Japanese phrases.'[2] The troops were taught nine phrases, and Larry and his fellow officers and the Intelligence Section learned an additional twenty-one, ranging from 'halt' and 'who goes there?' to 'pick up your wounded' and 'bury your dead here'.

During the evening of 24 November, the convoy passed within five miles of the Moroccan coast and Larry gazed in wonder at the lights of Tangier blazing in the distance. Britain had been subjected to night-time blackouts for the past four years, but as a neutral country Spanish Morocco could safely shine. Someone started singing 'Till The Lights Of London Shine Again' and the solo voice was gradually joined by others. Larry's thoughts turned to home as they sang the sentimental words about wartime separation and he wondered whether he would ever see his loved ones again.

Later that evening, the convoy advanced past the Rock of Gibraltar, another beacon in the darkness, and dozens of local fishing boats weaved among the *Reina Del Pacifico* and her convoy companions.

Two days later, as the convoy cruised along the Algerian coast, the relative tranquillity and monotony was shattered. Just after four o'clock in the afternoon, the hum of approaching planes began to drown out the sound of *Reina Del Pacifico*'s choir practising 'Jesu, Joy of Man's Desiring' ready for the Sunday service. Those who had been strolling on the decks paused and peered up at the sky, those who had been reading closed their books and joined them, a member of the ship's crew, who had been doing a roaring trade as a barber, threw down his scissors and sprinted towards the nearest gun. As the hum grew louder, a formation of more than a dozen German Heinkel planes could be seen heading in the direction of the convoy. As the order was given for the top decks to be cleared, there was suddenly an explosion of noise as the booming anti-aircraft guns began to blast skywards. While the ships moved around, changing course so as not to become sitting targets, the guns continued to fire and RAF and USAF aircraft streaked across the skies, hot on the trail of the Luftwaffe planes.

There were plenty of near misses with great plumes of water rising around the *Reina Del Pacifico* and the other ships in the convoy, as bombs and damaged aircraft plummeted exploding into the sea around them. Suddenly, a small plane of a type witnesses were unable to identify started on a direct collision course with HMT *Rohna*. The aircraft smashed through *Rohna*'s side and blew up in her engine room, sending a fireball soaring into the sky.

Almost 1,150 of the men on board *Rohna* were killed and a veil of secrecy was immediately drawn over the incident. The unidentifiable aircraft that struck *Rohna* was in fact a guided missile – the precursor to the German V-1 rocket – and this was one of the first times the Germans had scored a successful hit with such a weapon. The US Government felt it would be reckless for such information to become common knowledge and this, combined with the heavy loss of life exacerbated by insufficient training and inadequate life-saving equipment, led to a cover-up that lasted for more than twenty years.

Eventually the all-clear sounded and with the Luftwaffe finally despatched and the *Rohna* a floating mass of flame and smoke behind them, *Reina Del Pacifico* and the rest of the convoy limped on.

Bren guns were mounted on the *Reina Del Pacifico*'s deck and were manned during daylight hours; for the next couple of days, Larry anxiously scanned the skies. Over on *Ranchi*, Bill Stoneman of 42 RM noticed that the sharks seemed to have singled out their ship and had been following them day and night – a portent of things to come.

8

A Passage to India

A few days later, just after teatime on 30 November, everyone was settling down to their books, letter-writing and card games, when an enemy aircraft warning was given and another formation of German bombers made its way towards the convoy. The decks were evacuated and the men gathered at their mess tables down in the *Reina Del Pacifico*'s hull, listening to a commentary of the unfolding events given over the ship's loudspeakers.

Once again, Larry and his fellow commandos on the *Reina Del Pacifico* made it through the experience unscathed but over on the *Ranchi* they were not quite so lucky. A bomb hit the ship's forecastle, penetrated the deck and then exited through the vessel's other side before exploding in the water. Amazingly, only one man was killed, struck by flying debris as it scattered inside the ship.

Once the Luftwaffe had been seen off again and the threat was over, all the ships in the convoy lowered their flags to half-mast and the *Ranchi*'s casualty was buried at sea, his white shrouded figure slipping beneath the waves. The sharks' escort of the ship came to an end.

The *Ranchi*, carrying the 3rd Commando Brigade's HQ together with No. 1 and 42 RM Commandos, was diverted towards Alexandria for repairs while the rest of the convoy continued on its way.

As the *Reina Del Pacifico* sailed into hotter climates, the men were ordered to wear their khaki drill uniforms in an effort to get them used to the high temperatures they would soon be facing. Some of them relished the heat though, and soaked up the sun on the decks whenever possible, their skins turning pink, then red, and finally brown. Larry's blond hair and fair skin meant that sunbathing was an activity only to be undertaken with extreme caution.

The convoy passed through the Suez Canal – one of the first to do so for more than two years – and then the *Reina Del Pacifico* dropped anchor at Aden, where she remained for five days. A request by the Commanding Officer (CO) for the commandos to go ashore was rejected on security grounds and so they were confined to ship in furnace-like temperatures. An RAF band was permitted to board and provide music for an all-ranks dance out on deck and the comparatively small numbers of Wrens and nurses on the *Reina Del Pacifico* were very much in demand. Larry and the other officers took full advantage of their rank to claim most of the dances.

Early in the morning of 13 December, the ship was under way again, part of a new convoy sailing for India. The sea breezes were a welcome relief after the Aden heat and made it easier for Larry, the other officers and NCOs to concentrate on the increasing number of lectures they attended now that their arrival was imminent.

On 18 December 1943, No. 5 and 44 RM began to make preparations for disembarkation and on the following day they docked in Bombay. Confined to ship once again, they were unimpressed with the view and decided that the 'Gateway of India' definitely looked better on a cinema screen.

At eight o'clock on the morning of the 20th, they finally disembarked and headed towards Bombay railway station to begin another journey to another unknown destination, although this one would last for only ten hours rather than the thirty-eight days they had spent at sea. Each man was presented with a twenty-one-page booklet to read on the train entitled 'Some useful hints for soldiers arriving in India'. It had been produced by W.D. and H.O. Wills, the makers of Wild Woodbine cigarettes, which according to the advertisement on the back cover were 'the soldiers' smoke'. Larry developed a heavy smoking habit during his war service, perhaps after being subtly brainwashed by the slogans printed at the bottom of each page of the booklet:

Never be without them: 'Woodbines'

Don't forget your: 'Woodbines'

Wherever you go – take: 'Woodbines'

Other than urging Larry to ensure he had a Woodbine to hand at every possible opportunity, his booklet did also contain a lot of helpful information. As well as details about the geography, size and climate of India and its three seasons – winter from November to February, summer from March until June and monsoon covering July to October – there were also sections about language, health and sport.

The 'Language' chapter had lists of useful words and phrases in Hindustani together with phonetic transcriptions of their pronunciation, such as 'Where is the cinema?' (*Bioscope kid-her high?*), 'Shut up' (*Choop ra-ho*) and one that everyone would learn very quickly, 'Tea' (C*har*).

Among other things, 'Health' covered how to avoid and treat sunstroke; how to determine whether you'd been bitten by a venomous or non-venomous snake by studying the shape of the fang marks; and how under no circumstances should you smoke everything that came your way but stick to the safe choice of the British Army's old favourite, Woodbines (of course!).

When not reading his 'useful hints' booklet, Larry passed his time on the train journey gazing out of the window at the contrasting tableaux: wide streets full of grand buildings gave way to howling beggars living in unbelievable filth and squalor, and as the train left the cities and towns behind, villagers could be seen toiling in the vast parched fields. Every time the train paused at a station the local people would swarm around the windows proffering a seemingly unlimited variety of fruits and nuts, and the chorus of the word 'baksheesh' (a plea for a charitable donation) would become almost deafening.

If witnessing squalor and reading about venomous snakes, dog bites, dysentery and malaria during the rail journey didn't exactly instil confidence in Larry regarding his destination, his feelings didn't improve when he reached Kedgaon and was transported by truck to the camp. It was set on a barren rocky plateau, or as a member of 44 RM described it, acres and acres of sweet nothing. Row upon row of tents stretched in all directions and the only smear of colour was provided by a distant Union Jack fluttering on a solitary flagpole. After everyone had been provided with a hot meal, they discovered that the beds were bug-ridden and so a miserable and uncomfortable first night was spent there.

The last few days before Christmas were taken up with getting the camp in order. Under a fiercely hot sun in a cloudless blue sky, they fumigated the beds and gave the kitchens and latrines a thorough clean so that things were at least a little better. They also discovered there was a camp cinema in operation – although it was housed in what was little more than a mud hut – showing films such as *They Flew Alone* and *River's End* starring Anna Neagle.

On his first ever Christmas Day abroad, Larry, together with the other officers, served Christmas dinner to the men in the time-honoured tradition. The meal was a vast improvement on anything that had been served up during their time on the *Reina Del Pacifico* and included roast pork, roast potatoes, oranges and bananas. Each man was also given three bottles of beer to celebrate the festive season. The day was rounded off with a carol service and it was a much happier group of commandos who went to bed that night.

No. 5 and 44 RM quickly settled into camp life. Their bodies began to get used to the climate, they continued to make visits to the mud hut cinema and they spent occasional leave periods in Poona, where there was a swimming pool, several 'proper' cinemas and some skilful tailors who ran up fancy new uniforms for Larry and the other officers. In a letter to his girlfriend Margery, Larry lamented that he was unable to get flannel trousers anywhere, and he found it 'highly depressing to say the least'.[1]

As an officer, Larry was provided with a canvas bath outside his tent and had to swiftly get used to the lack of privacy this arrangement meant; there was a constant stream of locals passing through the camp, eager to sell their wares, and they always seemed to appear, waving a bunch of bananas or similar, just as Larry was attempting to wash his more intimate parts. All the commandos grew to appreciate the services of the 'char wallahs' though, whose tea was the best they had ever tasted and who would even serve their morning cuppa to them in bed.

The bleakness of Kedgaon wasn't exactly the ideal terrain for jungle training but a specialised team spent several days at the camp giving the officers and NCOs lectures on the art of jungle warfare, Japanese tactics and their personal experiences of Burma. However, there was a break from the training and instruction and more focus on fun for Larry when he and the other officers from No. 5 were invited to a 'legendary' party at 44 RM's Officers' Mess on 10 January. The treats on offer included a lethal punch, which was almost strong enough to remove tooth enamel and was described as being more suitable to fill petrol lighters than to drink.

A week later, a visiting entertainment troupe from Poona gave a concert, but to the men's disappointment the 'entertainment' was decidedly below par. It wasn't the only thing: Larry's health was suffering and he was admitted to hospital the same day.

Four days later, while Larry was still in hospital, Brigade HQ, No. 1 and 42 RM arrived at Kedgaon after their Egyptian diversion and the whole Brigade was finally together. Another Commando unit had also arrived and taken up residence – a Dutch troop from No. 10 (Inter-Allied). Even though the camp was now in much better shape than when Larry had arrived at the end of December, the new arrivals were still none too impressed. A member of No. 1 remarked that the only thing he could find to recommend about it was its unlimited space.

The highlight of the month was on Sunday 23 January when Admiral Lord Louis Mountbatten, the Supreme Allied Commander of South-East Asia Command (SEAC), made an official visit to the camp. Every aspect of his visit had been planned, right down to the tiniest detail – the Kedgaon rocks had even been painted white. The Admiral was introduced to all the Brigade's officers and NCOs, an opportunity that Larry unfortunately missed, due to his spell in Poona hospital.

By 26 January 1944, he had recovered enough to be discharged but another member of No. 5, Private Haydn Walters, died of 'some noisome disease'[2] and became the unit's first fatality. The commandos were experiencing a radical change in diet and environment in India and it took a lot of adapting to. Many of the officers had been complaining of upset stomachs and put this down to the young cooks failing to adhere to basic hygiene rules. Time in hospital became an expected part of life, and dysentery, typhus and heatstroke were common ailments. The commandos tried to make the best of their hospital stays, as a letter Larry later received from one of his officer friends, Ken Waggett, demonstrates:

Had a blank sheet for six days and finally they gave me one of those damned stirrup pumps. Imagine it – eleven orderlies queuing up with bed pans!! They tell me I won the Silver Cup with my brilliant performance... Every other day they let some blood out of a clot I have contracted in some peculiar (and no doubt underhand) manner. During the process a nurse holds my pulse and asks me if I feel faint. If I do, they dose me up with brandy so I (naturally) feel faint all the time and come out quite whistled![3]

A fully recovered Larry settled back into life at Kedgaon Camp and around this time he was appointed No. 5's Entertainments Officer. This was very much a secondary duty for him, but it was an incredibly important role as it was imperative to maintain the morale of everyone in the unit and organising regular entertainment was one way of doing this.

The commando officers as a whole were always in search of amusements and diversions for their men and one of the ideas the Brigadier came up with was to produce a Brigade magazine which he thought would help 'the hearts of the four Commandos to beat as one'.[4] As a consequence of this suggestion, the officers spent several evenings making plans by lamplight, all the while swatting mosquitoes away, until the *Third Jungle Book* magazine began to take form.

Eight issues of the magazine were produced between April 1944 and September 1945, followed by a special souvenir edition in March 1946. Only 400 copies of the first two issues were printed and the price ranged from two annas for other ranks up to one chip for officers. By the third issue, the magazine had begun to gain in popularity and almost 1,000 copies were produced; anyone who was willing to pay an extra one anna to cover the cost of a stamp could have a copy despatched to their friends and family back home. As well as regular features such as 'The Padre's Column', 'Nature Diary' and 'Music', content was provided by the Brigade's men – stories, articles, poetry, drawings and photographs – together with news roundups from each of the troops. A submission in issue 2 to a regular section called 'George's Live Letters' from 'Optimistic' of 1 Commando read, 'Suggest Jungle Mag. on lines of Razzle, not Piddlehinton Church Magazine.' Included in the fourth edition was a letter from Nobby of Brigade HQ, who wrote, 'Your magazine is becoming too much like Razzle. Can't you make it a little more refined?'!

Most of the work in battling the Indian printing presses and getting the first issue to bed ended up in the hands of the officers from No. 1 and 42 RM as the other two units were due to leave camp and see action against the enemy as part of 'Operation Screwdriver'.

On the morning of 20 February 1944, an advance party comprising Larry, Lieutenant Kenneth Pammenter and their two batmen left the Kedgaon camp for the local railway station where they set about making the necessary arrangements for the rest of the unit's move towards action. In the evening they were joined at the station by the majority of their No. 5 comrades as well as the bulk of 44 RM and five members of the No. 10 (Inter-Allied) Dutch troop. They all boarded an overnight train for an eleven-hour journey to Bombay and from there they transferred onto the river steamer HMS *Keren* in preparation for an early voyage the following morning. It was a notable day for Larry as he was awarded his second pip and promoted to Lieutenant at an increased pay level of 640 rupees per month. He was ready to shoulder the additional responsibilities that would fall to him in the action that lay ahead.

9

Into Action in Burma

HMS *Keren* set sail as part of a convoy at midday on 22 February 1944, bound for a port in Bengal called Chittagong. During the journey, everyone was given a cholera inoculation, bush jackets and trousers were issued and it was announced that all items of kit would have to be dyed jungle green, leaving no doubt as to the sort of environment they were heading into.

In years to come, Larry would remember the eleven-day sea voyage as a happy time of his life and one of the points at which talents would emerge, sowing the first seeds of an idea for his post-war career. In his role as Entertainments Officer, he arranged a concert party to entertain those on board the *Keren*; it was so noteworthy that it was mentioned in the History of No. 5 Commando that appeared in the final souvenir edition of the 3rd Commando Brigade magazine when the war was over. This concert was apparently 'made remarkable by the wide range of "Irvingesque" talent' on display. It seems rather likely that this article describing No. 5's experiences in the East was written by Larry himself, especially as photos of two of the troops he served with were also included.

After a two-day stop in Madras, punctuated by air-raid warnings, an announcement was made that the destination had been changed to a small port to the south of Chittagong called Cox's Bazar, a place which has since become known for having the longest natural beach in the world and, at the time of writing, is the site of the Kutupalong refugee camp sheltering Rohingya refugees. When the men of 5 Commando arrived there on 4 March, they were greeted by the smiling locals, who had prepared vast quantities of sugary tea with which to welcome them. Suitably refreshed, the commandos then had to march for just under a mile through soft sand to meet the trucks that would ferry them to their overnight camp. The following morning they were taken by lorry to board a vessel on the Naf River from where it was a short journey to No. 5's base for the next week: Nhila, sixteen miles from Maungdaw in Burma.

The week in Nhila was spent in making preparations for the forthcoming action, known as Operation Screwdriver. The goal of the operation would be to occupy an area of high ground and thus prevent Japanese reinforcements and supplies from moving northwards. On 7 March, Brigadier Nonweiler arrived at the camp for an evening conference attended by Larry and his fellow No. 5 officers. At the time, Larry was one of the leaders of 6 Troop – the heavy weapons troop – and he was informed they would be allocated three walkie-talkie sets compared to the single set the other troops would have. He was also told he would need to carry field dressings with him and it was left to his discretion as to whether he armed himself with a rifle or a Colt automatic. Recognition signals were established, which would be used between troops and also with the 81st West African Reconnaissance Regiment, who would be located on 'C' beach. The conference concluded with a stark reminder that 'once shot at, no Jap must get away. Dead men tell no tales.'[1]

Green battledress and green berets would be worn for the operation but all badges of rank and cap badges would have to be removed. RQMS Sam Hartley lit bonfires and boiled up his own concoction of dye in some old oil drums and then everyone soaked their white underclothes, towels and handkerchiefs in the mixture.

As the time for action grew nearer, 'first night nerves' obviously began to play a part for some. An unnamed officer managed to drop his .45 Colt from trembling fingers into the latrine and lengths of bamboo were plunged into the murky depths until it was eventually fished out. The officer was grateful for the nearby Naf River as it made it easier for him to wash the filth from his handgun.

The commandos ran through landing rehearsals and practised moving across country and forming 'boxes', the defensive positions they established. Although they were called boxes, these formations weren't always square box-shaped. A series of slit trenches was dug, each large enough to hold two men. The rifle bearers were located in the trenches around the outer perimeter and the more vulnerable sections in the middle. Further protection was offered by strategically placed booby traps located outside the box, often something as simple as a concealed sharpened stick.

Larry received his final briefing and orders, escape kits were issued and lectures were given on the Japanese positions, all accompanied by the sound of shelling from across the river. Finally, on 11 March, a day behind 44 RM, No. 5 boarded the steamer *Elsa* and departed south along the Naf River as far as Teknaf, where they disembarked. Larry spent the next seven hours on standby, waiting to hear whether No. 5 would be needed to go and support 44 RM's landing on 'B' beach.

He had been issued with American 'K'-type rations for the run-up to the operation but once they went into action, he would switch to his usual British mess-tin rations. While he was waiting for news of 44 RM, Larry passed the time investigating the contents of these novel US rations. There were separate packs for breakfast, dinner and supper, although the contents of each didn't differ wildly. The things that would probably have been of most interest were the ones he wasn't accustomed to: instant coffee, chewing gum, tinned cheese and Spam. There were even four cigarettes and a book of matches with each meal pack.

At eight o'clock in the evening, No. 5 began boarding four river steamers and two and a half hours later, after hearing that 44 RM's landing had been successful, the commandos continued on their journey. Private Rudy Blatt, one of the Dutch commandos who had been attached to No. 5, described what happened next in his memoirs:

All of a sudden we felt a shock in the boat. A few seconds later there was another shock, and then the boat came to a complete stop. The captain was all excited. He shouted commands to his native crew. We could hear the old engine making strange noises. He threw her into reverse, then forward, and into reverse again – with no luck. The boat did not move. Finally he gave up.[2]

Unfortunately, three of the steamers had become grounded on sandbanks in the middle of the river in the early hours of the morning. It was a nerve-racking time for Larry and the others on board as the vessels were in full view of the enemy. Rudy Blatt wrote, 'It started to get lighter then. This was the time we might come under Japanese fire. The minutes were hours. Finally we could feel it. There was movement in the boat. The new tide was coming in.'[3] By half past seven on the morning of 12 March they re-floated and an hour and a quarter later all of No. 5 had arrived in paradise.

When people close their eyes and try to imagine a tropical island, the images they conjure up are generally a very close match to St Martin's Island where the river steamers had moored. Coconut groves lined the white sandy beaches and the island's turquoise waters were clear enough to see the multi-colours of the darting fishes and the surrounding coral reef. With a two-day stay at the island, there was plenty of time for swimming and sunbathing. The islanders were incredibly friendly, probably because they were charging their visitors the inflated price of one rupee for a coconut.

When darkness began to fall, Larry spread his blanket out on the soft sand, wrapped himself in his mosquito net and lay down to sleep. What he hadn't realised was that he and his fellow commandos had chosen to settle down on top of a labyrinth of crab burrows and so their night's sleep was somewhat disturbed as the tetchy crabs kept attempting to break through their blankets and get to the surface.

On the morning of 14 March, No. 5's attention was turned back to much more serious matters as the time had come for them to relieve 44 RM. After all the months of training and preparation, Larry would finally be leading his men into action.

10

Operation Screwdriver

On 14 March 1944, at half past nine in the morning, the commandos began to board landing craft, manned by Royal Indian Navy crews, and head away from St Martin's Island. Rather than landing on one of the beaches, as 44 RM had done, they were to be set down on the muddy banks at the mouth of the Ton chaung (creek) in three waves. Larry's 6 Troop together with rear HQ, 5 Troop and the unit's stores would be the middle one of these three groups to land.

The first wave of 1 and 2 Troops arrived at eleven o'clock and formed a beachhead to give cover. Fifteen minutes later, Larry's group began to disembark, closely followed by the remainder of the Commando, who all landed safely and without incident. Then 1 and 2 Troops pushed on to Dodan village to take up another defensive position and Larry's troop followed behind with the heavy stores and equipment. Once the supplies had been securely stowed in Dodan and were under the guard of a party from 4 Troop, they moved off again, towards Kanyindan, and had their first sighting of a Japanese soldier, although he was quite some distance away. Their final destination was Alethangyaw, where the unit assembled and formed a defensive box just south of the village, close to the beach.

While they were in Alethangyaw, Larry was introduced to Major Denis Holmes, commanding officer of V Force, who was to assist them during the operation. V Force was a paramilitary unit comprising local men, who gathered intelligence about Japanese activities and carried out daring raids and rescues behind enemy lines. V Force scouts and members of the Burma Intelligence Corps would be attached to No. 5 and would be offering them valuable help and information.

The commandos' arrival had not gone unnoticed and their box came under occasional enemy fire during the evening from 75mm rounds and mortar bombs. They set about trying to pinpoint the enemy's position, somewhere over on a hill which had been designated 'Point 211'. Thanks to basic language lessons from the men of No. 10 (Inter-Allied) who were with them, 5 Commando took to passing radio messages to each other in Dutch, which meant that the Japanese – who had rapidly discovered the English network – couldn't understand what was being said.

It was only the following morning, when a patrol from 2 Troop came under fire from two machine guns at the base of Point 211, and Lieutenant Colonel Shaw's request for an air bombardment of the hill had been refused, that things began to develop.

At midday on 15 March, a section from Larry's 6 Troop, armed with a Vickers machine gun, left their Alethangyaw base and headed towards Hill 211. While they were advancing in single file over one of the raised bunds of the open paddy fields they came under heavy mortar fire but Larry's section managed to make it to the edge of some nearby woods, mount their Vickers gun facing the enemy and fire off a belt of ammunition towards the suspected position of the mortar. Meanwhile, the Demolition Officer had moved over to the left and let off a smoke screen to try and confuse the Japanese as to where the commandos' attack was coming from. Under the cover of the smoke, Larry's 6 Troop moved further into the woods.

They held their position for two hours, returning the enemy's fire and coming under repeated shelling. The decision was then made for all the troops to return to base. The CO's party and 3 Troop went first, taking the dead and injured with them – one man had been killed outright, one died of his wounds and fourteen had been injured – and 6 Troop followed soon after.

No. 5 Commando continued to come under attack throughout the following days. The stretcher-bearers were fired on while evacuating the wounded and troops all over the area were subjected to further enemy assaults, but the commandos held firm and fought back with great ferocity.

During a night-time mission as they crept stealthily through the darkness in single file, the silence was only occasionally broken by the rustle of the bamboo thickets or the howls of nocturnal animals. After about an hour of slow progress, several of the commandos suddenly threw themselves flat on the ground and the rest quickly followed, like a line of domino tiles toppling from one to the next. Soon everyone realised what had caused this reaction as the shrill chatter and heavy footsteps of a column of Japanese soldiers approaching from the right began to grow louder.

It wasn't until they were within just a few paces that the Japanese became aware of the commandos' presence and they barely had time to get down before No. 5 opened fire. Streaks of orange from tracer bullets and bursts of flame from grenade explosions gouged their way through the night-time darkness as an intense battle developed. Although the commandos had been ordered to fix bayonets, their incessant fire kept the Japanese far enough away that their use didn't become necessary. No. 5 managed to stand their ground until the Japanese eventually retreated. V Force reports started to come in suggesting that the enemy's losses had been high.

Larry and other officer representatives from each of No. 5's troops went to meet the second-in-command of the 81st West African Recce Regiment so that plans could be put into place for No. 5 to relieve their positions. It was arranged that all moves would be completed by the early hours of 18 March and Larry's 6 Troop would begin moving from their base, through Kanyindan and on to Dodan village at half past seven on the evening of the 17th.

As well as learning about their forthcoming objectives, Larry also learned why the Japanese seemed to be so frightened of the West Africans. It turned out that after having captured some Japanese soldiers, the West Africans took them to one of their *bashas* (Burmese thatched bamboo structures), where they had animal bones bubbling away in a large cooking pot. Licking their lips, the West Africans convinced them that they were the remains of former prisoners. They then let one of the Japanese soldiers 'escape' so that he could share this horrific tale with his comrades.

Thankfully the evacuation of No. 5's base on the 17th went according to plan and by ten o'clock Larry and his troop were in Dodan. An hour later, a standing patrol of four men was sent northwards and early the next morning they made a thorough search of the Dodan woods.

No. 5 were soon to be relieved by 44 RM and just before they left the area, RAF support finally arrived. A squadron of Hurricanes flew in low across Alethangyaw and strafed the enemy positions in an unrelenting burst of cannon fire that lasted for twenty minutes. As the Japanese began fleeing to the hills, No. 5 withdrew from Dodan, leaving 44 RM to take over, and headed towards Nahkaungdo, known to everyone as 'no can do'.

Just after four o'clock on the afternoon of 21 March, Larry boarded one of the first landing craft to depart from Nahkaungdo and by six o'clock he was in Maungdaw. He and his comrades from 2, 5 and 6 Troops formed a defensive box and by eight o'clock the following morning the whole unit was back together again. The rest of the day was spent in cleaning their weapons and enjoying some well-earned relaxation.

They barely had time to settle into their new surroundings when 4 and 5 Troops were ordered to go and help extricate a gun battery which was coming under machine-gun and rifle fire and was in danger of being overwhelmed by the Japanese. They succeeded in their aim, but while passing through a narrow valley on their way back to base they were ambushed by the Japanese and came under significant machine-gun fire. Some of the commandos were killed instantly, others received horrific injuries. 'Captain Kerr was badly wounded having his arm practically severed by machine-gun fire. Everywhere lay dead and wounded commandos. Those who could move tried to reach the cover of the jungle but were shot down immediately. Captain Kerr was again shot in both legs and lost consciousness. 4 Troop coming to the rescue brought 2-inch mortars into play and, after a while, they seemed to be having some effect. Just before dusk, Lieutenant Noble brought a stretcher party out into the open and, at great personal risk, took Captain Kerr to cover.'[1] Lieutenant Noble then returned alone a further five times and carried Rifleman Mick Collins and the other wounded commandos on his back to safety.

Although No. 5 had suffered heavy losses during Operation Screwdriver, the CO, David Shaw, was rightly proud of his men and in a covering letter enclosed with his official report of the part they played he wrote, 'I should like to put on record the fact that during the whole of this period the morale of the unit was first rate under the most trying conditions. The display of guts and the cheerfulness of all ranks was beyond praise.'[2]

No. 5 needed a chance to mourn their dead and to revive their spirits. They returned to Nhila, where a memorial service was held for the twenty-five who had been killed and prayers were said for the forty-three who had been injured. Larry's 6 Troop had suffered fewer casualties than the majority of other troops in the unit: Trooper Morris and Driver Perkin had been injured and Private Sanson had died of his wounds.

The focus then turned to relaxation and the rebuilding of morale. The men swam in the river, listened to the wireless and were entertained by a visiting concert party. But everyone knew that the rest period would soon be over.

11

Patrolling in Assam

At the beginning of April 1944, No. 5 rejoined 44 RM and boarded a train bound for Silchar in Assam, their new base. The train journey was long and uncomfortable with the men vacuum-packed into the dirty carriages. As well as the transfer to this new location, transfers were also being made among the personnel, with the result that Larry was moved from 6 Troop to 1 Troop.

Larry's new base was a riverside camp in the Kasipur Tea Gardens, seven miles east of Silchar, where the only amusements on offer were a canteen, a cinema and a Chinese restaurant. Further to the east of Silchar, the Japanese were battling the 14th Army at Imphal, putting Assam, with its important communication links, under threat, so the commandos had been brought in to patrol the tea gardens of Cachar and safeguard the area's railway line and the Bishenpur jeep track.

Larry's new 1 Troop was sent on detachment to the Digun Tea Estate to carry out the first round of patrols in the hills north-east of Silchar. Although there was little chance of him having to take on the enemy, Larry may well have embarked on his first patrol with some trepidation as he would be entering the domain of the Naga people, a tribe who were rarely mentioned without the epithet 'head-hunters'.

A series of stories had appeared in *The Times* between 1923 and 1927 claiming that the Nagas had a 'strange craving' for human heads. The newspaper described how several villages would join up to form a raiding party to go in search of their victims. All heads were considered to be of equal value, whether of a man, woman or child, and they were often obtained as a result of murder rather than through a fair fight. Although these articles were written twenty years before Larry arrived in the area, the practice continued – albeit on a smaller scale than described – and reports of head-hunting continued until as late as 1970.[1]

Looking at a contour map of the patrol area is a little like looking at a cross-section of the folds of chocolate in a Cadbury's flake. The hills rose up to heights of between 650 and 4,500 feet – slightly higher than Ben Nevis, which had become so familiar to Larry during his time at Achnacarry Castle. There were few other similarities with the Highlands of Scotland though, and the area was covered in thick jungle with a tangle of creepers knitting the tall trees together, and a network of fast-running streams. It was home to tigers, snakes, gibbons and leeches. The air was clammy with humidity and heavy with the weight of the approaching monsoon.

Larry's 1 Troop had to negotiate the terrain as far as Mahur, twelve and a half miles to the north, where they were to rendezvous with the 18th Battalion of the Mahratta Light Infantry, and then south to Urabil, where 5 Troop's patrol group were to be based.

Each patrol lasted for between three and five days. When following trackways they expected to average around twelve miles in a day. Any forays into the jungle itself significantly reduced the distance they could cover and became a slow hack through the dense foliage.

Dressed in a bush hat with a face veil, shorts, unbuttoned bush shirt and ammo boots or SV boots (lace-up army boots with vulcanised soles) with gaiters or puttees, Larry would rise at dawn and aim to have his patrol group on the move by six o'clock in the morning. He carried most of his equipment in a backpack but there were a number of items he needed immediate access to, including a razor blade for dealing with snake bites, which he kept in his hat band, salt for sprinkling on leeches and a watch which, if carried in his pocket, had to be covered with a condom to prevent moisture from seeping in. The commandos also took to wearing condoms in the more conventional location after word reached them that a member of 44 RM, based seven miles south of Silchar, had suffered a leech in his penis.

Each member of the patrol kept a lookout for leeches on the legs of the man in front of him and they would pause every fifty yards or so to thoroughly check their own legs and boots in the hope that they would be able to remove any leeches before they had the opportunity to bite. The commandos found that they could usually prise them off using the blade of a knife, but sometimes they would burn the leech with the end of a cigarette or sprinkle them with salt. The last two methods would cause the leech to drop off quickly but weren't the best idea from a medical point of view, since this caused the leech to regurgitate its stomach contents into the wound, potentially leading to infection. The US War Department released an Intelligence Bulletin in September 1943, in which they gave a little more information about leeches, writing that they 'try to reach mucous membranes and frequently enter the rectum or penis without attracting attention until an itching sensation begins. Urination usually removes them immediately from the penis, but medical help may be needed to remove one from the rectum. However, after satisfying their hunger, leeches frequently leave the rectum during defecation. This may produce a certain amount of blood flow, which may be mistaken for the beginning of dysentery or piles, but its short duration will remove all fears on that score.'[2]

Larry's group would take a five-minute break after each hour of walking and would try and avoid marching at the hottest part of the day, between half past ten in the morning and half past three in the afternoon; they would probably have used this time of day to rest and to eat. The rations they carried, which included tea, powdered milk, sugar, raisins and curry powder, were supplemented with whatever the jungle could provide. They would shoot monkeys and deer, skin them, cut them into small chunks and stew them with jungle fern and bamboo shoots, or they would buy cobs of corn from the villagers and eat them raw. Monkey wasn't always the most palatable meal, as Des Crowden recalled:

> I took this patrol out into Nagaland and found a village... I saw this lovely little hill with about six huts on it, two quite large. One was a Christian church and the big one was where most of the natives lived and they had a fire inside with no chimney... We had to stay a day longer and ran out of food so I took three chaps down into the jungle... and we shot two monkeys, a male and a female, one black, one golden brown, and took them back and the natives carved them up and cooked them over this fire with no chimney and it ended up like pieces of black leather. One chap refused to eat it but the rest of us were so hungry that we ate this monkey and it was awful![3]

The commandos' rations were often boosted by the Nagas who, far from being fearsome warriors, lurking in the undergrowth and waiting to murder them for their heads, were 'not only helpful but extraordinarily hospitable – embarrassingly so at times – to the infinite confusion of more than one patrol leader!'[4]

The Nagas were handsome and muscular and wore earrings made of brightly coloured feathers and necklaces of shells and flower petals. Their picturesque villages of thatched houses, made of bamboo, wood and cane, were planted on the breezy hilltops. The people were intensely loyal to the British and their help in the fight against the Japanese proved invaluable. An Indian Army observer provided details of some of their activities to *The Times* newspaper in 1942. He described how the Nagas waited patiently to ambush the patrols of Japanese soldiers and were so nimble and stealthy that they could wipe out the rear of a line of soldiers while the front group continued on their way, completely unaware that anything untoward was going on. Some of the Nagas set up camps close to where the Japanese were garrisoned and would sell chickens to the officers every day, enabling them to report back later to the British with detailed information about the enemy's troop numbers and movements. The patrols from No. 5 said of the Nagas that they would 'not easily forget the cheery people who killed the fatted calf for them and whose one hate was the Japs'.[5]

Once the midday heat had subsided, Larry's patrol group would get under way again and would continue moving forward until around six o'clock in the evening, being sure to stop for the night at least an hour and a half before dark. At the end of the day's march, everyone inspected their clothes and skin thoroughly for leeches and once they were sure they were clear, they could begin cooking or bedding down for the night.

The commandos had a strict anti-malaria discipline in place and before dusk Larry would hold a 'mepacrine parade' to make sure everyone swallowed a double dose of the anti-malaria tablet they took on a daily basis and which gradually turned their skin yellow. They all smeared their faces with anti-mosquito cream, changed into long trousers, rolled down their sleeves and settled themselves under a mosquito net.

When speaking to the Danish *Weekendavisen* newspaper in 2012, Danish volunteer with 5 Commando Frede Pedersen related that one of the best weapons he had while out on patrol in the jungle was an affectionate mongoose. The mongoose snuggled down next to him at night but it remained alert enough to chase any snakes away while

Frede slept. 'We should have had two or three more of them. A few soldiers were bitten by snakes. They were immediately given injections – it had to be fast if they were to survive,' he said.[6]

At the end of April, just before Larry's troop was relieved, he had a spell in hospital in Silchar. Whether his reason for being there was a snakebite, a wound infected by leech vomit or a dodgy monkey curry hasn't been recorded, but it was only a two-day stay and he was soon back at the Kasipur Tea Gardens HQ.

Life at HQ was rather dull, despite the fact that the ladies from the plantation used to bring chocolate cake to the commandos once a week. The rainfall was steadily increasing as the monsoon season gathered strength and the drip, drip of the rain rose in tempo while the mud levels crept up to ankle depth. There were few entertainments to be had and swimming was stopped when it was thought the river might be infected with cholera bacteria. However, Larry and No. 5's other officers had managed to find a new diversion at one of the neighbouring tea estates while out patrolling.

The Balladhun Tea Estate had a rather unfortunate history. In 1880 it had been raided by the Nagas, its houses burned and the manager, Peter Blyth, and several of his labourers had been killed; then, on the night of 11 April 1893, the house of the planter, at this time a Mr Cockburn, was attacked by a group of men. They killed the watchman who was asleep on the veranda, entered the house and murdered Cockburn, and chased the local woman he was cohabiting with into the jungle, injuring her so badly that she too died a few days later.

By 1944, the planter at Balladhun was James 'Jimmy' Sinclair, a man who hailed from country very familiar to the commandos: the Highlands of Scotland. Larry and the other officers enjoyed dropping in on Jimmy whenever they had the chance, to chat about the homeland, listen to his jungle tales and enjoy more civilised surroundings than they had back at the camp or out on patrol.

Sinclair's white bungalow stood on top of a *tillah* (hillock) about forty feet high, and if he was sitting out on his large open veranda, he could see if anyone was approaching through the patchwork of surrounding tea bushes. One day he caught a glimpse of someone making their way along the path leading to his bungalow and assuming it was one of his new commando friends he called out, 'What's the hurry? How about a cup of tea?' The man who climbed the steps up the *tillah* towards him wasn't from No. 5 though; he was Lieutenant Colonel James Williams, better known as 'Elephant Bill'.

The rangy, suntanned Williams had settled in Burma in 1920 after leaving his native Cornwall for a job with the Bombay Burma Trading Corporation as an elephant manager in the teak forests. In February 1942, he had helped to evacuate twenty women and fifteen children from Burma to India, leading the party to safety and using a train of elephants to carry their supplies. It was after this that he was invited to become elephant advisor to the Eastern Army and eventually he became commander of the 14th Army's Elephant Company.

When Elephant Bill Williams arrived at Jimmy Sinclair's bungalow at the end of April 1944, he had just completed another epic journey. His party, which had departed from the foothills to the west of the Imphal Plain on 5 April 1944, comprised forty-five elephants, forty Karen people, ninety elephant riders and attendants, sixty-four refugee Ghurkha women and children and four officers. Their 170-mile journey had involved them crossing mountains around 6,000 feet high, similar to the heights Hannibal's elephants were said to have climbed when they crossed the Alps on their way to Rome.

It must have been during a visit to the Balladhun bungalow that the officer in charge of 4 Troop learned of Elephant Bill's presence in the area, and realising what a unique opportunity it would be, he arranged for representatives from 1, 3 and 4 Troops to spend some time undergoing jungle training at the Elephant Camp, now settled a couple of miles from the tea estate. Larry was among those who attended and they learned more about feeding themselves in the jungle, shot, skinned and cooked giant tree squirrels, pigeons, barking deer and monkeys and foraged for edible vegetation. They also spent time with the Burmese Karen people, learning about their customs and their way of life.

As another change from patrolling in the hills of Assam and in an effort to relieve some of the tedium, the unit took part in a training exercise called 'Exercise Alethangyaw'. It was designed to practise what had been learned during Operation Screwdriver and to see if anything could be improved on for the future. Half of the troops acted the part of the Japanese enemy forces and took on the other half, who played themselves. Supporting roles were given to the locals, Jimmy Sinclair and the other tea planters, who had given their full cooperation in organising the exercise.

The 'Japanese' were to patrol an area around Lakhipur, which had been designated as the sea coast, and keep a continuous watch for the 'British', who would be making a fictional beach landing at another of the villages in the area before attempting to discover their enemy's position. Both sides were warned that they should avoid damaging the tea gardens and that under no circumstances should they interrogate or in any way interfere with the native women.

At the end of May, Larry and the other officers underwent a two-day 'Training Exercise Without Troops' (TEWT) to discover what lessons had been learned from Exercise Alethangyaw and what further training needed to be implemented. They found that recce patrolling was poor; information was passed back too slowly; interrogation skills were poor (but despite this the 'prisoners' still gave away too much information rather than just their name, rank and number); positions were given away easily and camouflage was poor. The exercise had served its purpose and No. 5's future training had been identified.

By the beginning of the following month, Larry was unwell again but this time there is little doubt as to what was wrong with him.

12
Malaria

On 9 June 1944, Larry was admitted to No. 9 Indian Malaria Forward Treatment Unit (MFTU) and spent two weeks there.

The mobile MFTUs had been established to provide a quicker turnaround in the treatment of men with uncomplicated cases of malaria. Previously, they would have endured a journey to a hospital some distance away to undergo around three weeks of treatment, followed by an additional period of convalescence, before travelling back to their unit, meaning they could be absent for as long as two months. The MFTUs were positioned closer to the battlefields and aimed to get men fighting fit again within a maximum of three weeks.

Malaria is transmitted by the bite of female anopheles mosquitoes and the symptoms usually begin to manifest themselves approximately two weeks after a bite. This would suggest that Larry was infected around the end of May, perhaps even during the two-day TEWT. At first he would have had a headache and muscle pains as his immune system kicked in and began to fight the parasites that were multiplying in his liver and travelling around his bloodstream; then he would have felt an icy chill snapping through his body and would have shivered and trembled it away as his temperature rose and rose, possibly beyond

100° (38° Celsius), at which point he would have started sweating profusely and may have begun to hallucinate. As his temperature began to drop again he would have felt the chill descending over him and the cycle would begin again.

No. 9 MFTU had opened on 27 May, just two weeks before Larry's admission, and was situated on the fringes of the jungle at a place known as the Dimapur Downs, seven miles from Silchar. Larry wasn't the only officer from No. 5 at the MFTU – Captain Housden followed him three days later, and Lieutenant Salt had arrived a week earlier – and they were accommodated and treated in the officers' ward, which was a large tent with stretchers spaced out on either side of a central gangway with mosquito nets draped over signal wire and hurricane lamps to provide the lighting. There were only fifty beds on site and these were reserved for the more serious cases, so most patients slept on stretchers which lay on top of bamboo frames to raise them two and a half feet above the ground. Larry was probably lucky enough to have had sheets on his stretcher bed, a luxury that was discontinued soon after, as the monsoon conditions were making it impossible to get the sheets dry after they had been washed.

When Larry was discharged from the MFTU on 24 June, he rejoined the men of his troop who had moved to Urabil and were carrying out patrols in the surrounding area. The weather was oppressively hot and humid and prickly heat rashes developed in folds of skin and crept under waistbands. Powerful and dramatic thunderstorms did nothing to clear the air.

In July, the patrol troops began to be recalled to the Kasipur Tea Gardens HQ and Larry and his troop were back there on the 10th. So it was in this malaria-ridden tea plantation of Assam, ankle-deep in mud and with the incessant splash of monsoon rain drumming in his ears that Larry reached the official mark of adulthood with his twenty-first birthday on 16 July 1944. He would have to wait for almost a month before he could celebrate properly though, as a Movement Order had been received and the unit had to pack up and be ready to leave Silchar on 27 July for a move south-west to Bangalore.

The 1,800-mile trip to Bangalore was incredibly boring and the monotony of the week-long journey was only broken up when transferring from one train to another. They finally arrived at six o'clock on the morning of 3 August and were taken by truck to their camp forty miles away at Thondebhavi.

No. 5 spent the next few days organising and settling into their new base camp, carrying out kit and arms inspections and ensuring all the administration was up to date, at which point they were granted fourteen days' leave. While some headed for the relative coolness of the hills, most had had enough of travelling and preferred to spend their leave in nearby Bangalore.

In the 1940s, Bangalore was very different from the metropolitan sprawl of India's 'Silicon Valley' today. Back then it was a large town with only one main street but it still offered far more opportunities for entertainment than most of the places No. 5 had been based since leaving Liverpool. While the men headed to Funnel's or the nearest Chinese restaurant to fill up with 'big eats', Larry and the other officers made their way towards the Bangalore United Services Club known as the 'Bus Club'.

Within the walls of the elegant Bus Club it was almost possible for Larry to believe himself to be back in the England of an earlier era. Sir Winston Churchill had made use of the club when he was stationed in the area in the late 1890s and had left behind an irrecoverable debt of thirteen rupees. After passing under the porte cochère, where memsahibs would have alighted from their carriages, and closing the entrance door behind him, Larry could forget about the war and India, even if only temporarily. When he wasn't sipping iced tea on the edge of the immaculate lawns, playing tennis or cooling off in the swimming pool, he could attend one of the regular dances held in the magnificent ballroom and flirt and waltz with young English roses (to misquote Major Bloodnok, 'let's live our moment, in Bangalore cantonment'[1]). One dance was organised especially for the officers of No. 5 and 44 RM and seventy-five ladies were invited to ensure there were plenty of dancing partners for all.

Another place that held particular interest for Larry was a music shop owned by Jose Mariano Dias. In the days of silent films, Mr Dias had been a violinist with the orchestra that provided background music at the Globe cinema in Bangalore but in 1927 – the same year as the first 'talkie' appeared – he went into business and opened his shop on Promenade Road. The shop was a treasure trove for serious musicians where an impressive array of instruments was available to buy or hire as well as scores for all the latest Western hits. As a music-lover and performer, Mr Dias welcomed fellow musicians into the shop and encouraged them to give impromptu performances, and it is not difficult to imagine Larry sitting down at one of the pianos and playing a medley of jazz tunes.

Music was never far from Larry's mind. He took advantage of his rest period to catch up with his letter-writing, and to his band leader, Dennis Hinton, he would generally write 'a long screed upon technicalities connected with tunes or arrangements'.[2]

On 22 August, the leave period was over and Larry and the rest of No. 5 returned to the camp at Thondebhavi. The men swapped stories of their drinking exploits and counted up all the pet monkeys they had managed to acquire while under the influence of alcohol.

While they had been away, memos had been flying backwards and forwards between various high-level acronyms – the CIC of this, the

GHQ of that and the DQMG of the other – to organise their next move. The twenty-six officers and 500 other ranks were to journey from Thondebhavi Camp back to Bangalore railway station on the morning of 2 September, where at midday they would board a train for a twenty-four-hour trip to Trichinopoly.

With eight hours to spare on their arrival in Trichinopoly until the start of the next leg of their journey, No. 5 were allowed into town and the men used the opportunity to take baths at the YMCA in the shadow of the Rock Fort, an historic complex built on a 273-foot rock. At eight o'clock that evening, they boarded another train for an overnight journey to Dhanushkodi.

From Dhanushkodi they took a ferry to Talaimannar in Ceylon, then a train to Trincomalee and finally they were transported by lorry to their new camp at Nilaveli, where they arrived in the late afternoon of 5 September. Lieutenant Carryer of 44 RM described their journey in a letter to his mother, telling her how grim it had been. He found one part of the trip particularly taxing as it involved eight hours of travelling third class on a train without a corridor and packed with locals who were spitting all over the place and smoking the most obnoxious weeds he had ever seen or smelt.

Nilaveli, meaning 'open land of moonshine' in the Tamil language, was a picture-postcard perfect location of palm trees nodding lazily on beaches of fine golden sands and a shoreline tickled by the topaz-blue sea. Although it was an ideal setting for a holiday (if they managed to ignore the rats clambering over their mosquito nets at night), the commandos had to focus on work as their time was to be spent undergoing intensive training. This didn't stop Larry and the other officers from visiting the Trinco Officers' Club from time to time though, where the stone lions guarding the entrance were said to almost bristle whenever they saw someone from No. 5 approaching.

First of all they had to go through the usual 'settling into a new camp' routine – administration, kit and arms inspections and so on – and it was during this period, two days after they had arrived, that No. 5's CO, David Shaw, announced he was relinquishing command of the unit and returning to his parent regiment, the Inniskillings. The next few days were a round of farewell parties and speeches for him in the canteen, in the Sergeants' Mess and in the Officers' Mess, and when he left on 11 September, 'his jeep was pulled out of the camp by ropes'.[3] In his place came Lieutenant Colonel Charles Pollitt MC, transferred over from 1 Commando.

When the training got under way, every morning began with twenty minutes of physical training and swimming for all at quarter past seven and then, after they had breakfasted, each troop followed different programmes for the rest of the day. Larry and the other officers had to ensure that they incorporated the weak areas highlighted during Exercise Alethangyaw and the two-day TEWT held at the end of May into the training at every possible opportunity, as well as the lessons that had been learned during Operation Screwdriver. The instruction over the next couple of weeks included lectures, first aid, demolitions, passing verbal messages, observation, night exercises and route marches. The culmination of the training was a parade for the new CO on Saturday 30 September followed by a kit and arms inspection and then an evening concert in the canteen.

Throughout the month of September there had been quite a lot of sickness in the unit. Corporal Robert Hay Shields of the Royal Army Medical Corps, who was attached to No. 5, recalled that 'some higher up said this was a non-malarial area so stop taking our mepacrine. Within a fortnight we had 140 cases of malaria on our hands.'[4] Numerous members of No. 5 were despatched to the No. 54 India General Hospital in Trincomalee. Larry's turn came again at the beginning of October but rather than being admitted to hospital in

Ceylon, for some reason he was sent on a long journey to the British Military Hospital in Bangalore. Perhaps he had succumbed to a more complicated case of malaria.

Larry was only at the hospital for a week, and the day before he was discharged, his comrades back in Ceylon had been mobilised to move at forty-eight hours' notice. They were going into action again.

13

On Operation in Godusara

On 14 October 1944, twenty-one officers, 421 other ranks and their seventy-five tons of baggage left the camp at Nilaveli to begin the journey back towards India. Although reinforcements had arrived during their time in Ceylon, so many of No. 5 were in hospital that their numbers had been significantly depleted. On 15 October, seemingly unaware of these developments, Larry boarded a plane in Bangalore towards Ceylon and arrived at Colombo later that same day.

Larry didn't return to Nilaveli to see tumbleweed blowing across a totally deserted camp and to wonder where all his friends had gone as, fortunately, Lieutenant Beasley, Lance Sergeants Skelton and Connah and Colour Sergeant Blake had remained behind. For logistical reasons, 44 RM were also still at the camp as they were following the route from Ceylon to India a day later than No. 5. Larry was briefed, collected his kit bag and weapons, settled his Mess bill, removed all identifying badges from his uniform, swapped his green beret for a slouch hat and left on the following day's ferry, chanting the mantra that had been impressed on all ranks to maintain secrecy: 'We do not know what unit we are in, where we are going, how we are going to get there or where we have come from.'[1] He managed to catch up with his No. 5 comrades in Madras where they had begun boarding the SS *Rajula* during the morning of 18 October and at half past six the following morning they set sail.

Three days later, they arrived in familiar waters and anchored off Chittagong before transferring onto landing craft. They passed St Martin's Island, entered the Naf River, disembarked at Teknaf and then marched to camp a mile away, where they found No. 1 Commando and 42 RM waiting for them. All four units comprising the 3rd Commando Brigade were now together again for the first time in eight months. The arrival at the new location signalled another change for Larry and he was transferred from 1 Troop to 2 Troop on 25 October 1944.

The commandos were accommodated in bashas (temporary structures constructed from bamboo and jungle vegetation) rather than tents, so No. 5 set about making improvements to the rather primitive camp. Once 'matchets had been sharpened and bamboo craft been brought into play discomfort was a thing of the past',[2] although the washing facilities still left a lot to be desired as there was just a single stream to be used by all.

They managed to get everything in order just in time for three important visits: on 27 October the new Deputy Brigade Commander, Colonel Peter Young, paid an inspection visit and the following day Brigadier Nonweiler arrived to discuss the latest operational instructions. The Commando Brigade units were to be dispersed across the Teknaf area and would be defending the Naf peninsula, preventing any attempts by the enemy to land. In addition, they would be undergoing their most intensive training to date. A few days later the Commander of the 15th Corps, Lieutenant General Sir A. F. P. Christison, also paid a visit to the camp.

Captain Norman Housden recalled that during a patrol training session, as he led Larry and his 2 Troop comrades along a paddy bund in single file, he was forced to make a sudden stop as a huge cobra was on the bund just in front of him, its head swaying as if it was about to strike. Captain Housden's knowledge of snakes was very limited so he shouted back for Lieutenant John Salt to come and help him. Lieutenant Salt had lived in Southern Rhodesia before the war and so Housden felt sure Salt would have much more experience with the reptiles and would know what to do. Lieutenant Salt took control and rapidly assessed the situation. He raised his rifle and took aim at the cobra's head and then emptied an entire magazine but failed to hit it once. The snake looked at him with disdain for a while and then slithered off the bund and disappeared. The following day, some musketry practice sessions were hastily arranged and as each troop underwent separate daily training programmes, Larry found himself out on the firing range, teaching his 2 Troop men all the intricacies of hand-held two-inch mortars and the Garand rifles they had recently been issued with.

They continued with their planned schedule and No. 5 'earned a vigorous back clap from the Brigade Commander for the enthusiasm and skill which they put into all their training'.[3] As well as the usual lectures, demonstrations, drill and exercises, Larry and the other officers attended meetings with a variety of high-ranking visitors and had regular conferences with No. 5's CO.

During a conference held on 16 November, the officers were given brief details of a forthcoming operation and were told that they should prepare themselves and the men for an imminent move for a raid on Buthidaung, where they would try to establish how many Japanese were in the area, what units they belonged to, what the names of the officers were, what their recent movements had been and what armaments they possessed.

While they waited for further instructions, they passed the time as best they could. Larry settled down in his basha and began writing a letter to his girlfriend, Margery. Five of his letters to her are held in the archives at the Imperial War Museum and give us a rare opportunity to read about his life in his own words.

Larry described to Margery the different ways in which he tried to keep himself amused:

> I pass my spare time nowadays in the most ridiculous pursuits (I mean those other than drinking, of course). Included are writing the beginnings of novels, operas, ballets, symphonies, swing tunes and poetic epics and then tearing them up. It is all quite pointless of course but I have lost the ability to amuse myself by reading and I have no piano so I have to do something. It stops me from going utterly screwball. My greatest effort so far was a full-blooded opera which brought in a boogie, a fan dance, a murder, rape and green beer. The hero was a left-handed tea addict named Gunsbury F. Gunsbury. Unfortunately I grew tired of the whole affair during the second act so I threw it away. The only thing I retained was the music for the fan dance. I will bring it back and play it and you shall do the fan dance. If you haven't got a fan it doesn't matter as you can do the dance and I will imagine the fan. We might even tour the music halls together. We should be a great success, especially without a fan.[4]

Larry's letter-writing was interrupted by the sound of firing close to his basha. He crept cautiously outside to investigate but it turned out to be Freddie Hoyle, a fellow officer, attempting to shoot a stray dog that was wandering around the camp. Not long afterwards, more hullabaloo alerted him to a fire in the neighbouring paddy field. Major Bray, affectionately known as 'Woner', had lobbed a smoke grenade into the field and half a dozen officers were attempting to beat out the resulting blaze.

Thankfully, more gentle pursuits were on offer in the Mess later that day and Larry and Lieutenant 'Dicky' Dixon played draughts while drinking their tea. Not being a draughts player, Larry lost two games out of three but it didn't bother him too much as he had been beating Dicky at chess for a year. In preparation for the forthcoming action, Dicky was waiting for one pair of his shorts to be dyed green and his batman was in the process of washing his other pairs. Consequently, he had none to wear and so he 'appeared dressed in a bush jacket and a tiny pair of underpants and calmly sat down in the Mess. As the bush jacket reached down further than the underpants, the effect was rather startling and he had a series of improper proposals made to him by several of the officers present.'[5]

By 20 November, the unit was back on high alert and ready to tackle the mission that lay ahead of them at Buthidaung; the adrenalin was flowing and they were keen to get started, so the air well and truly fizzled out of their collective balloon of anticipation when Colonel Young announced that the operation had been cancelled.

The deflation was short-lived though, as another Warning Order was published just two days later ordering Larry and his 2 Troop to be at Teknaf jetty by midday on the 23rd. The total force would be composed of 1 and 2 Troops, the CO and his batman, the Adjutant and his batman and representatives from the Intelligence, Signals and Medical Sections.

The party left camp at eleven o'clock on the 23rd under the command of Major Stuart and headed for the jetty. Once there, they boarded a steamer to cross the Naf River, and when they reached land on the other side they piled into waiting lorries and were driven to the village of Nalpannya to spend the night.

The following morning, they rendezvoused with representatives from 44 RM and with the help of their Royal Marines comrades, they spent the rest of the day inching forward until they reached the hill that would become their base until the end of the month. This feature had been codenamed 'Breast' and although it was only a single breast it no doubt provided ample opportunity for double entendres. Larry and his comrades established their positions on Breast and dug in.

The daylight hours of the week-long operation were mostly passed either out on patrol or in laying ambushes. The cold damp nights were spent in their trenches and the attempts to keep warm combined with the noisy squeals of frightened wild animals made sleep difficult. They also seemed to be under constant shellfire, day and night.

The lack of sleep resulted in frayed nerves and jumpiness. Some of the commandos began to fire or throw grenades towards any noises they heard. The 'trigger-happy' problem had also been exacerbated by general boredom as the men didn't have enough to keep them entertained. Larry and the other officers were told that for future operations they would need to ensure there were plenty of books and writing materials to go round and that rest periods would have to be enforced. Larry had more to fill his time as he had to 'supervise routine cleaning of weapons, taking of mepacrine, salt tablets, shaving, foot inspections...'[6] The general malaise had manifested itself in other ways among the officers and NCOs though, and they were later told by their superiors that they needed to put more effort into writing their patrol reports.

They were relieved by the Oxford and Buckinghamshire Light Infantry Regiment on the last day of November 1944 and were all glad to get away. There was only so much Breast they could handle. The return journey was mostly on foot: four miles back to Nalpannya for another overnight stay, a six-mile march the following day as far as the Naf River and then they were transported by steamer as far as Teknaf, covering the final mile back to base camp on foot again.

Back in his basha, while Lieutenant 'Dicky' Dixon lay fast asleep on Lieutenant Bill Stockton's bed, stark naked and undisturbed by the occasional burst of machine-gun fire on the range, Larry took the opportunity to write another letter to his girlfriend, Margery, although, as he admitted to her, he began writing with no idea of what he was going to say. He started off with a general muse on whether or not it would be possible for him to commit his stream of thoughts to paper. He asked if she had read James Joyce or Virginia Woolf, both of whom had tried to represent the endless train of thought of an individual. In Larry's opinion, Woolf's 'stream of consciousness' ended up being rather stylised and Joyce's technique became more and more abstract until he was almost completely unreadable. He suggested Margery get in touch with his sister, who had all of his books on the subject:

> I think you should meet Margaret (my sister) sometime, darling and establish Diplomatic Relations with the family. I think you would like Margaret and I can easily arrange for her to contact you. She is only fifteen (or sixteen, I forget which) but is a lot older in mind. She has passed School Cert and as far as I can gather, is going on to Varsity eventually and taking bio-chemistry (or something equally fantastic). Her interests are biology, literature and people. Her attitude towards the latter is somewhat cynical but that will change. Just as I was at her age (and for many years later) she is very intolerant.[7]

Larry complained that his creative inspiration had dried up and this meant he hadn't started writing any more operas or ballets. He felt sure that a fortnight with Margery would get his juices flowing again! He imagined their post-war future together:

> I shall run a night club and you will live in a luxury flat and do nothing except maybe bring a few suckers to the club to be rooked. The idea is that you raise their hopes just far enough to

make them follow you round to the club and only when they have spent about twice as much as they can afford impress gently upon them that you are a virgin white as driven snow and bid them goodnight. It's a great system – we should be able to retire at a very early age.[8]

He rounded off his letter with an extract from his 'famous melodrama', echoes of which would later appear in the *Goon Show*, most notably in the first programme of the second series:

VILLAIN: The time has come; the rent is due; the cottage is mine and so are you!! (He ends the speech with a terrifying laugh)
HEROINE (THE VILLAGE MAIDEN): I could never fall for you; because your chin is rough & blue – You should use Whisto, the wonder shave-cream!!
TRIUMPHANT FANFARE FROM THE ORCHESTRA. THE VILLAIN QUICKLY SHAVES WITH WHISTO THE WONDER SHAVE CREAM AND THEY EXECUTE A RHUMBA WITH CONSIDERABLE VERVE AND DEXTERITY. HE WHIPS HER THROUGH A DOOR MARKED 'BEDROOM', BOWS TO THE AUDIENCE AND FOLLOWS, SMIRKING IN AN ANTICIPATORY MANNER
(CURTAIN)[9]

Series 2, episode 1 of the *Goon Show* included a sketch entitled 'Broadcasting in 1999' in which adverts for fictional products such as Lurgi loaf, Sludge vitamin spread and the Bolohackenbrack hydrostatic razor were inserted into the dialogue in much the same way as Whisto had been in Larry's letter to Margery.

* * *

For the rest of December, Larry's thoughts began to focus on a much-anticipated Christmas. Three hundred ducks had been delivered to the Brigade at the end of November and they were being nurtured and fattened in a wire-fenced enclosure, upon which hung a sign reading, 'No sniping: this is your Christmas dinner!' There was an anxious moment two weeks before Christmas when 'Air Dispatchers in Dakota aircraft, which dropped the SEAC newspapers to camp, tried to "bomb"'[10] the ducks, and the men and officers of No. 5 could only pray that they missed as they had no way of protecting them.

Christmas dinner was greatly anticipated as the commandos' everyday meals weren't so much cordon bleu, more a déjà vu style of cuisine: soya link sausages and 'train smash' (tinned tomatoes) for breakfast and dehydrated potato and bully beef for dinner. They were so bored with their repetitive diet that one member of the Brigade felt compelled to compose a poem on the subject:

… And as for the food,
I could be really rude
And mention that bloke 'Soya Link'.

Sometimes it's in batter
But it really don't matter,
It's subject to no camouflage.

It's really disgusting –
My 'tum's' nearly busting
Through eating the old bread and marg![11]

The unit played host to more VIPs during December: Major General Robert Laycock, the Chief of Combined Operations, spent a couple of days with them and by the middle of the month whispers that Admiral Lord Louis Mountbatten would be visiting them again began to circulate.

The rumours were true and Lord Louis swept into camp for an overnight stay on 19 December, surrounded by a scramble of reporters, photographers and film crews. Larry managed to miss him yet again as the day before Mountbatten's arrival he had been admitted to a casualty clearing station – a type of mobile field hospital. A new Medical Officer, Captain Goldstone, had been posted to No. 5 on the 18th so it was probably he who insisted Larry receive treatment for whatever wound or condition he was afflicted with.

A couple of days before Captain Goldstone's arrival, another new officer had come to the camp in Teknaf to join No. 5 Commando. Lieutenant Sidney 'Nick' Bryant was five years older than Larry but the pair hit it off straight away and quickly became close friends, always making a point to seek each other out in the Officers' Mess.

Larry had now been overseas for a year and had covered almost 10,000 miles by road, rail, air and water with a large proportion of these miles on foot. He had spent time in three different countries and four different hospitals.

He returned to camp on 23 December, just in time for the festive celebrations. When the dinner gong – fashioned from a shell casing – was struck on Christmas Day, Larry entered the Officers' Mess, which had been decorated with strips of coloured fabric and cotton-wool snowflakes. After a tomato soup starter, the plump ducks were served up with stuffing, sausages, roast potatoes, Brussels sprouts and peas. This was followed by a brandy-soaked Christmas pudding containing three silver sixpences, jelly, fresh and crystallised fruits, nuts and raisins and was all washed down with plenty of beer. Halfway through their meal they paused to listen to the King's eight-minute speech on the wireless, which he addressed to the millions spread out across the world. After dinner, the officers toasted their loved ones and raised a glass to their wives, sweethearts, parents and siblings. They continued raising glasses until the early hours, resulting in 'half an inch of gin on the floor of the Officers' Mess the morning after!'[12]

The break continued over the next couple of days. On Boxing Day, 44 RM's officers held a party and invited their counterparts from the other units of the Brigade. A dance band provided the background music and the nibbles on offer included chocolate, nuts and raisins, and sausages on toast. On the 27th, No. 5 spent a day of recreation at the beach but they got back to the business of training the following day.

It soon became obvious that the latest training was in preparation for more action and sure enough, on 31 December 1944, details were announced. An assault on Akyab Island, codenamed 'Operation Lightning', was set to take place on 3 January 1945.

14

Operation Lightning and Operation Pungent

The target date for Operation Lightning had originally been set for mid-February but during December intelligence had been received to suggest that the enemy were withdrawing, leaving Akyab only lightly defended. It was therefore decided to strike as soon as possible. This meant No. 5 had less than three days to clear their hangovers and prepare.

On New Year's Day 1945, Brigadier Hardy and No. 5's CO, Charles Pollitt, briefed all ranks on the forthcoming operation. It was believed that a battalion of the Japanese 111th Regiment was on the island, their troops numbering around 700. Recent air reconnaissance flights suggested that most of the enemy's defences were in a dilapidated state, but the beaches were believed to be mined and there were wire fences close to where the commandos would be landing, as well as five machine-gun bunkers connected by trenches.

Half an hour before sunrise on the following day, the commandos moved out of their camp and in the sheltered waters of the Naf River at Teknaf they embarked on two destroyers, Larry boarding HMAS *Napier*. They anchored off St Martin's Island for a few hours and then at six o'clock in the evening, they set sail again.

While they were at sea, an artillery air observation officer carrying out a further recce of Akyab was unable to see any sign of the enemy. He landed in a paddy field and was greeted by the local inhabitants who presented him with garlands of flowers and told him that the Japanese had evacuated the island. As this meant the commandos would be landing unopposed, it was decided to cancel the preliminary bombardment that had been planned. Despite forecasts of stormy conditions on the way, the commanders wanted the landing to go ahead.

Back on HMAS *Napier*, Larry first heard the news in an announcement made over the tannoy: 'Well chaps, it looks like this will be nothing more than a ruddy club run. We have just received a report that the Jap has left Akyab Island. The aerial and naval and artillery bombardments have been called off, but the rest of the operation will go on as planned. Watch your step just the same – there are reported to be mines and booby traps all over the place and there might be a few snipers.'[1]

At half past ten on the morning of 3 January, the commandos transferred into assault landing craft (LCA). Larry was the officer in charge of craft number six which contained the thirty men of 2 Troop's number 3 Section. While Larry and the men crouched down low inside, the LCA moved away from HMAS *Napier* and joined a line of others, unfurling like a long ribbon and then fanning out as they approached the shore. The sound of bagpipes bobbed across the waves from one of the other craft.

As the first LCAs touched down, the commandos ran up the soft sandy beach, wriggled through the wire fence and headed towards the line of bushes and trees just beyond. They pointed loaded rifles into the slits of bunkers that had been sunk into the sand dunes and checked the crumbling trenches that snaked between them but all were empty.

Five minutes later the next wave of LCAs landed, together with a film cameraman who shot footage of the commandos smiling into the lens as they waded ashore. Three of the men drove a branch into the sand and tied a white ensign to it, before joining their comrades who were now assembling on the beach and getting ready to box in for the night. Colonel Young recalled it as being a very gentlemanly operation, as even though he couldn't describe it as a dry landing, he had the time afterwards to sit on the beach in peace, remove his boots and socks and let his feet dry.

For the next two days, No. 5 cautiously made their way towards Akyab Town. They marched across open dusty ground and through corridors of long grass that waved either side of them in the breeze. Film from the time shows them passing the camera in single file, looking bored and chewing gum. Larry stands out as one of the few commandos wearing sunglasses.

By the time they arrived in Akyab Town and succeeded in 'liberating' it on 5 January 1945, they had passed scenes of devastation and neglect. There wasn't a single building that hadn't been ravaged by the Japanese and they had stripped them of their corrugated-iron and wooden roofs. The jungle had started to reclaim some of the land and was in the process of swallowing up roads and sticking leafy tongues through broken windows. Peeling painted notices and signs hanging precariously from crumbling buildings pointed to the past: 'Akyab Hotel'; 'Exit – Saloon Passengers'; 'Mackinnon, Mackenzie and Co'. Stone lions roared at creepers winding their way around pagodas and felled Buddhas lay on beds of brick and rubble. The town clock had stopped at five minutes past three.

Small groups of locals began to come out of hiding, waving white flags but greeting the commandos with open arms, proffering an occasional egg or chicken. The Japanese had poured paraffin over all the supplies of rice they had left behind so there wasn't much else to offer.

Larry and his No. 5 comrades took up residence in bungalows on the waterfront and spent a quiet few days until a Japanese air raid on the harbour blew the peace apart. Four of the planes were shot down and thankfully little damage was done.

Whereas the capture of Akyab Island had turned out to be little more than a training exercise, the next operation, codenamed Pungent, wouldn't be such a breeze. The Brigade was to seize and hold the Myebon Peninsula, a five-mile gnarled finger of land, thirty miles south-east of Akyab, which pointed down through the Bay of Bengal towards the teardrop-shaped Dog Island. Once captured, the peninsula would be used as a base to launch further attacks against the enemy. A motor launch carrying Brigadier Campbell Hardy and a small party had come under fire while carrying out a reconnaissance of the area so it seemed there was little chance of another unopposed landing.

At quarter past nine on the morning of the 11th, No. 5 boarded HMIS *Jumna*, an Indian Navy Black Swan class sloop. Plans for the operation hadn't been finalised until the previous afternoon, leaving only twenty hours for the unit to prepare, embark, issue orders and brief the troops.

Hardy's recce party had identified a sturdy fence of coconut stakes along the coast just above the low water mark with the eight- to ten-inch-diameter stakes spaced about ten feet apart. As this would prevent the approach of landing craft, a Combined Operations Pilotage Party (COPP) was sent in at low tide to deal with the problem. At quarter to three on the morning of the 12th, the COPP team paddled three canoes towards the line of stakes and connected time-delayed charges to them so that they would detonate before H Hour – set for half past eight – and blow a gap wide enough for the craft to pass through. At half past six the charges successfully detonated and cleared a twenty-five-yard opening.

After a night on board HMIS *Jumna*, No. 5 disembarked into mechanised landing craft (LCM) at quarter to seven and began the approach to 'Charlie Red' beach, which was situated along the fingernail at the bottom of the Peninsula. Each commando carried twenty-four-hour jungle rations and an Australian Emergency Ration pack containing around 1,400 calories-worth of sweets, chocolate, tea, sugar and salt. Once again Larry was to command 3 Section in landing craft number six, but this time 42 RM would land first. As there was a shortage of available vessels, the operation commanders had had to choose between sending guns or tanks to support the commandos. They opted for tanks and consequently a troop of the 19th Lancers would be landing fifteen minutes after 42 RM to give support. The plan was for 5 Commando to land ten minutes later and for the support of the 19th Lancers to then switch to them. No. 1 and 44 RM would follow.

A preliminary air and naval bombardment of the coast took the Japanese completely by surprise and then, under the cover of a smoke screen, 42 RM landed on time. The first of the 19th Lancers' tanks began to trundle out of its landing craft, but despite being fitted with wading apparatus, it became bogged down in the mud hidden below the surface of the water. The attempt to land further tanks was abandoned.

By quarter past nine, No. 5's LCMs had begun to touch down just off Charlie Red beach close to Agnu village. The beach was 700 yards long with a line of rocks on one side and the path to it from the landing point involved thick mud, a strip of sand and then a row of trees reaching to a height of about forty feet.

Larry and his section disembarked and plunged into chest-high water. They began to wade gingerly ashore, their feet being sucked down into the mud, holding hands every now and then to help keep each other upright and ever conscious of the 'many shell craters that were covered by the high tide'.[2] Enemy machine-gun and artillery fire tried to pick them off as they made their slow progress towards dry land and shells exploded in front of them, clouds of smoke billowing up above the treetops. Clusters of mines waited for them further forward, looking like metal 'space hoppers' that had been buried up to their necks in the sand. As they laboured towards the shore, Larry watched in horror as the Royal Naval Beach Master, who had already made it onto the beach, walked a few paces before sitting down. There was a loud explosion and the Beach Master disappeared; he had sat on one of the concealed mines. Larry and his 2 Troop men were lucky and made it through unscathed. They joined the other troops and began forming up behind 42 RM. No. 5 Commando's 3 Troop hadn't been so fortunate: Lance Corporal Toms had been killed outright, Lance Corporal Scobie died of his injuries and Private Sawyer was wounded by another of the beach mines.

Meanwhile, No. 1 Commando was landing. The tide had moved further out so the muddy path was getting longer. They plunged into what they thought was water but instead found themselves planted in three feet of glutinous grey mud, topped with a foot of water. Every step took an almighty effort as they wrenched a foot out of the sludge and swung it forward, only to feel it being sucked down again. It took them an hour to get from their landing craft onto firm ground and they considered themselves lucky when they reached the beach and realised that another Commando was setting off behind them.

The commandos of 44 RM, acting as the reserve unit, were directed to land at 'Dog' beach. Unfortunately the order was misunderstood and they too were taken to Charlie Red. It took them three hours to get through the soft, sticky, waist-deep mud.

Another attempt was made to land the tanks, this time at 'Baker' beach, but they came under heavy shell fire and only one of them managed to make it ashore. The tanks' landing craft changed course again and the tanks eventually managed to land at 'Easy' beach but then a road had to be cleared through the boulders by the Madras

Sappers and Miners before they could finally make it round to Charlie Red the following day.

The commandos could have had a much easier landing if the scientific advisors at HQ had taken heed of a warning they received about the mud. Instead, they simply studied aerial photographs of the area and declared that the beach was firm.

In the meantime, Larry and his No. 5 comrades had started to push forward. They headed north towards Myebon village and met little opposition until they were crossing open paddy just under a mile away from the village. Suddenly Larry heard an unmistakable 'brrratatat' and three machine guns opened fire on them from a hill codenamed 'Rose'. Before they could retaliate or take cover, 3 Troop's Fusilier Reeves fell dead to the ground and Sergeant Dalziel was wounded.

No. 1 Troop continued to work their way forward until they too came under fire – rifle shots cracked towards them from 'Pagoda Hill' alternating with bursts of machine-gun fire. Although Major Bray, Signalman Bridley and Fusilier Howard were wounded, the troop managed to kill two of the enemy and lay a smoke screen, enabling 3 Troop to withdraw from their exposed position and into the woods fringing the paddy field. Stretcher bearers then evacuated the wounded men and 1 Troop followed into the woods.

Larry's friend Lieutenant Bryant with 4 troop led a patrol around the right-hand side of Rose but they came under mortar fire, fortunately sustaining no further casualties. It had now become apparent that No. 5 would not be able to advance any further until Rose was captured and as it was too late in the day to mount a full-scale assault, the unit withdrew and formed a defensive box for the night.

They had a few hours of peace, which gave Larry and Corporal John Wall, who were on 'stag' (sentry duty) together for some of the time, a chance to chat. Larry had always struck John as being quite a straight-laced young man and certainly not as boisterous as the majority of the other officers. He was well known for his skill in playing the piano and clearly passionate about music. Their conversation turned to football, a subject that elicited a strong reaction from Larry as he detested the sport. Even though John was more of a rugby league man, he put up a stout defence for football and eventually brought their good-natured verbal spat to an end by pointing out to Larry that even though he didn't like piano-players, he didn't criticise them all. Luckily Larry took the comment in good part.

It was back to business just after half past two in the morning when the Japanese directed a long burst of machine-gun fire towards No. 5's box and continued to do so for the next hour and a half. During this time, plans were being finalised for the assault on Rose and at quarter to eight the commandos moved 300 yards further back into the woods in preparation for the preliminary air bombardment that was set to take place. After a twenty-minute airstrike, No. 5 charged forward and with the support of two tanks from the 19th Lancers, quickly succeeded in seizing the hill from the enemy.

By 14 January, No. 5 had moved slightly north of Rose to 'Onion', a hill that had been gained by 1 Commando the previous day. From here they would be moving further up the peninsula to assault hill features codenamed 'Father' and 'Brother'.

At nine o'clock on the morning of the 15th, 3 Troop began the assault of Brother under covering fire from Larry's 2 Troop and the 19th Lancers' tanks. The only resistance they encountered came in the form of grenade dischargers fired from over on Father. While 3 Troop consolidated at the southern tip of Brother and sent a recce patrol towards the northern perimeter, 2 Troop moved across to the bottom of Father without meeting any opposition. They began to edge their way up the jungle-clad hill, with Larry's 3 Section taking the left-hand side and Lieutenant John Salt's 4 Section on the right, pausing when they reached the now strangely silent Japanese trenches at the crest of the hill. The CO, Charles Pollitt, together with Captain Charles Beard, then set off with a small recce party in the direction of the northern tip of the hill but they had progressed only 300 yards when the Japanese broke their silence and opened up with machine guns. The recce party threw themselves to the ground and began to return the fire while a runner dashed back towards Larry and his section with orders for urgent assistance.

When Larry arrived at the position, he pushed forward with a fighting patrol and for the next forty-five minutes they attacked and fought trench after trench. Thankfully the enemy resistance didn't appear to be very well organised. Eventually the Japanese were silenced again, and at the cost of only two injured men, Larry and his section had secured the northern segment of Father. He counted twenty-four enemy dead and surmised from the pools of blood on the ground and the discarded blood-stained clothing they later found, that a high number must have been wounded. In a personal letter, Lieutenant John Salt declared that they 'very definitely got their own back for last year'.[3]

By now it was half past five in the afternoon. Larry and the rest of his 2 Troop pals dug in for the night and were soon joined by the remainder of their unit together with other units from the Brigade. Lieutenant Carryer of 44 RM gave his impressions of the recent actions in a letter home to his mother and described how magnificent the support they received had been. He told her the combination of artillery, ships and aircraft produced more noise than he had ever heard in his life and commented how brave the Japanese were in the face of the onslaught. He saw one of the Japanese soldiers take out a bayonet and commit hara-kiri with it after being shot.

Larry ended up staying on Father for the next few days and had a grandstand view of air strikes over on features of the landscape that had been tagged 'Guinness', 'Sherry' and 'Gin', the ingredients for a lethal cocktail. He also had a perfect view of an assault by the Gurkhas of 74 Brigade on Feature 262, a pagoda-topped hill, and 'saw the earth covering which the Japs had used to conceal the pagoda being chipped away by the shells from the tanks and artillery, and… the Gurkhas steadily advancing to the top despite intense fire from the enemy'.[4]

Now that the Myebon Peninsula had been cleared of enemy forces and was in the hands of the Allies, the Japanese escape and supply routes in the Arakan had almost all been blocked. The one exception was the Myobaung–Tamandu road. The village of Kangaw, eight miles from Myebon, was at a key point along this road and was to be the next target for the commandos, but getting across the heavily defended area would not be easy.

15

The Battle of Hill 170

It was decided that rather than travel overland to Kangaw, 3 Commando Brigade would make the approach by water. First they would travel along the Thegyan River and then follow the meandering, narrow Daingbon Chaung (*chaung* means a small river or stream), a total distance of twenty-seven miles. Once there, they would form a bridgehead for 51 Brigade to pass through and into the village. At half past eight on the morning of the 20th, Larry and the rest of No. 5 left Father and set up camp near the beach at the south end of the peninsula.

COPP parties had been surveying the length of the Daingbon Chaung to find suitable landing points for the Brigade and No. 5 were allocated to 'George Beach'. The word 'beach' was a rather misleading description as the terrain comprised mangrove swamps leading into paddy fields, waterlogged by the spring tides.

During the early afternoon of the 21st, the commandos marched back to Easy Beach from where they were taken in LCMs to the minesweepers that would ferry them as close to the *chaung* as possible. They set sail the following morning and while the minesweepers anchored midstream in the *chaung*, the commandos transferred back onto the LCMs with 1 Commando setting off first. By the time No. 5 followed an hour later, the Japanese were expecting them and shelled them as they approached George Beach, but thankfully Larry and his comrades didn't suffer any casualties whereas 'small arms could have done untold harm'.[1]

After they had picked their way through the tangle of slippery mangrove roots and reached the paddy, they could see the main obstacle between the *chaung* and the village of Kangaw looming up in front of them: a wooded hill codenamed 'Brighton'. The highest point of the feature reached 170 feet and so it came to be more commonly referred to as 'Hill 170'. They arrived to discover that No. 1 had already cleared most of the hill and were now in trenches facing the enemy, who were stubbornly clinging on to the northern tip. No. 5 settled in the southern section, dug in and brewed up.

Overnight the Japanese on the extreme north of the hill attacked No. 1's positions but were repelled by every conceivable method and at first light No. 1 put in a fierce counter-attack and managed to run the enemy off the hill. The other units of the Brigade were having equal success with 44 RM established on a neighbouring hill tagged 'Pinner' and 42 RM over on 'Milford'.

The Japanese were not willing to give up these important positions so easily though, and over the next few days they bombarded the commandos with shell, mortar and small-arms fire. At one point, 160 shells landed on Hill 170 within the space of ten minutes. There were 'many lucky escapes and negligible casualties, largely due to a good many dud Jap shells... The lads all got up and cheered at each dud.'[2] However, 'with all-too-regular attention from the Jap artillery the Unit lost many old and valued friends and trenches grew palatial in depth and security'.[3]

From 28 January, Larry and No. 5 were moved from hill to hill in the area, helping out as and where they were needed, finally settling on Pinner on the 29th. The Japanese shelling was relentless and they suffered more casualties.

Plans were being made for the Brigade to begin withdrawing on the 31st for some well-earned rest and for a regiment of the Punjabs to gradually take over their positions. Little did they know, however, that around the same time General Miyazaki, commander of the enemy forces, had issued a Special Order of the Day:

> In the past battle opportunities have been lost because passive, conservative, slow-witted NCOs have been ineffectively commanding and controlling their men. The fact that the true worth of the Imperial Army was not in evidence at this time is the responsibility of every Division Group Commander and every Battalion Commander. This is extremely regrettable and is a state that cannot be tolerated. All combat is now to be carried out with careful planning and daring and the following action must be taken: If no order to the contrary is received, each defensive position must be held until the death of the last soldier. Those withdrawing without orders will be severely punished under the penal code. Reconnaissance and defence are of primary importance... The enemy is in the progress of moving and is extremely weak. Carry out immediate and determined attacks, regardless of your strength, whenever the opportunity arises. Infiltrate and block their path and make reinforcement impossible for them. To win a battle the enemy must be killed and every man must kill no fewer than three of the enemy: kill, kill, kill.[4]

As a result of this Order, 3 Commando Brigade's planned move didn't go ahead, as at around six o'clock on the morning of the 31st, a heavy barrage of artillery was directed at Hill 170 – at this time occupied by No. 1 and 42 RM – followed twenty minutes later by an attacking advance by the Japanese. Their first target was the three tanks that had been brought over the difficult terrain a few days earlier and were positioned at the west of the hill. The enemy used pole charges attached to lengths of bamboo and in what was effectively a suicide mission for the party of twenty involved, they managed to destroy one tank and damage another before they were stopped. The area was littered with their corpses; one whose pole charge had exploded prematurely had been 'very thoroughly' killed;[5] another had died with his finger through the ring of a grenade.

Japanese soldiers then swarmed onto Hill 170 towards the positions of 1 Commando's 4 Troop, the enemy being described by Colonel Young as 'mostly armed with their long, clumsy rifles like spears with their long French-style bayonets. Their dwarf-like figures under their mediaeval helmets, their revolting faces with glasses in two cases and many with gold teeth, look like creatures from another world.'[6] They attacked en masse again and again but 1 Commando fought them off with grit and determination. By half past eight, despite inflicting heavy casualties on the enemy, 1 Commando's ammunition was running low and the number of men still able to fight was dwindling. But they didn't give up until every member of the troop had been either killed or injured.

At half past nine, No. 1 Commando's 3 Troop and twelve members of 42 RM's W Troop put in a counter-attack but half of the 42 RM platoon were wiped out in one burst of machine-gun fire.

While No. 1 and 42 RM continued to battle and 'the skin was burnt from their hands and fingers from changing the red hot barrels of their Bren guns under the constant firing',[7] a Warning Order to return to Hill 170 was received by Larry and his No. 5 comrades.

At three o'clock in the afternoon, Colonel Young received a report to say the situation was now critical but fortunately the reinforcements from No. 5 had just begun to arrive. Brigadier Hardy gave an order that no more counter-attacks were to be made for the time being and that the commandos should concentrate on defending their current positions. Two troops from No. 5 were immediately moved forward in support of No. 1 Commando.

Another enemy attack stormed towards them shortly afterwards and TSM Ferguson 'dashed forward several times to the crest of the hill, throwing grenades which he carried in a bucket'.[8] The machine-gun fire was intense and grenades rained down on them. No. 5's CO, Charles Pollitt, was shot through the knee and had to be evacuated by the stretcher-bearers. Major Stuart moved forward and assumed command of the unit.

A communication was sent back from No. 1 to warn that twenty to thirty Japanese soldiers were on the move and beginning to install themselves with light machine guns on the right flank. Larry's friend Nick Bryant took two men from his section, Watson and Hubbard, and crept towards where the enemy had been spotted. Once he had them in his sight, he grabbed hold of Watson's Bren gun, fired off some rounds and killed one of the Japanese before directing Watson to take up a position on the left while he and Hubbard dashed for cover behind a large tree. Rushing across open ground towards the next bit of cover, Bryant was caught in a burst of machine-gun fire that unzipped his abdomen. He fell, mortally wounded, his blood seeping into the ground beneath him. With his last breaths, he called out for his young wife, who at the age of twenty-one and after less than two years of marriage would now be a widow.

Elsewhere, the intense fighting continued, but after two hours, the frenzied attacking of the Japanese abated and only the incessant jabbing of sniper fire remained. During the lull and as darkness began to fall, Larry's 2 Troop was sent to the frontline on the northern tip of Hill 170 to relieve 1 Commando, who had fought for the whole day without rest. As an officer, Larry would have needed to stay doubly alert as among the deception techniques used by the Japanese was the shouting out of senior NCO and officers' names, and even though all badges of rank had been removed, the enemy could determine who were the leaders by observing the commandos' behaviour and would target those in charge with their sniper fire. Larry was so, so tired though. He couldn't remember the last time he'd had a proper sleep. He had managed to grab an hour here and there but the cat-naps (or Jap-naps as the lads had renamed them) did little to recharge his batteries. Despite this, he had to stay strong, to ignore the fatigue, the dry throat caused by an almost constant raging thirst and the rank smell of his filthy clothes, spattered with the blood of his friends. To lose concentration could mean death for him or for his men.

The night passed relatively quietly with only intermittent gunfire exchanges and the occasional cry of 'withdraw commandos' or 'cease fire'[9] coming from the Japanese trenches in an effort to confuse the British troops. But at half past five the following morning, an avalanche of grenades bombarded Larry's position as an hors d'oeuvre to another fierce attack by the enemy, who were by now severely diminished in number. Corporal Taylor was killed and Privates Roberts, Birkett and Osborne were all wounded before the remainder of Larry's troop succeeded in crushing the attack with close-range fire.

By six o'clock on the morning of 1 February 1945, Hill 170 had finally been won, and as Larry's troop cleared the area, collecting weapons and searching for their wounded and dead comrades, they counted 340 dead Japanese scattered across the ground, some of them wearing green berets snatched from the heads of the men they had slain. The fallen commandos were shrouded in grey army blankets and buried in temporary graves. Nick Bryant's green beret was placed on top of the pile of earth beneath which he now lay, waiting for the team who would exhume his body and transfer it to Akyab cemetery after his friends had left.

After a breakfast of hard-boiled eggs, No. 5 were relieved by the 2/2nd Punjab Regiment and began the journey back to Myebon where they were finally able to eat a hot meal, bathe, change their clothes and have a good night's rest. Only then did Larry begin to absorb the fact that Nick had gone and he would never see him again.

The following weeks saw a memorial service for those who had been killed in action or had died from their wounds, plus a succession of visits from high-ranking officials, all keen to congratulate the Brigade on a job well done. As Lieutenant Salt put it: 'We get inspected now by every VIP under the sun. We've got three coming this week. We don't look at anyone below the rank of General these days. I must say they've all been so complimentary it's becoming highly embarrassing.'[10] In recognition of their success in the action, the commandos were awarded the battle honours of Myebon and Kangaw in September 1957.

On 17 February, Larry's 2 Troop, together with 1 and HQ Troops, set out on a journey back to Akyab with the remainder of the unit following the next day. Once they had constructed their bivouacs and settled in, Larry set about writing a letter to Margery back home in Quinton. He adjusted the flame of his dilapidated hurricane lamp and inserted a cigarette between his lips. The light from the oil lamp fell gently upon the features of Captain Charles Beard, who was seated opposite him. Away in the distance a radio was playing but it was all but drowned out by the insistent shrilling of the crickets. He sipped at the mug of hot coffee his batman had brought him.

In her previous letter, Margery had offered to visit the Beech Tree pub in Quinton and down a couple of pints on Larry's behalf. He described the effect this had on him: it 'caused my tongue to droop out thirstily in a manner which both alarmed and shocked my fellow officers who were present at the time. However, I was forgiven when I explained the reason for this frightful display of emotion. Custom allows a certain amount of visible excitement only where liquor or women are concerned. Otherwise a poker-faced display of honed stolidity must be sustained at all times. I usually manage this quite well by merely acting and looking normal.'[11]

He paused to light another cigarette from the end of the first before continuing to write. He apologised for not having been in touch for such a long time and hoped that he had now put Margery's mind at rest. The recent action must have had a deeper effect on Larry than he was perhaps willing to admit to his girlfriend or to himself as he used his letter as an opportunity to lash out at some of his fellow officers and criticised them for their years of low, hard living. He claimed they could tell wild tales of brothels around the world, boasted of nights of hard drinking and carousing and described how one could be found in the 'lower joints of London before the war, faultlessly dressed and consistently blotto'.[12]

The closing paragraphs of the letter had a melancholy air, and the final two sentences help to explain his frame of mind: 'A very good friend of mine in this unit – Nick Bryant by name – had many worldly sins for which to account. They were all washed away about two weeks ago when he died with a machine-gun burst in his stomach.'[13]

Writing to Margery and receiving letters from her helped to keep Larry in touch with normal civilisation and, he admitted, was about the only thing that enabled him to maintain his mental balance in the hell-hole of war. He often illustrated his letters with either an intricate sketch or a rough doodle, a habit he continued once he began writing the *Goon Show* after the war, when he would cover his scripts with drawings.

Larry's mood showed signs of improvement over the following days when he had the opportunity to relax and let himself have fun again. The unit was treated to two ENSA shows, and they had the pleasure of being entertained by the renowned beauties Frances Day and Patricia Burke within a fortnight of each other. Another visit – perhaps not quite so easy on the eye – was from the Brigade Commander, who took a salute at a march past, having inspected No. 5.

During the quiet period, Larry spent time in the Troop office, writing more letters and signing them off with a variety of 'Goonish' pseudonyms such as Lieutenant Tooting-Smythe and Bertie Hope-Flatwater. The Troop office table had been constructed using planks and logs of varying shapes and sizes in what seemed to be a totally haphazard manner. The five-foot-two Troop Clerk, Private Shoreman, known as 'Titch', had difficulty clambering up onto the bench. Larry watched him for a while, hard at work with his legs dangling a foot above the ground and 'his tongue following his writing like a faithful dog'.[14]

The sun shone unrelentingly but a slight breeze blew Larry's letters and papers off the table and hither and thither on the floor. He retrieved them, swearing softly, and decided to pop along and see Captain John Sergeant. It being a Sunday, he found him unshaven and undressed and writing letters. Larry picked up John's tom-tom drum and tapped out some noisy rhythms. The tom-tom was beginning to crack under the strain of being beaten by every officer who dropped in to visit John. The two squabbled about several unimportant topics for a short while and ended up having a brief tussle during which time John's mosquito net was torn and his towel dirtied. Larry made a rapid and strategic withdrawal. The serenity and idleness was starting to affect them all.

A couple of diversions relieved the tedium towards the end of February. A Brigade swimming gala provided an alternative to the favoured pastime of imbibing large quantities of rum and Larry swam for the No. 5 team, helping to lead them to overall victory.

Rum was back on the agenda again though when the officers were invited to a party at the Sisters' Mess of the local hospital. According to Larry it was:

the usual combination of liquor, food, liquor, liquor, small talk and liquor. I became enmeshed (I know not how) with a pudding-faced female who prefaced every remark with – 'well – I know you'll think I'm awfully bla-a-a-asé but...'

I was somewhat stinko, as usual, and she was sitting opposite me with her knees drawn up under her chin.

'Isn't it awfully chilly,' said she.

I remarked that I found it a little warm, too warm in fact.

'Oh well,' she said, 'I suppose you're wearing far more clothes than I am.'

'Yes,' replied I. 'For instance, I'm wearing pants.' After that remark she left me, thank God.

Larry later discovered that one of the other officers had been outside with her earlier in the evening to 'look at the stars' and still had her underwear in his right-hand trouser pocket. 'He always was absent-minded,'[15] Larry explained.

The party brought February to a close and with it came an announcement that the unit would soon be on the move again.

16

Intelligence Section

An advance party left Akyab Island on 3 March 1945 while those remaining behind paid a visit to a battalion of the Hyderabads who had fought alongside No. 5 at Kangaw and were now stationed in the same area. They entertained No. 5 with a display of 'Catch as Catch Can' wrestling, played them at football and volleyball, fed them an enormous meal and put on a concert. A few days later it was time for No. 5 to return the favour. A team comprising TSM Wilson, Privates Cumberbatch and Danes, Fusilier Hamilton and Lieutenant King took the Hyderabads on at wrestling but as they were practically clueless about the techniques of 'Catch as Catch Can', the Hyderabads won every bout. After the wrestling, No. 5 put on a display of water polo, served up an equally enormous meal and then put on a show that was organised by Larry, in his role as Entertainments Officer, with assistance from Lieutenant Andrew Scott.

The moving day eventually arrived on 12 March and after a few nights spent at Akyab jetty, the whole of the 3rd Commando Brigade was on board HMT *Dunera* by 15 March for 'a delightful four-day voyage to Madras'.[1] As No. 5's arrival in Madras was to be greeted with fourteen days' privilege leave, the unit's Medical Officer gave a lecture to remind the men of the wide variety of venereal diseases

.

they could encounter if they didn't take proper care of their sexual health.

Their leave began on 26 March and most of the Brigade opted to spend their free time in Bombay. Many took a stroll along Grant Road, a street lined with brothels where the women were displayed behind bars as if they were precious goods in a shop or dangerous animals to be gawped at in a zoo, but with the Medical Officer's lecture still playing back in their minds, how many were tempted to sample the wares? Bill Stoneman of 42 RM also remembered seeing 'children who had been maimed and blinded for the purpose of begging, for this was a growth industry in the east where poverty was rife. Everywhere the plaintive wail of the beggars could be heard: baksheesh, Sahib, baksheesh.'[2]

As the privilege leave coincided with a workers' strike in Bombay, British troops, including members of the Commando Brigade, took over the running of the public transport system to enable them to get around. 'Later it was announced by the Bombay Transport Authority in the press that their financial receipts had never been higher!'[3]

In mid-April, the officers and other ranks of No. 5 began to trickle back from leave and congregated at Pashan Camp in Poona, where they remained for the rest of the month. According to the unofficial diary of the activities of No. 5, the only thing worthy of note during this time was 'the second-hand booksellers who [plied] their wares on the veranda of the dining hall' with 'the most popular, but very dog-eared book [being] "The Escape of Erotic Edna".'[4] The official War Diary for the month, although not mentioning any such literary treats, was checked and initialled by Larry, and the covering letter sending a copy of the diary to the Officer in Command of the Commando Wing of GHQ 2nd Echelon, Allied Land Forces was also signed by him.

Captain Charles Beard was running a cadre for new recruits so Larry was Troop Commander for the week with a couple of subalterns under his command. He found it a little daunting despite spending most of the day sitting in the Troop office, looking frightfully important but doing very little. While pretending to work, what he was actually doing was writing to Margery again. She had spent some time undergoing treatment at the Ear and Throat Hospital in Birmingham and so when Larry wrote to thank her for the photos she had sent, he said he assumed she had now recovered since the 'microscopic note' she included with the snaps hadn't mentioned anything about it. 'If right, write a cross on the dotted line,' he wrote. 'If wrong, send a stamped addressed envelope and you will receive by return of post our pamphlet entitled "Advice to Young Brides" by Nurse McKickerly with an Appendix and Notes on "Treatment Of Spinal Fractures And Athletes Foot", the complete set of volumes, bound in bronze pigskin and painted on 8vo vellum (pink), entitled, "Sex And Why Cycling Is So Much More Interesting". Cost only 210 guineas, postage extra.'[5]

On the final day of April, with the news of the execution of Mussolini having just reached them, a Warning Order of an impending move to a camp at Ahmednagar Stud Farm was received. They journeyed there by rail and road, leaving on 4 May and arriving the following day. A series of transfers coincided with the move and saw Larry and his batman, Private Scott, transferred to the Intelligence Section of HQ Troop. Larry's previous position as second-in-command of 2 Troop was filled by one of the new reinforcements to the unit, Lieutenant Duncan.

A few days later, the war in Europe came to an end and the occasion was marked by a public holiday throughout India on 9 May. The next day, Larry was placed on the 'Sick in Quarters' list – perhaps his celebrations had been somewhat over-indulgent or perhaps he was suffering from a delayed reaction to the cholera inoculation he had been given on the first day in the new camp. Fortunately he was well enough to attend the Sunday VE Day (Victory in Europe) thanksgiving service and to join the officers and NCOs in waiting on the other ranks at the 'Thanksgiving Day' evening meal.

No. 5 Commando officers at Ahmednagar, 1945. Back row from left: John Salt;
John Gilbody; John Sergeant; John Bowyer; Ray Bolitho.
Front row from left: Ken Waggett; Larry Stephens; Ralph Noble.
(Courtesy of Captain Bowyer's grandson, Paul Gordon)

Arrangements were now under way for the unit to undergo a period of jungle training and a recce party under the command of Major Beard was despatched on 14 May. The chosen location was Astoli, thirty-five miles from Belgaum. An intense period of training followed, with new skills learned and old skills honed.

By 4 June, No. 5 were back at Ahmednagar Stud Farm and the following day Larry was once again admitted to the hospital in Poona for a two-and-a-half-week stay. During this time there was a high number of hospital admissions so it seems likely that conditions had reawakened the malaria parasites.

During his spell of sickness, Larry's comrades had undertaken yet another move and were now established at a camp in Kharakvasla, surrounded by 'almost familiar Highland scenery and with Lake Fife spread out below'[6] them. A series of parties were held to celebrate the fifth anniversary of No. 5 Commando and to say goodbye to Lieutenant Lee and the fifty-eight other ranks who were being demobbed. For his farewell party, Lieutenant Lee had recruited an army of helpers and between them they provided heaps of good food and plenty to drink. The canteen had been decorated with strings of coloured flags and an excellent marine band played for hours on end. Larry contributed to the entertainment by playing the piano and accompanying Gunner Reed while he sang a few songs.

The war in Europe may have been over but the war in the East continued. No. 5 had been earmarked to take part in the planned attacks on Malaya, which had been under Japanese occupation since 1941, as part of Operation Zipper and so once the party detritus had been cleared away, the commandos turned their attention back to training once again.

Now that he was part of the Intelligence Section, Larry's training was very different from what he had been used to up to this point in his army career. He had arrived back at camp just in time to join a two-week intensive intelligence course. Further instruction during the first two weeks of July focused on, among other things, map reading and enlarging; panoramic sketching; the preparation of sand tables; studying aerial photographs; learning about the Japanese language, weapons and organisation of their Infantry Division; and lectures on message writing and office procedure. There was also office work to keep up to date with as well as practical exercises such as a night compass march.

In mid-July, No. 5's CO at the time, Lieutenant Colonel Stuart, together with Larry, Captain Bolitho and Second Lieutenant Alting de Cloux led a party 150 miles away to Nasik, where they were to carry out a tank training course with the 45th Cavalry Regiment of the Indian Army. The party included five drivers, two cooks and two batmen – one for Lieutenant Colonel Stuart and one for Larry – and the Movement Order for the trip stated that they would be provided with 'sufficient cooking gear for the whole party' and 'the necessary crockery and cutlery for the officers'.[7] They were away from Kharakvasla for five days but unfortunately no records seem to have survived describing the visit itself, although it seems certain that Larry would have had decent china to eat off for the occasion of his twenty-second birthday.

Some of Larry's newly learned intelligence skills were put into action at the end of July when an Operations Order for the training exercise 'Completion' was published, with the Intelligence Summary for the exercise referring to a sand table model and aerial photography. The name given to one of the hill features, 'Snowdon', together with the password 'Welch' to be answered with 'Wales', perhaps hark back to Larry's school visits to Bryntail Farm in Llanidloes, although what the codenames for the other two features, 'Rupture' and 'Banana Ridge', refer to can only be guessed at.

No sooner had the troops returned from 'Completion' when an Operations Order for another training exercise, this time 'Lilliput', was published. The exercise was carried out in the fictional lands of Brobdignasia and Lilliput and involved the whole of the Brigade, therefore suggesting that the commandos would soon be going back into action. However, some significant events took place soon after No. 5's return to Kharakvasla which resulted in the postponement of an intended third exercise and changes in future plans for them.

17

Hong Kong

On 6 August 1945, the first atomic bomb was dropped, its target the Japanese city of Hiroshima, and three days later another was dropped on Nagasaki. On the same day Russia declared war on Japan and invaded its puppet state of Manchukuo. By 10 August Japan had offered to surrender, on condition that Emperor Hirohito be permitted to remain in power, but the offer was rejected by the Allies. Finally, on 15 August, Japan unconditionally surrendered. The Second World War was over. As soon as they heard the news, members of the 3rd Commando Brigade celebrated by firing two-inch mortars and letting off flares, since they had nothing else available with which to mark the end of the war. The bar in the Officers' Mess was opened, even though at that time they would usually have been tucked up and sound asleep in their charpoys, and as the drink flowed, Larry and his fellow officers kept running outside and firing their .45 Colts up into the sky. The CO was not at all pleased with them the next morning.

The following day, the Brigade left Kharakvasla and No. 5 reached Ghilpuri railway station at two o'clock in the afternoon. They had arrived with plenty of time to spare as their train to Bombay wasn't due to leave until four o'clock the following morning. They had been warned that on arrival in Bombay they would be boarding a White

Ensign vessel and that they must therefore present themselves looking smart and spruce. The muddy conditions they had left behind at Kharakvasla Camp meant that their appearance needed some work to get to the required standard and so they engaged the help of some little local boys who gave their boots and gaiters a good wash in pools of water and charged them a penny each. The Bombay train arrived at the station platform around twelve hours before its scheduled departure time and so once all the equipment had been stowed, the men were allowed into Poona on condition that they be back at Ghilpuri by the stroke of midnight.

At Bombay they embarked on HMS *Glengyle* and set sail for Penang as part of 'Operation Tiderace' with the plan that they would occupy the island and accept the formal surrender of the Japanese on the Georgetown racecourse.

The *Glengyle's* skipper gave Larry and the other officers access to his Mess. As the ship headed out to sea, a heavy swell caused much seasickness but this didn't deter them from taking advantage of the drinks provided at Navy prices. Back on shore, a Top Secret Cypher Telegram was sent to Admiral Lord Louis Mountbatten from the Chiefs of Staff:

1. It has now become most urgent to get a land force to Hong Kong as quickly as possible.

2. Australia are unlikely to be able to help.

3. Accordingly you should arrange for earliest despatch of one brigade from forces under your command in order to reach Hong Kong as soon as possible after the arrival there of units of the British Pacific Fleet...[1]

On 19 August, Mountbatten replied to say that he could make 3 Commando Brigade available and providing he received approval by 21 August, they could reach Hong Kong around 5 September.[2]

As a result, HMS *Glengyle* was diverted to Trincomalee and remained moored in the Ceylonese harbour for just over a week. During this time, the *Glengyle*'s skipper withdrew the privilege of being able to drink the Navy Mess's entire stock from No. 5's officers and so they had a whip-round and despatched Captain Balchin and his batman to replenish the stocks of alcohol from the NAAFI onshore instead.

Arrangements were made and briefings given regarding the new destination and eventually, on the last day of August 1945, No. 5 and 44 RM on board HMS *Glengyle*, together with No. 1 and 42 RM on board HMIS *Llanstephan Castle*, set sail for Hong Kong.

The *Glengyle* entered the Strait of Malacca and sailed along the coast of Malaya. As they passed a strip of beautiful, white sandy beach, the Captain announced over the tannoy that it was Port Dickson – the beach No. 5 had been scheduled to land on and lead the assault, had Operation Zipper gone ahead. It had been a lucky escape; the Venerable Basil Stratton, Chaplain General of Field Marshal Slim's 14th Army, had been involved in the planning of the operation and had been horrified by the barbaric suggestion that the high number of casualties expected on this beach should be bulldozed out of the way so as not to dent the morale of those who were due to land after them. He asserted that he would land with the first wave to ensure all those who were killed would instead receive a proper Christian burial.

On 11 September 1945, HMS *Glengyle* made its way into Hong Kong. Larry stood out on deck and immersed himself in the new sights, sounds and smells as the ship made its way into Victoria harbour. A series of low buildings squatted along the waterfront and Victoria Peak rose up behind them. There was one structure the commandos were not pleased to see though: the Japanese had erected an ugly victory monument at the top of one of the hills which they called the 'Pagoda of the Loyal Spirits'. It was claimed that the Japanese had planned to use it as a mass hara-kiri site in the event of what they considered to be the almost inevitable return of the British.

The harbour contained a real mishmash of vessels: battleships and aircraft carriers shared the water with local junks and sampans, bedecked with strings of washing and with plump-cheeked children peering over the sides. Larry unknowingly passed within yards of his cousin, Michael McKechnie, a naval gunner who was on board HMS *Anson*, already at anchor in the harbour.

After another night on board ship, No. 5 disembarked and together with the rest of the Brigade, they paraded through the streets led by the pipe band of 42 RM, 'the first band to do so since the fall of Hong Kong'.[3] A front-page article from the *China Mail* described the scene:

'The stirring echoes of martial music, bringing office work in the Central District temporarily to a complete stoppage signalised the landing in the Colony yesterday of the 3rd Commando Brigade...

The march of the commandos through the city streets provided a stirring spectacle, particularly for the remaining British residents of the colony, who were getting their first glimpse of men of this famous military organisation, the stories of whose daring and resource under the most hazardous conditions had percolated through to Stanley despite the Japanese.

The bearing of these particular commando units as they marched through Des Voeux Road Central was endorsement enough of the stories of the gruelling training course demanded of volunteers accepted for service with the commandos. Perfect physical specimens, tough as they make them!'[4]

Following the pomp and ceremony, No. 5 marched to Mody Road in Kowloon and took up residence in a modern block of flats. Although the building itself was in an overall good condition, it was almost entirely bereft of furniture, but at least it was somewhere for them to get their washing done. Three Chinese barbers visited the flats and from first thing in the morning until late into the evening they cut the hair of everyone in the unit. Feeling clean and dapper once again, every now and then a troop would take to the city's streets for a smart march. It gave them the opportunity to stretch their legs and also to indulge in a bit of preening as Hong Kong's inhabitants seemed to be tremendously impressed by the displays.

While most of the commandos were enjoying this brief period of time off, Lieutenant Colonel Stuart and Captain Oliver took a recce party to Fan Ling, to meet the Japanese commander there and make arrangements to take over from his troops.

The following day, No. 5 packed up and prepared themselves to move. They marched through a torrential downpour and boarded a train at Tsimshatsui station, which then gingerly made its way as far as Fan Ling. It was the first train to travel along the route, which had been abandoned by the occupying Japanese after Chinese guerrillas had taken to destroying the engines and removing sections of the track, for quite some time.

Having made it safely to Fan Ling, the Commando initially moved into barracks that had been inhabited by the Japanese during the occupation; furniture was once again in short supply. Once settled, they made contact with Major Hurota of the Japanese 67 Battalion and his sixteen officers, ninety-four NCOs, three hundred and fifty-eight other ranks, and eighty sick personnel who had been stationed in the area.[5] The Japanese POWs were strip-searched to make sure they weren't carrying anything that could be used as escape apparatus or that had been looted, a task Larry was almost certainly involved in for the gathering of intelligence, before being sent to the Shamshuipo internment camp in Kowloon. Over the next few days, around a thousand more Japanese soldiers were rounded up, disarmed and escorted to the camp.

No. 5 now set about trying to find more comfortable billets for themselves and began to commandeer suitable residences in the surrounding area. As Fan Ling had been the weekend retreat for the wealthier members of Hong Kong's society, many of the commandos now found themselves living in grand houses. Les Aucott recalled that he was responsible for making sure the electric lights at the Officers' Mess in Fan Ling were in working order. He helped Sergeant Eric Price to install a Lister's diesel engine to provide the power and then scrounged light bulbs and telephone wire from everywhere possible so that Larry and the other officers would be able to enjoy electric lighting.

By 18 September, No. 5 were confident to report that the New Territories, a stretch of country behind Hong Kong that extended about thirty miles to the Chinese frontier, had now been cleared of the Japanese, with the exception of a group of eighty POWs who had been retained at Fan Ling to perform fatigue duties. There were now a new set of challenges to face, though: to prevent looting; to bring a more settled and ordered way of life back to the district; and to control those who wished to cross over from the Chinese border.

Life was busy for Larry. On 19 September a report was received by the Intelligence Section to say that a band of 400 Chinese had crossed into the New Territories. Contact was made and they were escorted back over the border with a warning not to cross into the British-held Territory under arms again. Later that afternoon a delegate from a Chinese guerrilla unit arrived at the Intelligence Office and was escorted on to Brigade HQ in Kowloon. A more illustrious visit on the same day had been that of Sir Bruce Fraser, Admiral of the British South West Pacific Fleet, who visited the unit's headquarters and lunched with the officers.

A piece of information that would have reached Larry around this time and which may well have sparked inspiration for future Goonery was the news that responsibility for the military administration of Kowloon had been handed over to the 3rd Commando Brigade's Brigadier Hardy by none other than Captain Eccles, RN.

As the days went on, more visitors had been arriving at No. 5's HQ, including Captain Chan Hon Leung of the Chinese Forces' 13 Army Group and two delegates from the Chinese National Comintern Irregulars, and it was decided to find a new building to better receive the increasing number of callers. On 23 September, the HQ was transferred to Lena Lodge.

Lena Lodge was built around 1921 as a clubhouse for the expatriate employees of Jardine, Matheson & Co. and during the war had been used as a Japanese military hospital. Of roughly Italianate style, the two-storey building had an arched, rusticated, grey-stone ground floor contrasting with the smooth-finished upper floor with its portico balconies and balustrading. A covered walkway connected the main building to a single-storey structure at its rear.

As September turned to October, groups of displaced people continued to move through the area. The East River Columnists had been ordered to return to China by their Commanders and the Chinese National Army passed through the Territory en route to Kowloon, where they were due to embark for Korea. Members of the National Army were apparently 'a terrible sight to see. Very old men and young children in uniform and carrying arms.'[6]

Throughout October almost 10,000 members of the various Chinese forces flooded through the New Territories, some disguised as peasants. There were problems with piracy, with contraband goods and with night-time raids on the local villages. Eventually it was decided that the villagers should be armed for their own protection and each village was issued with a stock of rockets to be fired at the first sign of any intruders. Lieutenant Bob Preston recalled that 'the very first night it was like the Crystal Palace, each village fired their entire stock of rockets, and the commando patrols were soon running round in circles. Needless to say, the rockets were never replaced.'[7]

On 28 October, news reached Larry of an announcement made by the War Office that the Army Commandos were to be disbanded. Major General Laycock had delivered the news to the 1st Commando Brigade in an Order of the Day stating that 'the Green Beret shall be worn no more. It is a thing of war but not of peace... To you, the wearers of that Beret who have made it a symbol of honour and bravery unsurpassed, I send you the unbounded gratitude of those whom you have served. Your country is justly proud of you – your spirit and your valour will live for ever, in the annals of our nation.'[8]

Despite the shock announcement, life and duty had to continue for the time being and for Larry this duty meant additional responsibility. On 10 November, he was promoted to the rank of Acting Captain and transferred out of the Intelligence Section and back to 2 Troop, which he now took charge of.

Unknown Lieutenant with Captain Larry Stephens, Hong Kong
(Larry Stephens Estate collection).

Although No. 5 were still working hard, they seemed to be finding more time for leisure activities too. A major event in their calendar took place on Sunday 25 November. A Victory race meeting was organised by the unit at the Hong Kong Jockey Club's Beas River race track to raise funds for H.E. the Commander-in-Chief's Hong Kong Distress Fund. The programme of events included flat races, steeplechases, sideshows, jumping and gymkhana events, and special trains and ferries were laid on to convey people to and from the course. Nearly all the jockeys were members of No. 5. The horses and ponies that competed were described in an article in the *Hong Kong Sunday Herald*:

> They are affectionate and grateful beasts. They had very much of a thin time through the last few months of the Japanese occupation and many of their brethren ended up as horse-meat. Since the commandos have occupied Fan Ling, however, they have been generously fed on every conceivable delicacy in the horse-diet... All 30 horses and 10 ponies have been meticulously groomed.[9]

It is not known exactly what part Larry played in proceedings but there is no doubt he would have been involved in some way, as the Unit's Entertainments Officer. The local newspaper reported that every event had a humorous side so it seems that he stamped his mark on the occasion.

A 'totalisator' had been specially installed to calculate the amount due to those who backed the winners, and as well as the horse racing there were sideshows and refreshment stalls all around the course.

The star of the day was Silly Billy, a stallion that won three of the six flat races. Silly Billy had been christened 'Willy-one-ball' by those in the know and had a reputation for giving his all to chase down and catch a mare. Silly Billy's winning streak was thanks to someone conveniently placing a mare near the finishing post.

The press gave a glowing report of the day's entertainments and congratulated No. 5 Commando on the magnificent job they had done. It was remarked that, for once, people paid little and had a wonderful time rather than paying a lot and having an indifferent time. Every sector of the community took part, both military and civil.

In December it was proposed to speed up the rate of demob, but this was of major concern to the Commander-in-Chief in Hong Kong. He sent a telegram to the Chiefs of Staff outlining his worries, which included the fact that in his opinion the military strength in the colony was already below what was required 'for the proper maintenance of law and order'[10] especially given that 45,000 Chinese soldiers were expected to pass through the New Territories en route to Kowloon during the following two to three weeks. It was eventually decided that reinforcements drawn from the Royal Marines Commandos in Europe would be shipped to Hong Kong as soon as possible.

As for No. 5, it was suggested that it should amalgamate with No. 1 to form 1/5 Commando. The Chiefs of Staff concluded that 1/5 Commando would remain under the command of 3 Commando Brigade until the depletion of numbers rendered it non-operational. This meant that Larry and his comrades in No. 1 and No. 5 would have the honour of being the last of the Army Commandos, although they weren't to learn of this for another few months.

On the first Thursday in December, the officers and men of No. 5 received what had become a regular weekly visit from a truckload of children from the Fan Ling Babies' Home. The commandos had found an abandoned baby girl when they first moved to Fan Ling and their close association with the orphanage had built from there, so much so that they now gave a tea party for the toddlers once a week.

'It's like a bit of home to have kids about the place,' said Corporal Fred Musson of Ellesmere Port, Cheshire, speaking for his mates and himself. 'It's certainly a treat to see how they enjoy themselves here on

Thursdays. They always get a good tea and our chocolate ration and we give them rides on horses we took off the Japs. Then they sing us songs and hymns and they sing very well for such little toddlers.'[11]

When No. 5 had first arrived in September, many of the children had been suffering from malnutrition, but by providing them with vitamin pills and chocolate and with treatment and advice from the Medical Officer, their health was now much improved. The commandos had repaired the Home's water pump, provided a stock of firewood and carried out numerous repairs. In return they could always be sure of a warm welcome and a cup of tea whenever they visited.

The next event in the calendar that was now receiving a lot of focus was the festive season, and as it would be the first Christmas since the war had ended it was set to be a particularly joyous occasion. Larry sent so many Christmas cards on behalf of 2 Troop that his handwriting became quite a scrawl, although still legible: 'Wishing you a merry Christmas and a happy and prosperous New Year from all of 2 Troop, Fan Ling. L. G. Stephens, Capt.'[12] For once there was plenty to eat and drink (although shortages of sugar icing and almonds had been reported) and each Mess had its own party. Boxing Day had been designated a unit holiday so everyone was able to thoroughly over-indulge without worrying too much about the next day.

It would seem that Larry and the other officers had been taking the over-indulgence very seriously across an extended period and had been spending rather a lot of time living the high life in the Colony's nightspots. On one particular night out, a small group of the officers, which included Larry, David King, Ray Bolitho and Nick Grose, arranged for Captain King's driver, Bill Elliot, to transport them in his jeep the twenty miles or so from their base in Fan Ling to Kowloon. The officers had a whip-round for Bill and when he dropped them off at the Star Ferry pier, they handed over the pot of cash and asked him to stay sober and return to collect them from outside the Peninsula

Hotel at one o'clock in the morning. It's possible they took a ferry over to Hong Kong Island and spent some time in the bar at the Gloucester Hotel there, but at some point in the evening, they were definitely back in Kowloon and strolled along the Salisbury Road from the pier towards the Peninsula Hotel. The neoclassical building was still wearing its overcoat of camouflage paint, which the Japanese had daubed over its exterior walls during the occupation, but as Larry and his friends headed through the vast entrance doors, aside from the fact that many of the clientele wore service uniforms, most of the reminders of the war had been expunged.

The group made their way up to the Officers' Club in the Rose Room on the top floor and found themselves a table beside one of the chunky square pillars with geometric designs carved around its base and ornate plaques weighed down with gilded plasterwork swags and festoons at the top. As the evening wore on and the alcohol began to take effect, the party of officers became more and more boisterous and their raucous conversation began to drown out the gentle clink of glasses and the whirring of the fans overhead. Their focus became fixed on an American admiral at one of the neighbouring tables, or more specifically, on his hat. It didn't look out of place in the opulent surroundings with its abundance of embroidered gold oak leaves and acorns on the peak. They knew they had to have it. Larry checked his watch. It was already one o'clock and Bill Elliot, the driver, would be waiting outside for them. They huddled together and planned what they were going to do. After settling their bill, they began to saunter towards the exit but as they drew level with the admiral's table, one of them grabbed his cap and roared 'NOW!' Breaking into a run, they tumbled out of the Rose Room, hurtled down the stairs and tore through the lobby, their yells and shrieks reaching all the way up to the coffered ceiling. Waiting outside in the jeep, Bill could hear the pandemonium and looked up to see them erupting into the street. They sprinted towards him, flung open the doors and as they piled in, yelled, 'GO! GO! GO!' With a screech of tyres Bill sped away and was soon flying along the Nathan Road at close to sixty miles per hour. As soon as they were a safe distance away, he slowed down and asked the officers what had happened. With their eyes glittering like naughty schoolboys they told him about their prank and showed him their prize.

Since arriving in Hong Kong, Larry seems to have been embracing the 'low, hard living' he had been so judgemental about after the Battle of Hill 170, but having survived the terror of war, he was keen to erase the grisly images that haunted him every time he closed his eyes and tried to sleep – passing out in a drunken stupor made it much easier to do.

On the final day of 1945, Larry and the other officers were all hauled up in front of the Brigade Commander or, as the official War Diary described it, 'Brigadier HD Fellowes, DSO addressed Unit officers.'[13] 'Busty' Fellowes, formerly of 42 RM, didn't approve of the behaviour of No. 5's officers and had told their CO, Robin Stuart, that he intended to do something about it as soon as possible. Captain Dennis Buckle recalled the event very clearly. To his complete amazement, as adjutant, he was ordered to march in all the officers as if they were in jankers (official military punishment). After they had been given a thorough roasting, they were so incensed by their treatment that they stormed into a nearby room and wrote out their resignations. 'As if they could!' said Dennis.[14]

It is to be hoped that the officers were back on their best behaviour when the unit received another visit from Lord Louis Mountbatten at the beginning of February 1946. For once, Larry wasn't in hospital and so he was finally able to be introduced to him. After inspecting the troops, Lord Louis gave his thanks to the assembled men for the outstanding part they had played in the Burma campaign and for the way in which they were now carrying out the reoccupation of Hong

Kong, which he described as being one of the most important tasks of the post-war world. The Supreme Allied Commander was then taken up to one of the frontier posts by Major Waggett where, standing under the Union flag, he was able to look out over China.

Military life continued throughout 1946 for Larry, and his rank was amended from Acting Captain to Temporary Captain. He also had the opportunity to indulge his passion for music when his comrades managed to find a piano for him, enabling him to play for them regularly.

There were also occasional ENSA shows to keep everyone entertained, one of the most notable being a visit by Gert and Daisy Walters in mid-February. Gert and Daisy were comic cockney characterisations created by Elsie and Doris Waters; prior to 1946, they had appeared in three films. During their visit to Fan Ling, the Waters sisters autographed the Mess motto belonging to No. 5's officers including Larry, John Sergeant, Phil Donnellan and Terry Skelly, and which read, 'work is the curse of the drinking classes'. Terry Skelly had created the motto in his best calligraphy and it had been given pride of place on the wall behind the officers' 'illegal' bar where it acted as an aggravating provocation to the CO. Eventually it was confiscated by HQ... and displayed there instead.

At the beginning of March 1946, No. 5 moved south from Fan Ling to Stanley Fort Barracks on Hong Kong Island. Nearby, at Stanley Prison, war criminals were being hanged and each execution was signalled by the tolling of the prison bells. This was undoubtedly part of the reason why Stanley was described by members of No. 5 as a 'grim place'.[15]

Things didn't improve when, just under a week after the move, the announcement was made that 1 and 5 Commandos were to be amalgamated by the end of the month. On 23 March the officers, warrant officers and sergeants held their final party as No. 5 Commando and from that point on they became part of 1/5 Commando, reorganised with 'HQ and six troops, personnel of 1 Commando and 5 Commando being mixed within troops'.[16] It is not known which troop Larry was allocated to.

Records for the remainder of Larry's time in Hong Kong are scant but he would have moved from Stanley at the beginning of April 1946 when 1/5 Commando's positions were relieved by 42 and 45 RM Commando and the unit would have been sent either to Kowloon or back to the New Territories.[17] Nothing else is known until 5 October 1946 when a farewell dinner party was held to mark the disbandment of 6 Troop, and the remaining members of 1/5 Commando feasted on cream of tomato soup, fried garoupa fish, roast chicken and ham, roast potatoes, French beans, banana trifle and mixed fruit sundae.

On 12 November 1946, Larry boarded the SS *Empress of Australia*, which had arrived in Hong Kong the previous day. On the way to Hong Kong, the ship had made a stop at Kure in the Hiroshima prefecture to pick up nineteen Japanese suspects who were being taken to Singapore for trial in connection with Burma–Siam 'Death Railway' war crimes.

Three days later, the *Empress of Australia* left Hong Kong and Larry began the month-long voyage back home, together with 1,826 other British and Indian troops who were scheduled for demob and 600 Chinese cadets who were due to undergo training in the UK. One hundred and eighteen berths had also been set aside for British civilians in Shanghai who were to be repatriated following several years of internment.

The ship made its first stop in Singapore and from there the *Empress* called at Colombo, Suez, Port Said, Malta and Gibraltar and finally arrived in Liverpool on 13 December 1946. Larry was on home soil once again, but he was still not free to go home. He was posted to the north-east, to No. 6 Infantry Holding Battalion at Hartford Bridge near Morpeth, and spent a month there before being sent to the Royal Warwickshire Regiment's Depot at Budbrooke barracks in Warwick. Budbrooke barracks was also home to No. 6 Primary Training Centre and Larry would have observed young men undergoing the Basic Training for their National Service, no doubt providing material for *The Army Game*, the television comedy series he would write for in later years.

Larry was now just twenty miles or so away from home but still had another three months to serve before he could return there. The day he left Hong Kong, he had enjoyed a temperature of twenty-one degrees and more than six hours of sunshine, but his arrival back in the UK coincided with the coldest winter since 1813–14. February and March of 1947 were particularly harsh. Sunshine in February was around 40 per cent of its average total and for twenty-two of the month's twenty-eight days, the sun didn't make an appearance at all. In March, a snowstorm deposited almost sixteen inches of snow on Birmingham and caused drifts sixteen feet high.

Larry was struck off the unit strength in Warwick on 8 April 1947 and his service records show him as being on leave at Perry Hill Road on the 9th and 10th.

On 11 April, back in Hong Kong, a silver salver was presented to the 3rd Commando Brigade, engraved with the following inscription:

Presented by
THE GOVERNMENT OF HONG KONG
to
3 COMMANDO BRIGADE, ROYAL MARINES
In Grateful Recognition of the valuable services rendered to the
Colony during the period September 1945 – April 1947

The singling out of the Royal Marines over the Army Commandos didn't go unnoticed by Brigadier Wills in the colony and to his official report of the occasion he added, 'I do feel that the greater part of the credit in achieving the high reputation with which 3 Commando Brigade leave the Colony is due to my predecessors and those officers and men both of the Army and Royal Marines, who have left the Brigade and are now scattered widely over the world.'[18]

Larry probably wouldn't have learned of this great honour until at least September 1947 when the details were published in the newsletter of the Old Comrades Association of the Army Commandos, of which he had become a member. Very diplomatically, the newsletter didn't reproduce the actual inscription though.

On Friday 11 July 1947, five days before his twenty-fourth birthday, Larry was released from the Army and began his first weekend free of military life for five years.

His childhood friends in Quinton were startled at the change in him. Gone was the confident young man who used to organise their youthful games and in his place was a quieter, more reflective man who seemed somewhat disorientated by his experiences. It was as if he had closed himself off from everyone. He was frightened to let anyone get too close to him – he had seen too many of his friends die.

When the joy he felt at his 'welcome home' party had faded, he found that Quinton village life was quiet and dull in comparison to the sights and sounds he'd experienced in the previous five years. He had held a position of responsibility and been respected by his men and now he was back home at his parents' house, almost as if he had been demoted to the rank of Private again and was now under their authority.

So much had changed since he'd been away. His former bandleader, Dennis Hinton, had remained in Handsworth throughout the war, working in a reserved occupation. He had found replacements for the musicians who had gone away to fight for King and country and had continued with the band. Larry's place at the piano had been filled by an older man called Ron Hardy. As well as a change of line-up, the name of the band had undergone several changes over the preceding five years – Dennis Hinton and his Championship Band, Dennis R. Hinton and his Orchestra and Famous Dennis Hinton's Broadcasting Band being just three examples. The band had won the 1944 Birmingham District heat of the *Melody Maker* dance band competition and then the 1945 Midland Counties contest, which earned them a place in the 1945 All-Britain finals. By the end of 1946, Dennis was boasting of 'great success' on stage at Manchester and Blackpool as well as on the radio. By the time Larry arrived back in the country, the band were on their way to another All-Britain final in which they would take the runner-up position. Larry was now surplus to requirements.

Margery left no mark on the available archives from the period so it is impossible to determine what became of her or to know whether or not she was reunited with Larry. The letters he wrote to her were donated to the Imperial War Museum following her death in 2013 but the fact that she kept them all her life suggests she always held him in her heart.

When Larry had enlisted and left his job at the estate agent's in Birmingham, he was still a junior employee and the position is unlikely to have been held open for him. The thought of returning there and starting at the bottom again was inconceivable anyway, so as soon as he was able, he escaped south for London, keen to try and rediscover life and excitement.

Part Three
GOONS

HANCOCKS AND MUKKINESE

18

The Grafton's Crowd

There is no record of exactly when Larry arrived in London or what he did when he got there but his niece, Laura Brown, recalls her mother mentioning that he worked for an advertising agency after he left the army so this seems to have been one of the reasons for his move to the capital.

By late 1947 he was living in a flat at 8 Cheniston Gardens, close to High Street Kensington Underground station, and not long afterwards he moved to the south of Kensington, to 33 Redcliffe Square, where he took a flat in a grand Victorian villa with polished granite columns framing the entrance porch and a mansard roof. It was a short stroll away from the Coleherne Hotel public house in Old Brompton Road and Larry would often chat to another of the regulars, a young man of similar age called Ben Cleminson, who lived in nearby Redcliffe Gardens.

The two stayed in touch when Larry moved again in 1949, to 17 Broad Court in Covent Garden, a location which would be very significant in influencing his future life. The Broad Court flats were built as artisans' residences in 1897 and Larry's flat was number 18 in the building. Close to the Bow Street Magistrates' Court and Covent Garden markets, the area was bustling and lively. But Larry had become more interested in a venue that was a ten-minute walk away: the Nuffield Centre.

The Nuffield Centre had opened in the former Empire Restaurant and the neighbouring, bomb-damaged Café de Paris in Wardour Street in 1943, as a recreational club for servicemen and servicewomen. In July 1948, the Centre moved to new premises at 8 Adelaide Street in what had formerly been Gatti's restaurant. It offered a snack bar and cafeteria; a hall for dances and other entertainments; a billiard room; a games room; a tailor; a barber; a first aid post; rooms for writing or lounging in; an information desk and an entire suite for women's services. Various recreational activities were also laid on, including orchestral music every afternoon and dancing every evening.

Among the entertainment provided was a twice-weekly variety show, and every Tuesday and Friday evening anyone who fancied themselves as an entertainer could stand up and do a turn alongside established stars such as Gracie Fields. Lurking in the shadows at the back of the room would be agents and BBC talent scouts, who frequented the Centre in the hope of discovering the 'next big thing', or at the very least someone they could 'book, take 10% and push… round the music halls',[1] recalled BBC producer Dennis Main Wilson in an interview with the Tony Hancock Appreciation Society in 1991.

As a commissioned officer, Larry probably shouldn't have been there as the club was supposed to be for other ranks only, but during one of his visits in 1949, he met Phyllis Rounce, an agent from International Artistes who was representing an up-and-coming star called Tony Hancock. As Phyllis got to know Larry better she came to believe that he had 'something special' in his mind and decided to introduce him to Hancock.

The pair hit it off straight away and almost immediately Larry began writing material for Tony to perform on stage. The routines he created for him often began with a monodrama involving an improbable storyline and finished with a spoof commercial. By the end of the year they were sharing the first of several flats. They initially set up home in a disused book warehouse but also lived together in the Bayswater and Primrose Hill districts. Phyllis remembered visiting the boys at their warehouse residence, which was approached along a gloomy corridor and then down through a trapdoor. She never ventured into the depths of the flat itself though, so she had to crouch down on her hands and knees and talk to them through the hatch.

'Goodness knows what they got up to in there,' she later recalled. 'I couldn't see inside and Tony would only talk to me through the trap – it was almost something Larry would have written.'[2]

In another of their flats, located just off Trafalgar Square at 17 St Martin's Street, they shared with Larry's friend from his Redcliffe Square days, Ben Cleminson. The terms of their tenancy agreement specified that they were not allowed to engage in any business on the premises, a clause Larry in particular flouted. Not only was he writing scripts for Hancock in the flat but he was also providing material for Dick Emery. Dick became one of their more frequent visitors and closest friends; when he wasn't there in the role of customer for Larry, he was looking for a bed for the night after performing in one of the London clubs.

The landlord tried to catch his tenants out by pretending to be other people when he called round, so they had taken to hiding all their typewriters, scripts and props from view. Sporting paraphernalia was strewn about and they concealed the tools of their trade under cricket bats, tennis racquets and rugby balls, in an effort to convince the landlord they were outdoorsy types. But whenever possible, they would pretend to be out when he made one of his unexpected visits, a ploy which backfired spectacularly on occasion. One day, Ben's very respectable father, a Methodist minister, came to call and became increasingly infuriated when no one would answer his knocks at the door despite the giggling he could quite clearly hear from within.

The flat above was occupied by a lady they nicknamed 'The Groaner'. She had a humdrum day job but supplemented her income by entertaining gentleman callers at night. A great many gentlemen callers. Presumably *her* lease made no mention of running a business from the premises.

One evening, Tony took Larry to a pub in Strutton Ground in Westminster where a close friend of his, Jimmy Grafton, was the landlord. It was one of those glorious pubs with an abundance of gilt plasterwork and booths divided by mahogany partitions with etched and frosted glass panels. As well as running his family's pub, Jimmy had been writing for solo comedians for several years, among them Derek Roy, Harry Secombe, Peter Sellers and Alfred Marks. The comics brought their friends along to Grafton's, and they brought their friends in turn and the pub had steadily become a hangout for up-and-coming comedians. Larry was soon spending a lot of time at Grafton's and struck up friendships with most of the regulars. It was there that he first met Spike Milligan, who was lodging in one of the attic rooms of the pub. Spike remembered that 'Larry and Tony were like brothers. I don't know how or where they met. They seemed to have come from nowhere. They shared the same digs and the same women and they both drank. They both liked to laugh at the human race and they'd have hysterical laughing bouts.'³

Jimmy Grafton, Spike Milligan, Peter Sellers, Harry Secombe and Michael Bentine had been working together for some time on a comedy act that they called *The Goons*. In 1948, Jimmy had approached the BBC on behalf of the group with an idea for a 'storyline comedy'⁴ called *Sellers Castle* but the project didn't progress very far.

When Larry arrived within their circle, Jimmy soon discovered that as well as sharing a sense of humour with the Goons and having a similar taste in music and the arts, he also had a natural aptitude for writing comedy scripts. So while Larry continued to work on material for Tony Hancock and Dick Emery, he also began to collaborate on what was to become the *Goon Show* with Jimmy and Spike (who Jimmy considered to be virtually illiterate back then but who was undoubtedly a comic genius, thanks to his extraordinary imagination).

By early 1950, Ben Cleminson had gone to live in Southern Rhodesia and Larry and Tony had moved again and were now sharing a flat in Craven Hill Gardens in Bayswater. Speaking in the late 1960s, Milligan remembered an incident from around the time:

> Larry was in a car with me and we had a crash and he hurt his leg and had to go to hospital. I telephoned Tony and told him. There was this hysterical laughter and I said, 'it's serious, he might have broken his leg', but he couldn't stop laughing. I went round to the flat in Craven Hill Gardens and he asked what had happened. I said 'we were just on our way to see you in this car and we had a crash and Larry is in hospital'. Then I said, 'he was reading the *Daily Express* at the time'. I thought Hancock was going to die he was laughing so much.[5]

Despite his heavy schedule writing for and socialising with Hancock and the Goons, Larry had also found time for romance.

19

Oh, Diana

Larry had become engaged to a 5-foot-9½-inch blonde model five years his junior called Diana Forster. Diana worked with Rosemary Chance and Ellis & Goldstein, for whom she led a troop of 'mannequins' at fashion shows around the country. In 1949, her photograph had appeared in the national newspapers, including the *Daily Mirror* and the *Daily Express*, when she had been at a prestigious hairdressing competition held at London's Horticultural Hall. Diana's hair had been dressed for the 'Premier Craftsman of the Year' section of the contest and the photograph in the newspapers shows one of the judges, Madame Jean Black, peering through a lorgnette at this elegant and beautiful model's hairstyle. In later years Diana worked for the Rahvis couture house and had to parade around wearing gowns from the latest collection and then assist any of the clients who wanted to try on the outfits themselves. She came to notice that the richer a client was, the worse their underwear tended to be.

Diana's mother, Mildred Young, had married Master Mariner Osmonde Farrar at Whitburn Parish Church in January 1926, and the following month they had boarded the P&O ship *Devanha* at the Port of London, bound for Hong Kong. However, it appears that not long into her married life, Mildred's head was turned by another man.

Bernard Roy Forster had arrived in the colony a few months earlier as Private Secretary to the Governor of Hong Kong, Sir Cecil Clementi KG. A ladies' man, oozing charm, Forster had been born and brought up in India and had served as a Second Lieutenant in the First World War on attachment to the 5th Light Infantry.

Mildred and Bernard's 'friendship' shocked Hong Kong society and the pair were forced to flee separately, an event which is reminiscent of a reference in the *Goon Show* episode 'Drums Along the Mersey':

BLOODNOK: In – out, in – out, oooooooohhhhhhh – cast adrift in an open boat with only the sea to keep us afloat.

HARRY: You're the cause of all the strife, getting caught with the captain's wife.

BLOODNOK: It's a lie – we were just good friends...[1]

In September 1928, Diana was born in Newcastle upon Tyne and a month later her birth was registered in the name of 'Diana Forster'. By January 1929, Osmonde Farrar had filed for divorce.

During court proceedings it was alleged that Mildred and Bernard had 'lived and cohabited... at divers places and at The Green, Whitburn... and finally at Peak Hotel Hong Kong',[2] that while in Hong Kong during the period December 1927 and March 1928 they had 'frequently committed adultery... and from the 1st day of November 1928... at the St Margaret's Hotel in the City and County of Newcastle upon Tyne and later at 169 Lauderdale Mansions, Maida Vale, London'.[3] Diana's paternity was also called into question. Mildred and Bernard denied the charges of adultery but a jury found them guilty, the divorce was granted and Osmonde Farrar was awarded £500 in damages, equivalent to around £30,000 in 2017.

Although they had pleaded not guilty, Mildred and Bernard, travelling as Mr and Mrs Forster, went with Diana to Southampton in March of 1929 and embarked on the *Montclare*, which was sailing for Saint John in the Canadian province of New Brunswick. Bernard was now describing himself as a merchant and the family declared that Canada was to be their country of permanent future residence.

They arrived back in England in April of 1930, together with a three-month-old brother for Diana named Jeremy Clive. The family spent a fortnight at the Kensington Palace Hotel before moving again, this time to Shanghai, where they spent three years, with Bernard now stating that his occupation was engineer. Once back on British soil in 1933, Bernard attempted to carve out yet another career for himself. Writing under the name Roy Forster, his novel *Joyous Deliverance* was published by Thornton Butterworth in 1939. The novel seems to have been largely autobiographical.

The central character, Tony Blake, is a successful cricketer, but weary of his life and of Western culture. He decides to escape abroad and takes up a post as private secretary to Sir Theodore Lancet, the Governor of Hongloon. He finds that the Chinese philosophy and way of life is much more in line with his own thinking and so becomes more and more immersed in the society of his Oriental friends.

The outbreak of the Second World War had prevented Diana's father from publishing any further novels for some time and on 1 September 1939, 'Bernard Roy Forster, late Ind. Army'[4] became a Major, just like Bloodnok. However, a 1944 announcement in the *London Gazette* shows that Larry's curry-loving future father-in-law shared more than a few things in common with the *Goon Show* character: 'Maj. B. R. Forster is cashiered by sentence of a Gen. Court-Martial. 24th Jan, 1944.'[5]

In the *Goon Show* episode 'Scradje', Bloodnok's misdemeanour is described but Major Forster's offence must have been somewhat more serious:

PETER: It was in the autumn of nineteen kwinty-kwodge –
the year Major Bloodnok was discharged from the army.
HARRY: Yes, it was the usual. Cowardice in the face of ENSA...[6]

Around April 1950, Larry had recovered sufficiently from his car
crash with Spike to accept an invitation from one of his fiancée's closest
friends. Cicely Romanis, one of Diana's fellow models, had arranged
to celebrate her birthday with a party at an ice rink close to Larry and
Tony's flat in Bayswater and both men were invited. The party was
certainly successful for Tony as the following day he announced to
Phyllis Rounce that he had met the woman he wanted to marry, and
he clearly meant it as he and Cicely quickly became engaged. Their
wedding was planned to take place on 18 September 1950 and Larry
was asked to act as Tony's best man.

From mid-June into September, Tony was appearing at Clacton-
on-Sea in the *Ocean Revue* summer show. The time he had available
between performances didn't give him long to pack everything up
and dash back in time for his wedding. He later recalled: 'In my
rush to catch the train to London I just dived into the wardrobe and
snatched together what I mistook for a complete suit. It turned out in
the unpacking to be the jacket of one striped suit and the trousers of
another. So there I was gawping at myself in the mirror in a ridiculous
ensemble of blue above the waist and grey below.'[7] Thankfully, Larry
was able to do his duty as best man and lent his friend a pair of trousers
to match the jacket. 'I felt it would be churlish to complain about the
cigarette burn just below the knee and so I covered it up as best I
could,'[8] added Tony.

The wedding took place at Christ Church, Kensington and
Larry had obviously already peaked in his role as best man with
the trouser-lending as things went rapidly downhill for him from
there. Sir Reginald Harland attended the ceremony with his wife

Doreen – Cicely's elder sister – and recounted events moments before the arrival of the bride: 'My sole memory of Larry is of him dropping Cicely's wedding ring down a grating in the church, just before the start of the service, and coming back to us to borrow Doreen's one. It gave Cicely quite a shock when Tony put it on her finger, as hers was to have been gold, but Doreen's was platinum, instantly recognisably different. Tony did not replace it for about six months!'[9]

Photos taken outside the church after the ceremony show Larry in the centre of the group – unsmiling as usual – flanked on his right by Cicely's father, Tony's stepfather and Tony's mother and on his left by Tony, Cicely and Cicely's mother.

Two days later, Larry attended another wedding in Kensington, but this time it was his own. He and Diana were married at the Kensington Register Office on 20 September 1950 and for once he even managed to smile for the camera. The newly-married Mr and Mrs Hancock acted as witnesses and also in attendance were Diana's brother Jeremy and Larry's best man, name unknown, but bearing a striking resemblance to 'DT', the trumpet-player from the Dennis R. Hinton band that Larry had played piano with in the 1940s.

Larry's occupation was given as 'Commercial Accountant' on the marriage certificate but there doesn't seem to be any evidence of his ever having trained as an accountant, nor are any of his surviving family members able to confirm this. Perhaps he feared that Diana's father wouldn't have approved of her marrying a writer and musician and so invented an impressive-sounding job title for himself to reassure his new father-in-law he could provide for his daughter. Or perhaps the Registrar misheard or misinterpreted what he said and his job was actually something to do with advertising commercials.

The group were photographed on the steps outside the Register Office looking relaxed and happy, with Larry and Diana holding hands. Diana wore a pale suit with a nipped-in waist and a spray of white flowers on the left lapel. A four-strand pearl choker, dark hat, gloves and court shoes completed her outfit. Larry opted for a dark, double-breasted suit with a pale tie and breast-pocket handkerchief.

Wedding day. From left: Unknown; Tony Hancock; Larry Stephens; Diana Stephens; Cicely Hancock; Jeremy Forster.
(Larry Stephens Estate collection)

The couple set up their first home in Larry's flat at 19 Craven Hill Gardens and shortly afterwards Larry took his new bride on a tour of the Midlands to meet his family. His then fourteen-year-old cousin, Helen Gibson, recalls that this visit made a great impression on her: 'I remember Larry bringing Diana to see us in West Bromwich and being totally overawed by her appearance, especially her make-up and clothes. I thought she was so glamorous!'

From left: Albert Stephens; Diana Stephens; Annie Stephens; Larry Stephens.
(Larry Stephens Estate collection)

Around the time of Larry and Tony's respective marriages, Spike Milligan, Peter Sellers, Harry Secombe and Michael Bentine – or the Goons as they had generally become known – began to perform regularly for their friends on a small, makeshift stage in an upstairs room at Grafton's, because the BBC were finally showing an interest in their material.

20

Those Crazy People, the Goons

The BBC had agreed to record a trial Goons programme as long as the cost didn't exceed £125. The quartet of friends were keen to rehearse their material and try it out in front of an audience before it was released over the airwaves and so the upstairs room at Grafton's had been converted into a temporary private theatre.

The Hancocks and Stephens were often members of the audience, as was BBC producer Dennis Main Wilson: 'We had a mate, who had a mate, who had a pub in Westminster and who didn't close his upstairs lounge after closing time, did he? So the *Goon Show* began upstairs in Jimmy Grafton's boozer. And we all went, the entire Goon Gang obviously plus Alfred Marks, Graham Stark, Benny Hill... There was a sort of gang of ex-service comedy types from whom I was the only BBC producer, the only one who had a regular weekly or monthly salary. Guess who bought the drinks?'[1]

Jimmy Grafton's children, James and Sally, were also allowed to sit and watch the performances and it was at this time that the eight-year-old James developed his first crush, the object of his desire being the attractive Diana Stephens. He also took notice of Larry though: 'I liked Larry a lot. Quite quiet. He used to go to the thirty-bob tailor to buy a suit and wear the same suit every day till it wore out. Then he'd go and buy another one... We had a piano in the bar and he'd play it. He was a very talented man.'[2]

Watching the Goons rehearse at Grafton's. Audience members include Cicely Hancock; James and Sally Grafton; and Larry Stephens, seated underneath the lamp.
(Courtesy of James Grafton and Sally Watson)

The trial recording of the *Goon Show* had originally been scheduled to take place on 19 December 1950 but owing to some legal wrangling over the availability of Harry Secombe, it was postponed until 4 February 1951. In the meantime, Larry continued to write material for Tony Hancock, including the script for his appearance on the BBC radio programme *Variety Bandbox* on 12 November 1950, in a sketch about Secret Agent Hancock being dropped into Ruritania, for which Larry was paid 10 guineas:

HANCOCK: It is dank, dark and dismal and he wishes he'd never volunteered. He wishes he was safe home in bed. And most of all he wishes he had a parachute. Luckily, beneath him is a hayrick. Unluckily, in the hayrick is a pitchfork. Luckily, he misses the pitchfork.

ORCHESTRA: Crash on drums.

HANCOCK: Unluckily, he misses the hayrick. Hancock picks himself up but after fifty yards finds himself too heavy and puts himself down again. He arrives in the capital where a great crowd of peasants are appealing to the Archduke for lower taxes. He turns them down but they are starving. They appeal to him, again and again, they appeal.

ORCHESTRA: Cries of 'Howzat?!' etc. etc.

HANCOCK: Not out! NO! [to audience] Oh, isn't it sickening! Never mind – back to work – nose to the grindstone… Bzzzzzz! – OO-o-oh! Where was I? Oh yes… On he goes and comes to the palace. A great mob is surging around the palace. The one-and-nines are standing only and the palace is littered with peanuts. Just above the town he spies a great castle and takes out his field-glasses, the better to espy it. [Repeats as for *Twenty Questions*[3]] The better to espy it. High up in the tower, he sees a tiny window and a little midget woman. He is enraptured by her loveliness, he is amazed by her tinyness. He is looking through the wrong end of the field-glassiness.

The date of the *Goon Show* trial recording was drawing ever nearer although the BBC were now referring to it as the *Junior Crazy Gang*, a title they felt was more appropriate. The BBC were alone in this opinion. The rehearsals and recording eventually took place from half past ten in the morning until half past three in the afternoon on Sunday 4 February 1951 at a cost of approximately £125, and despite the quartet being relatively unknown, it was considered newsworthy enough to make the national press. Entertainment journalist David

Lewin, writing for the *Daily Express*, felt that radio was becoming jammed up with one-man acts and favoured the decision by the four young comedians to join forces as a 'Goon Gang'.

The trial recording went well and plans were made to broadcast a series from the end of May 1951. Having baulked at the title *Junior Crazy Gang*, the Goons reached a compromise with the BBC and the programme was billed in the *Radio Times* as '*Crazy People* featuring radio's own Crazy Gang "The Goons".'[4] However before reaching this point they ensured there was plenty of pre-publicity for the venture. As he had experience of writing copy through his job, Larry was put in charge of placing a number of spoof adverts in *The Stage*. All gave thanks to a mysterious 'Arnold Fringe' and several included quotes from imaginary critics such as 'We are pleased to think Secombe was born in Swansea – *Cardiff Herald*.'[5] There was also coverage of a more conventional sort with various items in the newspapers. An article in *The Stage* on 17 May explained that the script was to be written by someone called Arnold Fringe, described as being the spirit of the Goons, but this was followed up a week later with another piece which gave the truth of the matter, that Spike Milligan had written the script for the programme with assistance from an ex-commando, Larry Stephens.

According to a piece in the *Daily Mirror* on 25 May, the BBC considered four different titles for the show and four different producers before deciding to give the job to twenty-seven-year-old Dennis Main Wilson, their youngest variety producer. As Dennis had been spending time with the Goon Gang at Jimmy Grafton's pub, he had the advantage of already being on familiar terms with the team of comics and writers.

Larry's role as co-writer with Spike had been officially sanctioned and was referred to in a memo Dennis sent to the BBC's Assistant Head of Variety (Productions): 'I feel that one man alone cannot write a half-hour comedy show – Milligan agrees with this and wishes to work with Larry Stevens [*sic*] (whom I thoroughly recommend) for further ideas and material. The script having been written, he then proposes to let James Grafton edit it from the point of view of continuity – and then finally pass it on to me.'[6]

At quarter to seven on the evening of Monday 28 May 1951, the first programme was broadcast:

ANNOUNCER: What is the zaniest comedy show on the air today?

SPIKE: Er – *Today in Parliament*?

ANNOUNCER: No, it's those *Crazy People*, the Goons.

(APPLAUSE)

ORCHESTRA: GOONS GALLOP (Up and under)

ANNOUNCER: At last here is a programme for listeners with three ears… one for Harry Secombe, Peter Sellers, Michael Bentine and Spike Milligan; one for the Stargazers, Max Geldray and the Ray Ellington Quartet; and one for Stanley Black and his Zulu Bubble Dancers!! So pull your chair up to the ceiling; fill up your glass with potassium cyanide and let the Goons do the rest![7]

All of those involved with the show quickly settled into their new routine. From ten o'clock every Sunday morning they would gather for rehearsals and script checks and the day would reach its climax at quarter to six in the evening when the programme was recorded in front of an audience. It would then be broadcast on the BBC's Home Service the following day.

Larry would often use the blank, rear pages of his copy of the script to doodle and jot down notes during the read-throughs. Judging by the intricacy of some of his sketches, he must have had some extended periods of hanging around. He was fond of drawing Goon characters, some of them generic and some of them more specific. There is a 'framed portrait' of Jim Spriggs, several sketches of Henry Crun and one particularly outstanding representation of Bluebottle, dressed in a pre-1950s Boy Scout uniform. Many of his non-Goonish cartoons show characters with large noses and he often signed his artwork as 'Larry "the nose" Stephens'.

In the early days, the *Goon Show* was a series of sketches, divided by musical performances by the Ray Ellington Quartet, the Stargazers and Max Geldray. The writing tended to be rather haphazard since some sketches were written by Larry and some by Spike with Michael Bentine and Jimmy Grafton both pitching ideas into the pot. Jimmy would then be responsible for editing this random collection of scribblings to try and bring a bit of consistency to the whole thing.

To begin with, the shows were listed in the *Radio Times* as having been compiled by Spike Milligan and an announcement to the same effect was made during the broadcast. By week 4, the *Radio Times* credit had changed to show that the script had been written by Spike Milligan with additional material by Larry Stephens and Jimmy Grafton and in week 7 it became fixed with a credit to all three of them as writers of the scripts.

Larry and Diana would generally join the studio audience for the programme recordings and they also attended the unofficial rehearsals, which continued in the upstairs room at Grafton's. A double-page spread appeared in the *Picture Post* magazine edition of 16 June 1951 and one of the photographs, captioned 'At Grafton's Pub, Victoria, They Are Definitely Amused', shows a group of people enjoying one of the performances, with a laughing Diana positioned in the centre of them.

Larry had very much been keeping his options open as he worked to establish himself as a scriptwriter. His name had been proposed as a writer with A. N. Other for a potential new variety programme suggested by producer Peter Eton at the end of March 1951. To be called *Pinhead's Gazette*, it would be 'a series about a badly run newspaper, the energies of whose staff are devoted to keeping the company out of liquidation and trying to get scoops and special features. The paper has a formidable list of creditors who are continually pestering the owner and threatening legal action. One of the principal characters is a writ-server who pops up in impossible places throughout the series. Each programme would consist of three regular spots separated by musical items.'[8] The programme does not appear to have materialised.

Larry was also mentioned in a letter written by Jimmy Grafton to the BBC towards the end of 1950 which showed that the two of them had been working together on more than just the *Goon Show*. In the letter, Jimmy set out the idea he and Larry had had for a 'light-hearted private detective series'[9] to be entitled *Shamus McKay – Private Eye*. The Variety Department at the BBC weren't averse to the idea but didn't feel that it would work as a standalone series, believing it to be more appropriate as a ten-minute spot in an existing programme. Although the BBC kept it in mind while waiting for a suitable programme in which to place it, nothing more seems to have come of the idea, although a sketch entitled 'Splutmuscle the Private Investigator' did subsequently appear in programme 9 of the *Goon Show*, which is notable for containing the following scene:

EFFECTS: (PHONE RINGS)
PETER: Hallo? Hawkeye Splutmuscle here. Ever vigilant.
MICHAEL: (WOMAN) Oh, Mr Splutmuscle! My husband's been shot! I've just come in from the front room and found him lying on the carpet here!
PETER: Is he dead?
MICHAEL: I think so.
PETER: Hadn't you better make sure?

> MICHAEL: Alright – just a minute.
> EFFECTS: (SEVERAL PISTOL SHOTS)
> MICHAEL: Yes, he's dead![10]

In 2001, Professor Richard Wiseman of the University of Hertfordshire embarked on a scientific study to discover the world's funniest joke. The winning gag, submitted to Professor Wiseman's LaughLab by Gurpal Gosall, bears a striking similarity to the Splutmuscle scene:

> Two hunters are out in the woods when one of them collapses. He doesn't seem to be breathing and his eyes are glazed. The other guy whips out his phone and calls the emergency services. He gasps, 'My friend is dead! What can I do?' The operator says, 'Calm down. I can help. First, let's make sure he's dead.' There is a silence, then a shot is heard. Back on the phone, the guy says, 'OK, now what?'[11]

Five years later, a BBC website article announced that the writer of the 'world's best joke' had been found and reported that Professor Wiseman had seen an archive clip of the Goons' sketch (probably from the 1951 film, *London Entertains*) and had noticed the similarity between the two. The script for programme 9 of the *Goon Show* is credited to Larry, Spike and Jimmy but, given the link to *Shamus McKay – Private Eye*, it seems likely that this particular sketch would have been the work of Jimmy and/or Larry. However, there is no way of knowing if it was their original work or something they had heard and adapted.

As the programme scripts for the first series were put together using contributions from several people, it is difficult to pinpoint exactly who wrote what but in his memoir in *The Goon Show Companion*, Jimmy Grafton mentioned one particular line of Larry's he remembered from the fourth programme. One of the sketches in this episode was called 'Parliament in Session' and the Goons had discussed the bouts of good-humoured banter and the fun and games that occasionally took place in the House of Commons. They tried to imagine what it would be like if the House was more like a theatre and the Members of Parliament were professional entertainers. The line Jimmy remembered Larry writing for this sketch was delivered by Peter Sellers, playing the part of a fictional roving reporter for the BBC called Jack Islott:

And here comes the Foreign Secretary now, tall and dignified, head and shoulders above his staff, moving smoothly and erectly on his one-wheeled bicycle.[12]

It is possible to see Larry's influence in other sections though, most notably in the opening sketch of programme 17 on the subject of piano lessons:

HARRY: ... But soon it became obvious that I was a musical prodigy... I had that little extra something that other children didn't have. I took up the piano and sat all day practising my six-finger exercises.
PETER: Five-finger exercises!
HARRY: Six. As I told you – I had that little extra something which other ch—

As the series progressed, the closing credits of each broadcast also became part of the overall Goon humour, ranging from:

The script cargo was swung aboard by Spike Milligan and Larry Stephens and lashed and stowed by Jimmy Grafton.

Producer Dennis Main Wilson was at the helm when the boat sank.[13]

... to:

> Regimental orders were scripted by Spike Milligan and Larry Stephens and the seal was affixed by Jimmy Grafton. Producer Dennis Main Wilson posted them up, shortly before deserting.[14]

... and also, in what can now be regarded as quite prescient in terms of the impact the show subsequently had on the development of British comedy:

> History was created by Spike Milligan and Larry Stephens and chronicled by Jimmy Grafton. Producer Dennis Main Wilson gave it to the world.[15]

There was certainly one person in the world who was witnessing this history in the making: the twenty-eight-year-old *Educating Archie* scriptwriter, Eric Sykes.

21

Writing and Farting with Spike

During the late summer of 1951, Eric Sykes was in hospital waiting to undergo an operation on his ear. He spent a lot of time dozing and listening to the radio through headphones and it was in one of the periods between snoozes that he happened to catch an episode of the *Goon Show*. After laughing himself to near exhaustion, he waited eagerly for the closing credits to see who was responsible for the dose of mirth: 'Script by Spike Milligan and Larry Stephens'. The names weren't familiar to him but he felt certain he would be hearing them again. What they had written was completely different from most of the comedy around at the time; it was inventive, energetic and it broke all the rules. It had such an electrifying effect on him that he decided to write a letter to the pair to congratulate them and to thank them for making his hospital stay more tolerable.

A few days later, propped up in bed with his head swaddled in bandages and still suffering from the effects of his operation, Eric glanced towards the door and saw a strange sight. Was he hallucinating? He squeezed his eyes shut, gave his head a gentle shake, opened his eyes and looked again. It was still there: two ghostly faces were peering around the doorframe, one about two feet lower than the other. Before he had time to work out that the lowest of the two faces must belong to someone who was kneeling, they'd gone. A couple of days later, he received a letter from Larry and Spike, apologising for turning up unannounced on his hospital ward. They had been so excited to receive his letter and were so grateful for his praise that they had wanted to thank him personally. A significant connection had now been made and within a year Larry would be working with Eric.

Larry's name was becoming more widely known and there was an attempt to make it even more so. During episodes 14 and 15, the Goons tried to introduce a new catchphrase:

SPIKE: More coal Larry. Larry − more coal.

PETER: Who is that?

HARRY: That is a catchphrase that we're trying to establish in the show.

PETER: Catchphrase? I say − you there, say it again.

SPIKE: More coal Larry. Larry − more coal.

PETER: (PAUSE) Hmmm. Is that supposed to be funny?

HARRY: No. Of course not. You have to repeat it several thousands of times before it catches on. But in a few years' time, you'll be able to switch on your radio and hear this −

EFFECTS: (DOOR OPENS)

SPIKE: More coal Larry. Larry − more coal.

ORCHESTRA: MAD LAUGHTER FOR SEVERAL SECONDS − THEN BREAK INTO THUNDEROUS APPLAUSE.[1]

The majority of the intended repetitions were cut from the script before broadcast so it didn't have quite as much impact as had been hoped; it wasn't mentioned in any of the future programmes either. If the Goons had persevered, the phrase 'More coal Larry. Larry − more coal' might have been as familiar today as 'the dreaded lurgi'.

This first series of the *Goon Show* came to an end with the broadcast of the 17th programme on 20 September 1951, the date of Larry and Diana's first wedding anniversary. Short of money, Larry had produced an oil painting to present to his wife. It was a portrait of Diana, wrapped in a fur coat and leaning against a tree on the right-hand side of the canvas. A chain of gold linked by brightly coloured gemstones is draped across the top and down the left-hand side of the picture. In the middle is written: 'A happy anniversary to Mrs Stephens!! With pitchers of oil-paint mink and oil-paint jewels on account of that's the only kind of mink and jewels I can afford but with a tankard (imaginary) full of love (real) from Baldy.'

Larry's artistic bent extended far beyond doodles on his scripts and the occasional oil painting; he also experimented with charcoal, watercolour, pencil and ink, and quite an extensive portfolio of his work still survives.

Now that the *Goon Show* had come to an end, the BBC were unsure as to whether another series would be commissioned or not. The show was being repeated on the Light Programme and on the General Overseas Service and the Corporation were waiting to garner audience reaction and opinion before making a decision. Spike and Larry had, however, been asked to submit a script for a Christmas Goon pantomime which would include original music and lyrics by the two of them.

The pair weren't idle though, and had other projects to keep them occupied in the meantime. They had apparently been writing material for Peter Sellers, who wrote letters to the heads of radio, television and theatre companies, trying to interest them in commissioning a show. First of all he tried Michael Standing at BBC Radio, telling him that he, Spike and Larry had come up with a great idea for a thirty-minute show and asking if he could send the details to him. Sellers stressed that he felt confident he could make a success of his own show and would definitely be able to handle the responsibility. He said that if Standing was amenable to the idea, he would prefer not to go into *Bumblethorpe* as he considered it would be too much for him to take on with his work on *Ray's A Laugh* too.

The show *Bumblethorpe* was an eight-part series which began on the BBC Home Service on 12 November 1951. Starring Valentine Dyall, Robert Moreton, Avril Angers and Kenneth Connor, it was a comedy thriller about a mysterious character whose lost diary had fallen into the hands of blackmailers. Each week, the title character was played by a different actor and Tony Hancock took the role in an episode broadcast on 31 December 1951. The series was written by Larry and Spike together with Peter Ling, a writer who is now best remembered as a co-creator of the soap opera *Crossroads* in the 1960s.

In the event, Sellers' appearance in *Bumblethorpe* was limited to a single episode. He was a last-minute replacement for Valentine Dyall, after Dyall – known to radio listeners as the sinister-voiced 'Man in Black' – failed to turn up for rehearsals.

This didn't make any difference to Standing's views on Sellers' suggestion for a new show, though. Standing replied that he would certainly be interested in seeing Sellers' proposal but added there was no opportunity for placing such a show in the near future. Sellers was clearly looking for something more immediate so his next attempt followed two weeks later in a letter to BBC Television's Ronnie Waldman. As with his letter to Michael Standing, he told him that he, Spike and Larry had been working together on some ideas. This time though, he changed the description to call them a series of short sketches that he felt were ideal for television. He suggested that if Waldman liked the sound of them, they could all work together and launch a new series.

Again, this seems to have been unsuccessful as the next reference to the material Larry and Spike had written was a brief mention in

The Stage on 11 October 1951: 'Peter Sellers... has a new stage act in preparation in which he will leave out impersonations. The script has been written by the writers of the *Goon Show*, Spike Milligan and Larry Stevens [*sic*], and will be presented in the near future.'[2]

In the event, the sketches didn't appear in the near future after all. They were eventually used in 1956, in the *Son of Fred* series made for ITV.

Spike Milligan and Peter Sellers photographed by Larry Stephens in 1953.
(Larry Stephens Estate collection)

As *Bumblethorpe* came to the end of its run, Larry and Spike's *Goon Show* pantomime, dubbed 'Goonderella', was broadcast on Boxing Day. As well as the four Goons, the cast included Graham Stark, taking the roles of the Second Ugly Sister and Prince Charming, and Lizbeth Webb as Cinderella. A *Radio Times* feature detailing programmes over the Christmas period confirmed that a second series of the *Goon Show* would begin three weeks after the pantomime had been broadcast.

The BBC had carried out a lot of audience research into the first series and the points raised in the listeners' reports (or 'Nosey Parker Listener

Research Reports' as they were referred to in programme 15 of the second series) were being taken into consideration before the new series of the *Goon Show* kicked off. Feedback suggested that a slower pace was desired and that the writers would need to ensure that the script announced which performer was playing which character. There were also plans to include a weekly running gag.

These listeners' comments must have reached Larry and Spike quite early on, as an item in episode 14 of the first series poked fun at them. In the sketch, a fictional elocution teacher and Dean of an Oxford College were invited to listen to the Goons' version of *Dick Barton, Special Agent* and to blow a whistle halting the presentation whenever they had a suggestion for improvement. The performance ended up as follows:

PETER: I am standing outside the front door of this house which conceals the fiendish Chinese crook Fu Manchu. Wishing to gain entrance, I shoot out my right hand and grasp a round brass object protruding from the woodwork. This is known as a door knob. I turn it sharply to the right –
EFFECTS: (HANDLE TURNING)
PETER: This releases a catch which strikes a nublet-pin, forcing the hurckle-block down into the sprunge-sprocket, which enables me to open the door – so –
EFFECTS: (DOOR OPENS)
PETER: And followed by my two assistants, I step inside. Now – quick, Jock – played by Spike Milligan and Snowy – played by Harry Secombe.
HARRY: Look out, Guvnor – played by Peter Sellers – there's a sliding panel opening in the wall![3]

One particular change, which was welcomed by all, was that the programme would now be billed as 'The *Goon Show* with those Crazy

People' rather than 'Crazy People featuring The Goons' because, as Dennis Main Wilson explained in a memo of 8 January 1952, 'everybody, both in and outside the business, refers to it as the *Goon Show* (or rather <u>that</u> *Goon Show*) but never as Crazy People (which quite frankly could be applied to almost any comedy show)'.[4] The cost of producing the show each week had now more than doubled from the £125 that was allocated in making the pilot and included £63 for the scriptwriters, equivalent to approximately £1,800 in 2017.

The first programme in the new series of twenty-five was broadcast on 22 January 1952 and the *Radio Times* credit had been changed to show that the script was now being written by Spike Milligan and Larry Stephens and edited by Jimmy Grafton.

At the end of February, Larry's work was heard not only in the *Goon Show* but also during Tony Hancock's appearance in the variety show *Calling All Forces* on the 25th of that month, with a monologue about family life:

My father was a woodchopper by trade but I never wanted to take up this profession, that is until I started working with Andrews. My father was a strange man, very fond of the open air. He loved exercising over the moors with dogs... in fact that is one of my earliest memories, the sound of father's heavy breathing as he ran steadily forward through the morning mist and behind him the baying of the bloodhounds and the shouts of the warders. He came to stay with us in the ditch for a while as there was a large reward out for anyone who turned him in... poor man. With the reward Mother bought a house. But this was no life for a spirited lad, no life for me with my great thirst for knowledge (INT. And gin!). Ah ah ah cheeky pupil. However, Dame Fortune smiled at us eventually. We had wealth and became people of leisure, able to ride on the downs whenever we wished. I remember one day I arose at six – rather earlier than usual but then it was such a lovely evening. I put on my riding boots, spurs, scarlet jacket and bowler and with one bound I mounted my thoroughbred chestnut bicycle. It was hard going, cycling over the downs. As I painfully pedalled along, one question burned in my mind: who had stolen the saddle? As fresh country breeze blew through my hair, caressing my curls with gossamer fingers, I began to daydream. I had always thought of myself as a city-dweller at heart but now I suddenly realised that deep down I was really a countryman, a man of the soil. I was close to the earth. I had fallen off my bike...[5]

Larry adapted the 'riding on the downs' joke for a 1954 *Goon Show* episode in which he described the amazing sight of the 230 pupils of Rottingdean, England's oldest school, getting astride their saddles to gallop over the downs. It was apparently an extraordinary scene because they didn't actually have any horses.

Larry, Spike and Tony were great friends during this period. They would go to a café in Chalk Farm every now and then and Hancock would order boiled rice with raspberry jam for the three of them. None of them particularly wanted to eat it but Hancock used to enjoy saying it. But this was very tame compared to some of the antics Larry and Spike got up to. Spike told John Antrobus about their 'writing practices':

Larry and I made a tape while we were writing Goon shows. A tape of our farts. When we felt one coming on, we would turn the machine on and record it. I put some introductory music to this fart tape and one night at home when we had company for dinner I put it on. The music was pleasant background to the dinner conversation and June was well pleased with the way the evening was going. Then the farting began. I said nothing. The people packed up and went home. Good riddance. Boring bunch of my wife's friends. They had no conversation anyway.[6]

Larry and Spike were spending more and more time with each other. Their days were full of work and writing but they enjoyed each other's company and so began to socialise together regularly too. When they were apart, they would exchange wildly funny correspondence in the style of *Goon Show* characters. Larry would also create drawings and sketches for Spike, one remarkable example being a huge colour composition entitled *The Fighting Milligans of India – A Panorama*. Along with portraits and descriptions of fictional Milligan ancestors it included the cap badges of their regiments such as the 2/7th Regular Army Deserters and the 3rd Mounted Bagpipes.

Larry Stephens photographed by Graham Stark.
(Larry Stephens Estate collection)

Spike delighted in Larry's talent as a jazz pianist and in the early days of their friendship he could often be found sleeping contentedly under the piano while Larry continued to play. The pair were very different characters; Spike was an extrovert, full of energy, and would let all of his thoughts and feelings escape. Larry was more introverted, would only open up to people he knew well and would generally suppress his emotions. They had different approaches in their professional lives to match their personalities too. Spike would sit at the typewriter and bash out whatever came into his head whereas Larry was more methodical and would plan and consider everything before committing it to paper. Dennis Main Wilson commented on their different strengths in a memo to the BBC's Head of Variety in 1952. He felt Spike was an ideas man who excelled at writing gags but had no sense of pure wit or any idea how to build situations or construct a plot. Larry he considered to be brilliant at writing situation and character and remarked that the more intelligent wit in the *Goon Show* tended to be his work. Larry had a weak sense of gag comedy though, which let him down. By ironing out each other's weaknesses and combining their strengths, the Larry and Spike mixture resulted in a well-rounded whole.

The pair's friendship was probably strengthened by the time the second series of the *Goon Show* reached programme 9, as they received something of a ticking-off from Dennis Main Wilson. He outlined a series of complaints and suggestions about their writing, in a letter which was copied to the Variety Heads at the BBC.

One of the main points raised was that Larry and Spike's scripts were too long. The producer gave several reasons for why this was happening:

We are getting a larger percentage of 'long build-up' gags than 'quickies'… These… gags take up much of the time which you tell me you need for the plot and action. This is one reason for your finding it difficult to keep the sketches down to the required duration... We must curb the tendency... to become a string of 'gags on a theme', rather than a Goon action plot with subsidiary gags adding to the comedy of the action. (And as all these extra gags take up time – here is <u>another</u> reason for your difficulties of overwriting.)[7]

Dennis Main Wilson also mentioned a lack of forward planning in the scripts' subject matter meaning they were missing out on topicality:

We are losing many chances of being 100% topical in the show. 'Olympic Winter Sports' was written for the show 10 days after the real thing had finished. The Irish Bloodnok sequence went out a week before St Patrick's Day. Having suggested to you weeks ago the idea of doing a circus routine to cash in on the topicality of 'The Greatest Show on Earth' – and everybody having agreed we should do it – it still hasn't been written. As a result 'Take It from Here' have scooped us on the idea. There must be more planning on the complete shows some weeks before settling down to work them out in full (in other words, meeting before rather than during scriptwriting, as I suggested to you before the series started)...[8]

Larry and Spike obviously took notice of this – at least for a little while – as they wrote a Grand National sketch which was broadcast on 1 April, four days ahead of the real event, although the circus routine didn't appear until the end of June.

Despite the reprimand, Larry and Spike were now considered to be among the elite of the scriptwriting profession. The renowned critic J. C. Trewin had been asked to provide Listener's Reports for the BBC's Variety Department and his report covering programmes broadcast in May was full of praise for the pair and for the *Goon Show*:

The Variety serials I have enjoyed most are *Bedtime with Braden*, *Just Fancy* and *The Goon Show*... All of these programmes are full of ideas... and they give what radio Variety never ceases to need: nonsense humour with an edge, with salt... *The Goon Show* takes us, of course, into a Never Never land under a green-cheese moon. ('What about a sub?' asks the Admiralty official. 'Not a penny until Friday' says the Admiral.) It does, I think, understand more than any other Variety programme on the air, the value of the sound effect. It is surprising that radio Variety should have been so unadventurous here... One of the great charms of such shows as... The Goons is that they are pure radio, the kind of hubble-bubble nonsense we can hear only on the air; they are in fact using sound-radio as it should be used.[9]

In order to see the BBC creating more programmes of this quality, Trewin suggested running a comedy scriptwriting competition to discover and nurture fresh talent. He did however add that there were 'unlikely to be many Nordens and Muirs, Milligans and Stephenses, Monkhouses and Goodwins'.[10]

Around the same time as J. C. Trewin was writing his report, another of Larry's spoof advertisements for the *Goon Show* appeared in *The Stage*; this one, placed in a prominent position, was in his own name:

LARRY
STEPHENS

wishes to announce that, owing to his heavy commitments as co-writer of 'The Goon Show,' he is unable to supply the following of his famous three-and-sixpenny Komedy Kameos:-

DAME	VENT
CURATE	CLUB PATTER
POLYNESIAN DIALECT GAGS	
KHURDISH FIREMAN	

Sole rights of 'Working Man with Stutter' have been sold to Alf Turley, the celebrated society entertainer, late of Turley and Perkins ('Unexpectedly Vacant').

However, Mr Stephens is preparing a new edition of his celebrated 'Dramatic Monos,' including those famous studies in pathos: 'Come Home, Fred Flange,' And 'We'll Light a Candle for You, Chester Suavely' – both dedicated to Harry Secombe.

ALL COMS: 18A Rue des Soubilles,[11]
Place de la Concorde,
Cardiff

P.S.:   WANTED, Tall attractive showgirls with two heads for summer season at Bearwood.[12]

Bearwood was a village located around two and a half miles from Larry's Quinton family house and was home to the Windsor Theatre. The theatre opened in the 1930s as a 'super picture and variety theatre', and after the war it was the base for Frank H. Fortescue's repertory company, known as his Famous Players. The company put on a wide variety of plays from domestic farces and grim thrillers to adaptations of works by Agatha Christie and Charlotte Brontë, but whether they were in the habit of employing tall showgirls with two heads or not is lost in the mists of time. Larry doesn't seem to have remembered the Windsor with any particular fondness and it received another mention in his script for 'The Missing Bureaucrat' episode from series 4 of the *Goon Show*. Playing the part of Dr Eidelberger, Peter Sellers was directed to 'ad lib' the following German curses while hysterical with rage:

> PETER: ... Undt den Windsor Bearwood – gedammt, geshleitung undt twice nightly! Mit all seats bookable...[13]

In keeping with his steady climb into the upper class of the scriptwriting world, Larry began looking for a new home that would be more befitting of his elevated status. He noted the details of a rental property on his copy of the *Goon Show* 'Grand National' script: '5 ½ per week. 3 months in advance. £10 deposit for gas, electricity etc.' and house-hunting became a theme in his scripts. In one of the episodes, Professor Osric Pureheart, played by Michael Bentine, takes part in the excavations at Pompeii and uncovers a Roman villa. He calls his wife to tell her the news:

> MICHAEL: ... after all these years I've found it!
> PETER: Wonderful, darling. Is it genuine Roman or just Neo-Pompeiic?
> MICHAEL: I don't care what the devil it is. The point is, it's unfurnished, self-contained, no premium, nothing to pay for fixtures and fittings... No key money – own bathroom – [14]

Not long after, Larry and Diana moved to the basement flat at 108A Regent's Park Road. The two-bedroomed flat was in a Victorian villa looking out onto Regent's Park and a short walk from Primrose Hill village. It was also ideally located, just across the road from the Queen's Hotel pub.

Larry Stephens outside Queen's Hotel, Regent's Park Road, 1953.
(Larry Stephens Estate collection)

Now that he was in a new home, no doubt at additional cost, Larry probably wasn't thrilled to receive a letter telling him that he had been overpaid. After its initial broadcast on the Home Service, the *Goon Show* was now being repeated on the BBC's Light Programme and on the General Overseas Service and Larry was paid a repeat fee for each additional broadcast. He had received a cheque for £13 2s 6d for a repeat of episode 5; however, this particular programme didn't end up being broadcast on the Overseas Service after all and so naturally the BBC wanted its money back. The Accounts Department simply deducted the amount in question from the next cheque due to Larry. Presumably, Spike had received a similar letter and the duo's resulting bad moods at the loss of their money may well have worsened a rift that had developed between them.

22

A New Series for Hancock

The BBC's Variety Department had noticed that for a few weeks there had been a decline in the quality of *Goon Show* performances and scripts, and had fired off a memo highlighting their concerns to Dennis Main Wilson. Dennis blamed the poor performances on a move to a new studio at the end of April 1952 but the script problems he put down to a falling-out between Larry and Spike. Spike had been off sick for a couple of weeks at the beginning of April and Larry had struggled to cope on his own, had got behind and submitted the scripts late. Even when Spike returned to work, there was still a battle to make up lost ground and get back on schedule. The pressure had made Larry irritable and snappy, and this, combined with Spike feeling out of sorts, had led to a squabble followed by a refusal to speak to each other. Instead of working together on the four separate sketches needed for each week's show, they had begun writing two sketches each as solo efforts. Dennis found the whole situation incredibly childish and ridiculous but was working to patch things up between them.

A month later, at the beginning of July 1952 and just as the second series of the *Goon Show* was coming to an end, Dennis announced that he wished to step down as producer. Peter Eton was approached and agreed to produce the show from the beginning of the third series, which was scheduled to start in November. Eton shared his recollections at a meeting of the Goon Show Preservation Society in 1976: 'I had some preliminary talks with Spike and also Larry Stephens who was working with Spike in those days; he was really the strong man in those days... Larry had come to me and said they wanted a drama producer on it to give the programme shape because in the early days it was just one-line gags and occasionally they were actually put into sketches.'[1]

Larry seemed to have been in the habit of making suggestions to Peter Eton and they often involved his friend Tony Hancock. Before he became involved with the *Goon Show*, Eton remembered that 'before anyone had heard of Hancock, he (Larry) came down to my office one day with this man and he said: "this is Tony Hancock who has an act on the stage... You should put him in one of your plays... because I think he's got great potential"... Larry had found this man – he was writing material for him.'[2]

By July 1952, Hancock was a much more familiar figure and now that Larry's name as a writer was regularly being mentioned in the same breath as the likes of Muir and Norden, Peter Eton took the latest suggestion they had for him much more seriously. He outlined their proposal in a memo to the Head of Variety:

> Tony Hancock and Larry Stephens have suggested an idea for a new Hancock series. As Tony is genuinely enthusiastic about Larry's idea I thought it might be a good thing to tell you about it, even while discussions are at a preliminary stage... Tony Hancock plays the part of an estate-agent-cum-bachelor-town-councillor who lives with his old aunt in one of those frightful semi-detached villas in a small South Coast town. Our hero is an unimaginative, unenterprising, charming idiot... Apart from the fact that each of the 6 or more half-hour programmes would consist of a complete story about Tony's pompous yet likeable blundering, there would

be no set formula. No audience – no orchestra – and no singers would be required. Recorded music would be used for opening, closing and links. Shall I encourage them to go further?[3]

The Light Programme expressed an interest in this new Hancock series, to be titled *Vacant Lot*, and asked to see a synopsis. Larry put together a 'brief synopsis' for the opening programme, a 'very brief synopsis' for the second programme and 'notes on the preceding'.

The setting for *Vacant Lot* was Churdley Bay, a fictional small town on the south coast of England, described as being neither modern nor 'olde-worlde'. What set it apart from other seaside towns was that whereas they were crowded during the summer and dull and deserted for the rest of the year, Churdley Bay was dull and deserted all the year round. We learn that campaigning is under way for the town council elections and Hancock is standing in one of the wards. He is regarded with amused tolerance by the local bigwigs, among them the Mayor, Ambrose Tripfield, and Dr Quince the GP, and is mocked and teased by several of the regulars at the Churdley Arms pub.

Churdley Bay isn't based on anywhere in particular but appears to be a pick 'n' mix of places on a small stretch of the East Sussex coast with elements of other British seaside resorts thrown in for good measure. Larry seems to have drawn a lot of inspiration from Pevensey Bay for his fictional setting though, and the two certainly share some features: both have a Martello tower and a shingle beach, for example. What's more, a former owner of the fictional Royal Hotel in Churdley Bay is called Mr Pevensey.

Registers from the real Bay Hotel in Pevensey Bay plus the memories of local people confirm that Tony Hancock, Peter Sellers, Spike Milligan and Michael Bentine spent holidays in Pevensey, and it crops up as a location in *Goon Shows* from time to time so it seems very likely that Mr and Mrs Stephens spent time there too.

Despite having a break from the *Goon Show*, Larry was kept incredibly busy throughout the summer and autumn. As well as writing the synopsis for *Vacant Lot* and working on scripts for other radio programmes, Larry had what was perhaps his first experience of writing for television when he was invited, along with Eric Sykes, to put something together for Jimmy James, one of the period's most popular entertainers. The 19th National Radio and Television Exhibition was set to open at Earls Court on 26 August and as well as displays of the latest technology, there would be a specially built studio for the production of full-scale television programmes. One of these was to be a comedy show with Jimmy James and Hermione Gingold on 4 September.

Larry and Eric travelled to Morecambe on 30 July with Producer Bill Lyon-Shaw to meet Jimmy James. They discussed scripts, not only for the Earls Court show but also for a new monthly series which was scheduled to start in October, called *Don't Spare the Horses*. As the trip involved an overnight stay, Larry and Eric were entitled to claim expenses, including the fare for their return journey, food and drink for one day, plus any money they would need for reciprocal entertainment.

Other programmes that Larry worked on during the summer months of 1952 included *Arthur's Inn* and *Forces All Star Bill*. *Arthur's Inn*, produced by Peter Eton, was broadcast on the Light Programme. Built around Arthur Askey, it harked back to the pre-war series *Band Waggon*. Askey's character was the proprietor of an almost poverty-stricken inn who was bossed around by a rich American with strong ideas on how he should be running things, played by Diana Decker. Askey was also joined by two of his co-stars from the stage production *Bet Your Life*: Brian Reece and Sally Ann Howes. Musical interludes were provided by the Revue Orchestra. The series had started in June with Bob Block and Bill Harding as the scriptwriters and had not at first proved very popular, either with listeners or with the BBC's management. J. C. Trewin had felt compelled to mention it in his report, even though it fell outside of his remit. He commented that no consideration seemed to have been given to how it would work on the radio; traditional slapstick that was effective on the stage didn't translate well into sound radio when there wasn't the visual element to rely on. He mentioned one scene from *Arthur's Inn*, involving wallpapering a room, as having been particularly tedious. The 'variety serial' as a genre, he felt, had become stale and was no longer the cosy family entertainment it had once been.

After seven programmes had been made, Block and Harding departed for Blackpool to take on another project and new writers had to be found. Peter Eton asked Larry and Spike to write a couple of programmes and also approached a pair of up-and-coming writers called Ray Galton and Alan Simpson.

Galton and Simpson remembered meeting Larry and Spike to discuss the programme and, as Ray recalled, 'the two of them came into the room, clutching their arms and pretending they'd just injected a strong drug. We thought this was part of the showbiz lifestyle we were getting into and didn't realise for quite a while that we were having our legs pulled!'[4] Ray and Alan admitted to having been slightly in awe of Larry, Spike, Tony Hancock et al. as they were only twenty-two; the others seemed so much older at around thirty.

Larry and Spike wrote *Arthur's Inn* programme numbers 8 and 10, for which they received seventy guineas between them. They were also called on to make some fairly significant alterations to programme number 9 as the writer, Eddie Maguire, was away on holiday at the time; for this they received twenty guineas.

Larry had now begun to represent himself and Spike in all dealings with the BBC and had been empowered to sign contracts on Spike's behalf. When they were asked to contribute some twenty-minute scripts for *Forces All Star Bill* at a fee of thirty guineas each per programme, Larry stepped in to do the negotiating:

> Mr Milligan and myself... have talked it over between ourselves and considering (a) the complicated format and continuity of the show and (b) the tremendous amount of work involved when an entirely new principal comedian has to be written for each time, we consider a basic fee of 40 guineas each would be reasonable. We agreed to write a certain number of these programmes only on condition that an adequate fee was paid; as we pointed out to Mr Wilson, many of the later *Goon Show* scripts were hurried and behind schedule merely because we were being forced to do other work in order to supplement our income. As you know, we lost our Overseas repeat and this cut down our fee considerably. We also pointed this out to Mr Peter Eton when he called us in to write No. 8 of *Arthur's Inn*. Incidentally, you mention that we have been asked to write *Forces All Star Bill* every other week. Although we are supposed to write approximately half the number of programmes, they will not be in strict rotation.[5]

The BBC agreed to meet them in the middle and they were subsequently paid thirty-five guineas each per programme. Larry did, however, request that separate cheques should be made out to him and Spike, explaining that, 'towards the end of the *Goon Show* we began to receive cheques made out jointly to both of us and this involved the business of joint endorsements which is difficult as we do not work together all the time'.[6]

They may not always have worked together but they generally collaborated with other people when writing for radio. However, in September, Larry was given the opportunity to create something on his own. His synopsis for the proposed Hancock series *Vacant Lot* had originally been rejected by the Light Programme 'as being unsuitable, not strong enough in character or sufficiently well developed,[7] but a week later the Head of Variety re-read the synopsis and disagreed with the Light Programme's verdict. He believed that it would be a good role for Hancock and therefore decided to commission a full script. Peter Eton contacted the Copyright Department and asked them to set the wheels in motion:

> Will you please commission Larry Stephens of 108A Regent's Park Road NW1 to write a half-hour script for a trial programme starring Tony Hancock called *Vacant Lot*. This is to be a first episode of a projected comedy serial. There is no music and the programme is not broken up by any musical acts or solo performances of any kind, therefore Mr Stephens will need to write 30 minutes of material.[8]

Larry must have seen this as his big break and he was so excited that he wrote the script without agreeing any fee whatsoever. He must have drawn material from his pre-war experience as an estate agent's clerk in Birmingham when writing the *Vacant Lot* script as Hancock's character is an estate agent and auctioneer who is elected to the Grimley Street Ward in the local council elections.

Grimley & Son had been in operation in Temple Street, Birmingham as auctioneers, valuers and estate agents during the period Larry was employed in the industry and in the 1930s they held weekly furniture sales as well as sales of pictures and antiques at the Grand Hotel. Although Grimley's set-up strongly resembles the agency Larry created for *Vacant Lot*, it is not clear whether he actually worked for them or for one of their rivals.

After reading through the script, Peter Eton handed it back to Larry with some suggestions for changes. The final version was completed on 15 October 1952:

Dear Peter,

I finished the script of *Vacant Lot* last night (Wednesday) and gave it to Tony, as so far he has seen no version of it at all. He said he would try to get it to you tonight, or perhaps tomorrow morning.

Just in case all is well and you want to go ahead quickly, I am enclosing a list of the characters, with my comments on them and their voices. I may have missed one or two as I am doing this from memory (in order of their appearance as far as I can remember).

In the second draft of the script, I have made some of the alterations which you suggested in your notes. As usual, I have completely agreed with some of your criticisms and violently and flatly disagreed with others. Where this has occurred, I have <u>not</u> altered the original script. There is, however, only one <u>main</u> point on which I disagree, and that is the question of broad farce versus comedy. I feel if this series is to be at all successful, each show must be compounded of (a) a fairly strong storyline – with, if possible, a twist in the tail (b) a certain amount of farce and (c) a certain amount of broad comedy, including at least two or more farcical characters. Otherwise the whole thing will degenerate into a beautifully written, slickly produced flop.

Incidentally – that guide-book section on Seaford is one of the funniest things I have ever read. Will return the book next time I'm in.

Yours,

Larry[9]

Eton must have been happy with the second version of the script as he arranged auditions for less than a fortnight later, on 27 and 28 October. Among those who tried out for parts in the trial recording were Arthur Ridley, Kenneth Connor, Sidney Vivian, Graham Stark and Spike Milligan. Charles Hawtrey didn't manage to secure a role but sent Eton a letter to say he hoped the new series would be popular and he wished Eton and Hancock the best of luck with it.

At the beginning of November, the script was sent to the Head of Variety, Eton describing it as 'a quiet, gentle, bumbling situation comedy with not many belly laughs – what a horrible word – but in my opinion it is almost perpetually wreathed in smiles. Nothing new or Ustinovian I am afraid – very simple and straightforward – I should imagine just what Light Programme need.'[10] This memo is the first known use of the term 'situation comedy' in British broadcasting but after it was sent, things went quiet for several weeks.

While the preliminary preparations for *Vacant Lot* had been under way, the names of the artists chosen to appear at the Royal Variety Performance on 3 November had been announced; among them was Tony Hancock. As Larry was responsible for writing the majority of Hancock's stage act, he had worked hard to produce something suitable; Larry's material was about to be performed in front of Her Majesty Queen Elizabeth II.

23

Royal Variety Performance

Just before eight o'clock on the evening of 3 November 1952, the Queen, the Duke of Edinburgh and Princess Margaret arrived at the Palladium in London's Argyll Street. Crowds lined the streets, eager to share a small part in Her Majesty's first attendance at the Royal Variety Performance as monarch and straining their necks to catch a glimpse of the royal party's outfits. The Queen wore a gold, silver and turquoise full-skirted silk gown with a diamond tiara, and Princess Margaret wore a red velvet full-cut gown.

The earliest known recording of Hancock on stage is this appearance at the 1952 Royal Variety Performance. He appeared quite early on in the first half and he presented three routines, written for him by Larry: a piece about Margate in the style of a 'James FitzPatrick Travel Talk' (a long-running series of short documentaries, filmed for MGM by American writer James FitzPatrick); a 'curtain speech' given by the foreman of a road-mending gang ('Next week we shall be appearing at the corner of Corporation Road and High Street in a little thing entitled *Getting the Drains Up*'); and a Royal Navy monologue, probably in deference to the Duke of Edinburgh, who was a Naval Commander at the time. At any rate, the Duke certainly seems to have enjoyed this section of Hancock's performance as he was described by the radio commentator as having disappeared behind the chrysanthemums, doubled up with laughter.

Well we couldn't leave England without a visit to the British Navy so let's look out to sea where the British Navy is on manoeuvres. Down below the surface is a British submarine commanded by Lieutenant Commander Pomfrit-Pomfrit,[1] Royal Navy, as he speaks to his men in his rough, sailor-like fashion:

Careful there Johnson. Don't bang yourself on that torpedo now. Come away, Jones! Jones, come away! You'll get your hands covered in grease. Up periscope. Put me down, Hathaway – no grog for you. Well it's half past four, I think we'll pull up for tea. As you will, yes yes. Put the kettle on Harmsworth. What's that? Oh you've put the kettle on. Yes I see you have. Yes I think it suits you too. All right men, prepare to submerge. Whoop whoop whoop whoop whoop. Submerge! Well let me get in! Fools!

Scriptwriter Brad Ashton recalls that Tony used the naval routine as a warm-up before recording episodes of *Hancock's Half Hour* in later years and it became so familiar that everyone in the audience would join in.

Hancock received a lot of positive press coverage for his part in the Royal Variety Performance, as did another artist on the bill at the Palladium that year: a relatively unknown blind singer called Gerry Brereton. Appearing towards the end of the show, he was described in the official programme as 'The Commando'. Gerry had served with No. 3 Commando and in 1943 his unit took part in Operation Husky, the Allied invasion of Sicily. During the operation, the commandos came under intensive mortar and shell fire, resulting in thirty killed, sixty-six wounded and fifty-nine reported missing or captured. Among the wounded was Gerry, who lost his sight in an explosion. Although he and Larry never served together, it is possible that they knew each other through membership of the Old Comrades Association of the Army Commandos.

Before the war, Gerry had a promising career as a footballer with Derby County but now, totally blind, he needed to find a new way to earn a living. In 1949 he received a fantastic reception from the audience when he took part in Hughie Green's *Opportunity Knocks* as a singer, and by 1950 he was described by one of his local BBC assistant senior producers as 'the North's leading vocalist'. His success growing, Gerry decided to move with his family from his home in Derby to see if he could hit the big time in London. He was a guest singer in a concert at the Royal Festival Hall, and then spots in several radio and TV broadcasts culminated in his invitation to appear at the Royal Variety Performance.

A few days after Hancock had appeared in the newspapers, Larry was in the press himself when a feature appeared in the *Radio Times* heralding the start of the third series of the *Goon Show*, along with a photograph of him looking serious and sitting very upright, his hands poised above a typewriter and a cigarette between his fingers while a smiling Spike looks on. It was very much a 'Goon' article rather than a totally factual one:

> 'We have been asked,' said Milligan, tapping the ash from his excellent cigar and toying with a glass of '97 crusted elderberry, 'to write a brief article for an obscure journal called... er... the "Wireless Advertiser", or the "Marconi Times", or the "Crystal-Set Observer". I forget which.'
>
> 'On what subject?' asked Stephens, yawning and closing his calf-bound copy of 'Confessions of a Gag-and-Bone Man'.
>
> 'On the subject of the *Goon Show*.'

'The...? Oh, that!'

'Yes. Apparently the readers of the "Churdley Bay Boot-Fanciers Quarterly" have voted us the most-hated show on the air.'[2]

The Churdley Bay reference means the article must have been written by Larry – perhaps in conjunction with Spike – at around the same time as he was working on the *Vacant Lot* synopsis.

One of the serious revelations made about the new series in the article was the fact that Michael Bentine would no longer be one of the Goons. The explanation given for Bentine's withdrawal from the show was that he was working in Variety for most of the week, often at great distances from London. His Sundays were spent rehearsing and recording the *Goon Show* and so he was left with hardly any time to spend with his family. Gossip among the people who worked on the show suggested that his departure was more a result of conflict between him and Spike. As Sound Manager John Hamilton explained, 'Spike and Mike both thought they were the greatest suggesters of ideas in history and it didn't always gel.'[3]

Despite the break of four months between the second and third series, the Goons had still worked with each other from time to time. Harry Secombe had appeared on the opening show of Jimmy James' new TV series *Don't Spare the Horses* while Peter Sellers and Spike Milligan were seen on show number 2. It is unclear whether Larry and Eric Sykes had ended up being involved with the writing or not, following their meeting with Jimmy James in July. If they had been responsible for the scripts, they perhaps wouldn't have wanted to admit it as the series was universally panned in the press. To be fair though, the criticism mainly stemmed from Jimmy James' unfamiliarity with performing to a television rather than a radio audience.

On 9 November 1952, the Goon gang congregated at the BBC's Aeolian Hall in New Bond Street to rehearse and record the first programme of the third series. Their new producer, Peter Eton, had been promised by the Head of Variety that the *Goon Show* would 'seem almost a haven of rest after *Arthur's Inn*'[4] but it wouldn't be long before he found that this was far from the truth.

24

Yo-ho-ho and Four Bottles of Rum

Series 3 of the *Goon Show* was beset with problems from the start. There were studio difficulties, a new conductor and an improvised orchestra to deal with, but the issue that had the most detrimental impact on the programme was the fact that Larry and Spike had fallen out again, weren't speaking to each other and certainly weren't collaborating on the script. Larry was writing half of the show from a small office he had taken in Shaftesbury Avenue and Spike was writing the other half in Eric Sykes' office above a greengrocer's shop in Shepherd's Bush.

During an interview in 2006, Eric Sykes told Goon Show Preservation Society researcher Mike Brown he considered that 'writing the *Goon Show* was the toughest job in comedy because of the pace'.[1] A couple of years after his falling-out with Larry, Spike would collaborate with Eric Sykes on a *Goon Show* episode and end up hurling a paperweight at him during a disagreement over the script. Spike and Eric never wrote the show together again after this incident.

Larry and Spike had only had a short break between series 2 and series 3 and had been working on other projects in the intervening weeks. The demand to keep churning out comedy was becoming a burden and they were struggling to agree on what was funny.

Peter Eton recalled that 'Spike used to have these mad paradoxical ideas and write them down in sort of one-line gags. Most of it was rubbish, utter rubbish and it was Larry who used to pull it into shape and make sketches out of it... He [Spike] was terribly sensitive, you only had to say, 'well that's a bloody awful line, let's cut it out' and he would go away and hide in a corner and you wouldn't see him for an hour. You had to treat him very, very carefully.'[2]

Relying on alcohol to help ease the stress, Larry had temporarily mislaid the kid gloves he usually handled his writing partner with. As a former officer, he was accustomed to having his instructions complied with, whereas Spike's natural instinct was to shout 'gibberish in the face of authority'.[3] Ray Galton explained how this was often a source of friction between them: 'Spike felt bitter that he was only a private during the war and Larry was an officer. He used to take the mickey out of Larry about it and not in a nice way.'[4]

Eton had been determined to take control right from the beginning and had arranged for the first six programmes to be commissioned and the fees paid to Larry and Spike back in July so that they would be written well in advance. He had requested that the scripts for the first two programmes be ready by 29 September, numbers 3, 4 and 5 by 27 October and number 6 by 7 November. Before they would agree to anything though, Larry and Spike wanted a pay rise. They had been offered thirty guineas each per programme, an amount they felt was inadequate. Larry wrote a letter to explain that the *Goon Show* was 'a fast, high-pressure show containing probably more gags per minute than any on the air and writing it is very hard work'.[5] He also pointed out the fact that the scripts now needed to be longer as there would only be two musical breaks rather than the three that had been usual in the first two series. They eventually agreed to accept a fee of thirty-five guineas each, on condition that they could renegotiate should the series run extend beyond twelve programmes. By the time the matter had been settled, the due date for the first two scripts had already passed and the late receipt of scripts would continue to cause problems for Eton.

After a few weeks of silence, discussions surrounding *Vacant Lot* had also started up again as preparations were made for the trial recording, something that would be the cause of more headaches for Eton and for Larry. Before Larry had written the script, both he and Hancock had been told that the programme would be recorded without an audience; however, the Heads of Variety were now umming and aah-ing over whether to invite a studio audience after all and even proposed recording the programme twice on the same day to try out both scenarios. Neither Larry nor Tony was happy. Larry had deliberately avoided writing lots of gags into the script as he had envisaged *Vacant Lot* as being more of a play with just gentle comedy. In addition, he didn't feel it would be fair on Hancock and the rest of the cast (who had mainly been selected for their acting ability rather than their comic timing) to have to perform in front of an audience, as it probably wouldn't get many laughs and the lack of reaction would have a bad effect on them all. Tony also made his feelings clear, saying, 'I want to do this as a non-audience show. If I am to play this story in front of an audience I would want quite a different script and cast.'[6]

The Variety Department bowed to the pressure and consented to the trial recording being a non-audience programme. But then a few days later they changed their minds again. The planners wouldn't agree to an amended date for the trial recording until they had seen a new script and an exasperated Hancock declared that rather than delay the project once again while an incredibly busy Larry rewrote the script as an audience show, he would prefer that it was dropped. The scripts were filed away and remained on the shelves at the BBC's Archive

Department for sixty-five years until they were unearthed and had their first performance in 2017 as a Birmingham Comedy Festival production for *Funny Things* in Wolverhampton.

Tony Hancock would have to wait another two years before he finally got his own show – *Hancock's Half Hour*, written by Ray Galton and Alan Simpson – but Larry would encounter *Vacant Lot* again in a different guise six months later.

Despite the lack of collaboration between Larry and Spike, the *Goon Show* had been steadily increasing in popularity. A journalist with the *Irish Independent* newspaper, who admitted to not being a fan of the Goons, unintentionally heard most of an episode when the programme he usually listened to irritated him so much that he switched stations. He commented that even though he was unlikely to become a regular listener, he had appreciated the lively writing of Larry and Spike. The BBC's Listener Research Reports were revealing a steady rise in the overall 'appreciation index' for the show from a score of 51 for the first week up to 67 by programme 5. It was now called simply the *Goon Show* in the *Radio Times* and all mention of Crazy People had been dropped. Jimmy Grafton's name had also been dropped from the *Radio Times* although he continued to play a major role.

As the series progressed and the end of the year approached, both Larry and Spike were showing increasing signs of strain. Larry was telling anyone who would listen that he was drinking more than four bottles of rum a week to cope with the pressure and Spike was becoming more and more difficult to work with. Things deteriorated, and after apparently threatening to kill Peter Sellers with a potato peeler, Spike was admitted to St Luke's Psychiatric Hospital in Muswell Hill. In 1999, he shared his recollections of that time in his book, *Spike Milligan: The Family Album*. A doctor gave him an injection of something and within ten seconds he was unconscious. He slept deeply for fourteen days and was only brought round occasionally so that he could drink some liquid food. It wasn't until February 1953 that he was well enough to leave hospital and go back to the 'slog of writing'.[7]

Although Spike had made some contribution to the scripts up to programme 8, while he was in hospital the main bulk of the writing fell to Larry with help from Jimmy Grafton. Larry drew on his wartime experiences for the first episode without Spike's input and wrote about a Combined Services exercise. BBC commentators were on location reporting on the exercise and Harold Secombe was interviewing the man in charge, Admiral Flowerdew, live from the operations room at HQ:

> HARRY: ... these wooden blocks they're moving around on the map – what are they?
> FLOWERDEW: They represent landing barges – and the smaller ones are the actual commandos.
> HARRY: And what are those being slipped <u>under</u> the map?
> FLOWERDEW: Frogmen.[8]

Larry Stephens photographed by Graham Stark.
(Larry Stephens Estate collection)

After programme 9 had been broadcast, the BBC's Copyright Department wrote to Larry in respect of the fees due, to confirm that, as Spike hadn't made any contribution to the script, Larry and Jimmy were owed the full payment. However, Larry and Jimmy wanted to ensure that Spike continued to receive a writing credit and that he was paid at least a share of the scriptwriting fees, so they rewrote sketches from earlier programmes and tried to make sure at least one of these was included each week for the period Spike was in hospital. Larry replied to the Copyright Department stating that the amount Spike would usually have earned should be divided equally between the three of them, rather than just go to him and Jimmy.

Recalling this period during an interview with the Goon Show Preservation Society in 1987, Spike remarked of Larry and Jimmy: 'They didn't have the same oblique insane comedy attitude that I had; I was starting to outdo them and they were becoming an encumberment to me,'[9] which shows a remarkable lack of gratitude and/or an incredibly selective memory.

Larry and Diana Stephens at the Café de Paris.
(Larry Stephens Estate collection)

As well as having the increased writing workload to deal with, Larry also seems to have been having some money worries. Gone were the days when he would wear a thirty-bob suit until it wore out; he was now always immaculately and expensively dressed and favoured pale silk ties or cravats, blazers and perfectly pressed trousers. He and Diana were photographed eating at London's top night spots including the Café de Paris and Al Burnett's Stork Room.

It seems he had either been living above his means or hadn't been planning his finances very well as he included a personal note with the letter he wrote to the Copyright Department in respect of *Goon Show* fees just after Christmas 1952:

> ... Should there be any delay over the fees for the programmes discussed, I should be very grateful if my fee for at least one of them could be paid as soon as possible. I am afraid the heavy expenses of the Christmas season (it seems to get more expensive every year!) have left me very short of ready cash. I hope you don't mind me making a personal request like this.[10]

This seems to give further weight to the theory that his previously declared occupation of Commercial Accountant was either invented for his marriage certificate or had nothing to do with finances.

As he was now having to write without any input from Spike, it seems rather unfair that he received a warning about the late delivery of scripts at the beginning of the New Year. The Assistant Head of Variety wrote to say it had been reported to him by Peter Eton that sometimes scripts weren't received until the morning of the rehearsals and recording and that this caused a lot of last-minute work for everyone involved. He asked that in future Larry deliver scripts no later than Thursdays weekly, finishing his letter with a very curt 'I trust you will not fail.'[11]

In order to submit his scripts on a Thursday, Larry would have needed to change his writing habits. Peter Watson-Wood, now a film producer, used to frequent the Duke of Wellington pub in Wardour Street, Soho and remembers Larry as another of the pub's regulars around the time of the falling-out with Spike: 'He would spend hours in the pub observing life, drinking (rather a lot)... and generally putting off going to his office to write that week's show.'[12] 'I don't recall Larry being a loner, he certainly joined in the social banter and fun in the pub, and often used material he gleaned from the bar, making notes if something amused him, and I always imagined, adapting this material into his script.'[13] 'Larry would finally leave the pub around three thirty in the afternoon on Friday, and go write his half of the show.'[14]

Even if Larry was going to struggle to alter his routine, Peter Eton was determined to make changes in the New Year. He made it his mission to resolve the quarrels that had broken out between various members of the Goon Gang: between Spike and Larry; Spike and Sellers; Sellers and Jimmy; and then he sought a promise from Larry that he would return to 'his old sober self'.[15] As Eton pointed out in a memo to the Head of Variety, 'only when these two writers really collaborate are the *Goon Show* scripts worth listening to'.[16]

While Spike was still out of action, Larry's importance as a scriptwriter was becoming more established. The duo had previously always been known as 'Spike Milligan and Larry Stephens' but now they were more commonly referred to as 'Larry Stephens and Spike Milligan'. This occurred not only on the *Goon Show* scripts and in the closing credits of the programmes but can also be seen in BBC memos, including one from the Script Editor to the Head of Variety on the subject of writers of major shows who had been discovered within the previous five years.

By the time Spike returned to writing and performing at the beginning of March 1953, the *Goon Show* had reached programme number 17. Larry suddenly remembered (or was reminded by Spike) that during negotiations at the start of the third series they had stipulated that their scriptwriting fee should be renegotiated if the run extended beyond twelve programmes. Larry fired off a letter to the Copyright Department to remind them and to explain why it had also escaped his notice: 'the pressure of work has been so much – during my partner's temporary absence – that I completely forgot the matter'.[17] He requested that their pay be increased to forty guineas each per programme and that it be backdated accordingly. It must have also suddenly occurred to him that he had never been paid for his work on *Vacant Lot* but in this matter he asked Peter Eton to deal with the Copyright Department for him. The result was some good news and some bad news: Larry was told that he was owed a fee of seventy guineas for *Vacant Lot* but he would only receive half of it, with the other half being paid if the programme was ever broadcast. As for the *Goon Show*, the BBC refused to increase the fee, citing late delivery of scripts for the decision. Furthermore, they made it a condition of payment for the future that scripts be received no later than Wednesday each week. Larry and Spike had little choice: they had to accept this, but in his response on their behalf, Larry explained what had caused the lateness: 'This of course was due to the prolonged illness of my partner, Mr Milligan. As you know by the balance of payments I was writing the scripts on my own for some time and as I was not prepared for this, it put me very much behind in my work. Now that Mr Milligan is well again, the scripts will be on time.'[18]

In this letter, Larry also made reference to a special forty-minute Coronation edition of the show that he and Spike had been asked to write. The cover page of the script for this show (which would be broadcast in June 1953) made a teasing reference to their latest ticking-off, describing the scriptwriters as being 'the late Larry Stephens and Spike Milligan'.[19]

Peter Eton remembered that the pair often teased him and played practical jokes on him:

> They got me drunk two or three times and then they rang up Michael Standing and explained where I was... Larry was a great boozer and Spike used to drink quite a lot in those days... I think

the script was due on the Monday for the show on the following Sunday and it wasn't there one day and I rang up Spike's office… and Beryl Vertue, who's now a very important film producer and was his secretary… said, "well, he left with the script this morning" – it was then lunchtime – so I thought "oh, he's on the booze with Larry", so I started looking for him and I started going round the pubs and clubs where I knew they might be and that night I got to a club called the Panama Club; I'd been round all these places… and was as tight as a drum. Spike and Larry came in sober as anything, picked me up, promptly rang up Michael Standing and said, "Peter's drunk, you know, there won't be a show this week," and I was lugged back and we just got it on actually.[20]

The final regular programme of the third *Goon Show* series was transmitted at the beginning of May but, luckily for him, Larry once again found himself with other projects to work on.

25

Horace Clabtrout and Friends

Back in mid-March of 1953, the BBC's Variety Department had begun plans to make a new programme called *Guide to Britain*, which would follow the exploits of Sonnie Hale and Claude Hulbert as they acted as tour guides to foreign visitors in Britain. By the beginning of April, it had been renamed *Coach Party* and a trial recording was being planned for the end of May. There seemed some doubt over whether the programme would ever reach this stage though, so the Variety Department began to look around for alternatives to feature Brian Reece and Wallas Eaton instead. Peter Eton remembered *Vacant Lot* and suggested it as a possibility. *Coach Party* was eventually shelved and a trial of *Vacant Lot* – now renamed *Welcome to Welcombe* (later changed to *Welkham*) was commissioned at the end of May.

Larry needed to completely rewrite his *Vacant Lot* script and he didn't have long to do so as the recording was scheduled to take place in early June. *Vacant Lot* had been written as the opening episode of a new series, whereas *Welcome to Welkham* would be a standalone play, needing a new storyline and some new characters. The rewrite at least meant that it was being treated as a separate assignment from *Vacant Lot* and Larry was paid seventy guineas for it.

Welcome to Welkham used some themes and characters from Larry's original *Vacant Lot* script but was mostly based on the plot he had intended to use in its second episode. Brian Reece plays the part of an estate agent and auctioneer who has recently been elected as a councillor in the seaside resort of Welkham. Welkham's mayor is keen to attract more tourists to the town and nominates Reece to take on the role of Entertainments Committee chief. Mayor Tripfield has reserved a large advertising space in one of the national newspapers and tells Reece that one of the first jobs in his new position is to provide the copy for this advert. He dutifully does this but he also writes another, more truthful version for his own amusement:

> Come to Welkham Bay. Sunbathe on the golden slopes of the Corporation Slag-heap! Lacerate your feet on the specially sharpened stones of the beach! Bathe in the cool waters of the Cabbage Lane Static Water Tank! Yes – forget Palm Beach, Florida where the turf meets the surf! Come to Welkham Bay where the drains meet the sea![1]

Of course, this is the version that ends up being printed in the newspaper, but to Reece's amazement everyone loves his unique slant and Welkham is swamped with advance bookings for the summer.

It was broadcast on the Light Programme on 19 July and some of the actors who had been booked to appear in *Vacant Lot* took parts in *Welcome to Welkham*: Arthur Ridley, Sidney Vivian and Graham Stark appeared alongside the newly cast Brian Reece, Wallas Eaton, Anthony Green, Dorothy Summers and Genine Graham. It had been listed among the 'Programmes to Note' at the front of that week's *Radio Times* but reaction following the broadcast was divided. The critic J. C. Trewin thought it 'had a nice curl of craziness and some rightly idiotic telephone-talks'[2] whereas the controller of the Light

Programme described it as carrying 'you gently along without at any moment exciting you'.[3] The BBC's Listener Research Report on the programme showed that it received an 'appreciation index' of 49 and comments ranged from a retired gentleman who declared 'With such a good cast I expected a roaring comedy but could hardly raise a laugh' to 'It's new and if I am not yet prepared to rave over it at least I can find no fault in it' from a crane driver. The Head of Variety had scrawled across the bottom of the report: 'Even if the Crane Drivers rally round I doubt if there is any future for W to W!!'[4] Consequently 'the gay life of the inhabitants of Welkham Bay – the seaside town with a difference'[5] was never visited again.

Larry and Spike had been asked to contribute some scripts to *Star Bill* for programmes to be broadcast during July 1953 while the regular writers, Ray Galton and Alan Simpson, were on holiday. Spike, however, would also be taking a holiday away from London at that time, so instead, Larry was commissioned to write the scripts with Eric Sykes. The programme's producer requested that they be offered a generous fee for doing so, given the dearth of alternative writers with the ability to generate material of the required quality. Towards the end of June, Larry and Spike had signed with Kavanagh Productions Limited, an agency that also represented Eric, so it fell to them to negotiate the contracts. Larry must have been relieved to finally rid himself of the burden of financial and other wranglings with the BBC, leaving him more time to concentrate on his writing.

Described as providing 'the best in Britain's show business', *Star Bill*'s compere throughout July was Tony Hancock, supported by Graham Stark. Galton and Simpson later explained that although they had by now built up a good working relationship with Hancock, they were still considered too young and inexperienced to write for the whole of the programme's run. Alan Simpson clarified that 'from Tony's point of view – he was the star and he'd been working with

Larry for a long time, and it served as a kind of insurance policy for him'.[6]

As it turned out, Larry only ended up contributing to the programmes broadcast on 5 and 12 July while Spike and Eric wrote those for 19 and 26 July. This may have been because Larry had also been asked to write another programme around that time, a forty-five-minute episode in a proposed series called *Fables of the Fifties*. It was suggested that Larry might also need to write two or three songs for this non-audience programme. His 'old legend with a moral' entitled 'Horace Clabtrout and the Beanstalk' was subsequently broadcast on the Home Service on 20 July 1953 and starred Charles Hawtrey.

The name Horace Clabtrout had made an appearance in *Welcome to Welkham* the previous day, as one of the people suggested as the new head of the Entertainments Committee:

TRIPFIELD: We need a new entertainments man. Any suggestions, Quince?

QUINCE: Er... Horace Clabtrout?

TRIPFIELD: Horace Clabtrout?!... He's over seventy! You're not seriously suggesting him?!

QUINCE: No, not really – I just like saying his name.[7]

Back in Goonland, Peter Eton once again attempted to resolve the eternal problem of late delivery of scripts. He had been authorised to commission scripts for series 4 in advance and to release immediate payments as and when he received them. He conveyed the news to Larry and Spike, telling them he would 'be in a delirium of delight'[8] to receive a script every ten days or so in the three months leading up to the start of the new series. However, in a memo to the Copyright Department on the subject of fees for the show, Eton explained that Larry and Spike would no longer be writing together. He suggested that their fees should perhaps be negotiated separately, adding: 'I anticipate no trouble in arranging fees with Milligan but you may have some trouble with Stephens.'[9] Eton also confirmed that Jimmy Grafton would no longer be involved in editing the scripts. At first glance, this may suggest that Spike and Larry hadn't settled their differences, but they were collaborating on other projects and also spending leisure time together so it seems more likely that they felt they could produce scripts more quickly if they worked apart.

One of the projects they had been working on together was a short film called *The Super Secret Service*, which was released in August 1953. Starring Peter Sellers, Graham Stark and Dick Emery, and with very Goonish character names such as Inspector Plungegroin, it also featured a performance of 'Teddy Bears' Picnic' by the Ray Ellington Quartet. The film was shot in a small studio in a Dean Street basement and ran for just under thirty minutes. It used a favourite theme of Larry's – a burlesque on MI5 – and followed the secret service in their attempt to track down a foreign spy called Q. Just as he would in 'The Case of the Mukkinese Battle-Horn', which would follow three years later, Sellers took on two roles – Sir Walter Smood and Reuben J. Crouch – and his wife at the time, Anne Hayes, also appeared in the film as Miss Jones.

Before the new series of the show started, members of the Goon gang spent a day together. They congregated at Larry and Diana's flat, crossed the road into Regent's Park and walked up to the top of Primrose Hill. As well as Larry and Diana, the party included Spike, Peter Sellers and a curly-tailed dog. Having recently returned from Southern Rhodesia with a new partner and her daughter, Ben Cleminson, Larry and Hancock's former flatmate, also joined them. One of the group – probably Sellers – arrived in a brand new Studebaker Commander Starlight Coupe, a stylish, left-hand-drive American car. Considering it was a romp in the park, they were all quite formally dressed, the men in blazers and ties and Diana looking chic and polished and wearing one of the latest trend 'waspie belts'. While they fooled around and posed, Sellers captured their day out on film and Larry took still photographs.

Diana Stephens and Spike Milligan photographed by Larry Stephens in 1953.
(Larry Stephens Estate collection)

Series 4 started out smoothly and although they appeared to be friends again, and were both being credited in the *Radio Times*, documents in the BBC's archives do seem to suggest that Larry and Spike were working apart rather than collaborating. The first two programmes were written by Spike, programme number 3 was a joint effort with

Larry and Spike working apart on different scenes, programme 4 was Larry's and programme 5 another of Spike's. Beyond that it is generally difficult to determine exactly who wrote what but by piecing together snippets of information from various sources there seems a very strong likelihood that they began writing on alternate weeks from programme 4 onwards.

The Listener Research Report for programme 3 reveals that the show had really begun to increase in popularity. It achieved an 'appreciation index' of 66 and had very few negative comments made about it. One listener remarked that it provided 'half an hour of frenzied but blissful inconsequence'.[10] This particular report also gives a glimpse into some written banter between the scriptwriters and their producer. Larry's name as one of the co-writers has been crossed through and handwritten in black ballpoint next to it is the comment, 'Correction! SM.' Underneath, Larry has written: 'Don't be so childish. LGS.' And finally Peter Eton has scribbled: 'Oh stop it you two. PE.'[11]

Larry had recently approached Eton with another of his suggestions. Eton explained that 'Larry quite rightly had the idea of actually doing small plays'[12] rather than dividing the show into sketches with different storylines, and series 4 is when this first begins to become the norm. 'Her' in series 2 had been an exception as were the Christmas specials.

The first programme in series 4 to carry a single plot was episode 4, 'The Building of Britain's First Atomic Cannon', which was one of Larry's solo efforts and he returned to his love of the piano for his inspiration in writing it.

The story concerns Britain's leading atom scientist, Henry Crun, who is obsessed with getting his piano moved to London from the Highlands as travelling there every day to practise his scales is costing him a fortune in platform tickets. The removal men won't touch it as it is too dirty so he builds an atomic cannon to blast it southwards.

As opposed to the more usual orchestra directions such as 'spooky music' and 'change of scene link', Larry opened the episode with a very detailed description of what he wanted the orchestra to play:

Long, complicated and flamboyant link on major 5-finger exercise, ascending in semitones from key to key. Start with full deep statement, Tutti. This continues – with slight variations – for three or four semitones. Then Pianissimo – one woodwind picks up the 5-finger exercise on the next semitone up. More woodwind and strings come in, in contrapuntal, pseudo-fugal style. This, as the keys ascend, becomes louder and more complicated until finally Tutti – now Sforzando – cuts out abruptly on the twelfth semitone (the leading note) – on an abrupt blast of suspense. (This cut-off must be devastatingly abrupt).[13]

Peter Eton was beginning to find out that working on the *Goon Show* was nothing like the 'haven of rest' he had been told to expect. When there was talk that the show would no longer be repeated on the Light Programme – and that Larry and Spike would lose their repeat fee as a consequence – it seems to have caused him some serious concern. He sent a memo to the Head of Variety which makes his feelings on the stars and writers very clear:

… This bunch of neurotics need all the encouragement they can get although at the moment they are riding high on the crest of a wave of delight caused by the kind things being said about them. I have managed to keep the sad news from Spike but as I told you it has already leaked out and Larry Stephens has categorically stated that he will be leaving the show when the Light repeat ceases as he wants to look for more remunerative work. Although I should be glad to drop Stephens, I must admit that Spike could not continue to write a weekly show on his own and so Larry, as far as the Goon Show is concerned, is irreplaceable. Apart from this I am afraid the news will upset Milligan's very finely balanced present mood of comparative sanity and Home Service may lose the programme as well. Can anything be done to find a 'repeat' for a programme that has recently been described on the air as the most refreshingly original comedy show since ITMA?[14]

The Head of Variety must have been equally concerned by the news and set about trying to find a suitable spot for a repeat, but despite these efforts on his behalf Larry still does not seem to have been satisfied and began to slip back into his old ways, not getting his scripts in on time. An official warning was issued through his agent, Kevin Kavanagh, making it clear that Larry would only be paid if his scripts were received by Peter Eton on the Wednesday before Sunday's recording.

As he was having trouble keeping up with his scriptwriting responsibilities, it seems odd that Larry was also given the task of clearing a backlog of letters that had been sent to the *Goon Show*. The reply to one of these letters was reproduced in a Goon Show Preservation Society newsletter and concerns a complaint over what a listener had considered to be the use of a risqué phrase during one of the broadcasts: a variation on 'the spirit is willing but the flesh is weak'. The tone of Larry's reply seems a little sarcastic:

I... have been distressed to discover – amongst the piles of letters from cranks and illiterates – a letter of yours dated 24th February which has apparently been neither answered nor acknowledged. How this oversight occurred we cannot imagine and trust that you will accept our apologies for the delay. (I have just re-read the above and realised with horror that I have given the impression that your letter was one of the 'cranks' letters: what I meant to convey was that it had become mixed in that particular pile by accident...)[15]

Larry didn't seem to be particularly enamoured with the *Goon Show*, its listeners or his colleagues around this time. As well as writing ambiguous replies to fan and critics' letters, he also scrawled his own descriptions of the show's three stars under a photograph which appeared in the *Radio Times* of 20 November 1953. The photograph bore the caption 'Three Smart Goons' but Larry's alternatives suggest he didn't feel they were very smart at all at the time:

> Spike Milligan – Prof Lance Schweizer, the well-known vivisectionist
> Harry Secombe – The inimitable 'Fatso'. 'With a ballad and a belly-laugh.' The whistling warble-monger
> Peter Sellers: Danny 'The Thumb' Martello, now serving seven to ten years for illegal bookmaking, extortion and dope-peddling.[16]

News had recently reached Larry that must have had a very deep effect on him. His upbringing and wartime indoctrination meant he was trying to keep a stiff upper lip and not display any emotion but it was clearly beginning to manifest itself in his surly mood and his waning concentration levels. The September 1953 issue of the Commando Association newsletter had carried two items of particular relevance to Larry. The first was that one of his fellow 1/5 Commando officers, from his time in Hong Kong, had been killed. Lieutenant Iain Milne had been on board a BOAC Comet flight to Delhi which crashed near Calcutta. There were no survivors. Larry also learned that the body of his close friend Nick Bryant, who had lost his life during the battle for Hill 170, had been exhumed and moved for a second time. He would have been aware that Nick's remains were relocated from the battlefield not long after the unit had left the area to be reburied in Akyab cemetery close by. But now, eight years later, Nick had been disturbed again. The bodies of all those who had fallen in the Kangaw area were to be reinterred in a new cemetery being laid out in Taukkyan, around twenty miles north-east of Rangoon. This would enable the Commonwealth War Graves Commission to ensure proper maintenance and commemoration. This information probably brought things Larry would rather have forgotten back to the forefront of his mind.

His mood was probably not improved by Spike's script for programme number 9 of series 4. The episode concerned 'Operation Bagpipes', a wartime mission to retrieve a set of bagpipes that had fallen into enemy hands. Captain Seagoon was told to report to Three Commando Training Depot and one scene described preparations for the exercise there:

> HARRY: So the intense training for Operation Bagpipes began.
> PETER: Up at the crack of midday;
> SPIKE: Bubble bath and perfume shower;
> HARRY: Paper tearing – blindfold;
> SPIKE: Floodlit fretwork courses;
> PETER: Coastal landings in armoured mess tins;
> HARRY: Inter-Battalion knitting contests;
> PETER: (FLOWERDEW) And last one home's a cissy.
> HARRY: Finally, the one thing that defeated me and ruined my health – seven days' leave in Piccadilly.[17]

As a former commando himself and having gone through the gruelling training to earn his green beret, Larry would have been entitled to gently poke fun at the elite force, but for Spike to do so was another matter entirely and it is completely understandable if Larry was riled by this, particularly given the news he had just heard.

Having been warned about the lateness of his script submissions, Larry was soon in trouble again – but this time unintentionally – when his script for programme 10 was broadcast.

26

Flying Saucers Over East Acton

The bulk of episode 10 concerned an unidentified flying object landing near the United Nations Weather Station at the North Pole, but the episode was interspersed with announcements about the route the UFO was taking, such as: 'We must apologise for interrupting the programme but a mysterious light – alleged to be a flying saucer – has been reported in the sky over East Acton. Will any listener able to confirm this report please telephone the defence board immediately at FITzroy 1136.'[1]

Unfortunately, a lot of listeners took these announcements to be real rather than part of the *Goon Show* and jammed the BBC's telephone lines to confirm they had seen the flying saucers too. The story made the headlines the next day and a BBC spokesman was forced to clarify that although these announcements had been taken seriously by some people, it had all been part of the crazy larking about that went on in the show.

Behind the scenes, the BBC were not as happy about the larks as the spokesman tried to suggest. Some of the department heads were apoplectic and a series of memos circulated between them. They mentioned occasions when similar things had happened: Ronald Knox made what purported to be a live report of a revolution taking place in London in 1926; and a radio adaptation of H. G. Wells' novel, *The War of the Worlds*, directed and narrated by Orson Welles, caused public panic in the US in 1938. As a result of these incidents, BBC policy had been changed to ensure that there were 'no broadcasts purporting to be official warnings, SOS messages, Morse SOSs from ships etc'.[2] but now that the *Goon Show* had seemingly flouted the rules, a directive was issued reminding everyone that no further pseudo-realistic announcements should be made and the majority were cut from the repeat broadcast of episode 10.

The publicity turned out to be a positive thing for the show though, and Larry and Spike were commissioned to write further episodes when the series' run was extended; however, this time it was made a contractual obligation that scripts should be submitted four days before the show was recorded.

The last rehearsal and recording of 1953 took place on Sunday 27 December for a broadcast on the first day of the new year. Entitled 'Ten Thousand Fathoms Down in a Wardrobe' it was written by Larry and he 'marked' the front page of his copy of the script like a schoolmaster. He ticked the details of the performers, announcer and producer but put a cross next to the scriptwriters' details and deleted Spike's name so that only his remained. At the bottom of the page he wrote '8/10 VG. Could do better.'[3]

Larry could be very finicky like this and Graham Stark, who spent a lot of time with the Stephenses, noticed that Larry was quite a slow worker and took time over his scripts, remembering that 'he would sit and type for hours at home or in his office'[4] to the exclusion of everything else. This apparently began to grate on his wife Diana and she took exception one day when, on her way out, Larry asked her to bring him back some cigarettes. According to Graham, she yelled at Larry and said that he spent all day either tinkering with his piano or tinkering with his typewriter and she didn't intend to be running around after him all the time any more. Conditions in the Stephens' house had become somewhat tempestuous and were about to get worse.

When he wasn't glued to his typewriter or piano, Larry began to disappear from home for days on end and spent the time drinking heavily. Something had snapped inside him and he was dissatisfied with everyone and everything, trusted no one and suspected they were all betraying him. There are hints of this in a series of doodles on his script for 'Ten Thousand Fathoms Down in a Wardrobe'. The first scene in the strip cartoon he has created shows a Fu Manchu-style character leaping through a window with a scimitar held aloft. Underneath where the little cartoon character is leaping and dashing about, Larry has written, 'Deceit. Her only mistake.' John Antrobus, one of Larry's later colleagues, commented, 'He was perhaps – I cannot vouch for this – a casualty of the war. He tried to laugh off the days when he had been engaged in the slaughter of his brothers and sisters who were officially called "The Enemy". But for a soul as sensitive as Larry not all his outpouring talents could compensate for the sorrow.'[5]

It seems quite likely that Larry was suffering from post-traumatic stress disorder (PTSD), possibly triggered by the news he had read in the Commando Association newsletter. He would probably have suffered mood swings, flashbacks and nightmares leading to extreme tiredness. His bouts of heavy drinking and increasing reliance on alcohol suggest that he was trying to numb himself. Naturally, this was damaging his relationship with his wife and having a negative effect on his ability to work.

Under his fortnightly writing obligations, Larry managed to submit a script in time for programme 16, but by the time programme 18's was due, he could only offer an incomplete script on the evening before the recording was due to take place. This was too little, too late and

Peter Eton had already cut and pasted material from previous episodes together so that there would be something to rehearse and broadcast. Despite previous comments about Larry being irreplaceable as far as the *Goon Show* was concerned, enough was enough. His scripts had been late eight times during series 4 and the latest fiasco meant the BBC now considered him to have broken the terms of his contract. Larry's agent, Kevin Kavanagh, who confessed that he could no longer do anything with him, was sent a letter confirming that the BBC couldn't continue to pay for scripts under the previous arrangements. The letter concluded with: 'If however Larry Stephens is willing to send in further scripts and if we find space in our programme schedules for them to be used, we would certainly consider them on their merits and if they are accepted, pay for them.'[6]

Larry had been reduced in status from one of the BBC's top writers to someone who was being invited to submit material 'on spec' with no guarantee that it would be used.

Larry's odd behaviour became the subject of gossip at the Kavanagh Productions offices. There was speculation that he'd discovered Diana was a lesbian (which sounds as if someone made a pass at her and was turned down). The rumour was embellished as it passed from person to person, Chinese whispers-style. Writer Brad Ashton was also represented by Kavanagh at the time and 'was told that Larry came home one day and found Diana on the couch making love with another woman'.[7] Graham Stark recalled that the attractive Diana was an object of desire and despite her clear devotion to her husband, she was often pestered with over-zealous flirtations and attempted seductions; Larry had to step in and put a stop to it from time to time. A talented photographer, Graham had appreciated Diana's beauty and taken portraits of her, pictures which Stanley Kubrick particularly admired. Graham claimed that, having seen the photos, Kubrick expressed an interest in making an erotic film, went on to obtain the filming rights to Arthur Schnitzler's novella *Dream Story* in the 1960s and eventually shot it in the 1990s under the title *Eyes Wide Shut*.

Whether PTSD-related or not, Larry had obviously had some kind of major breakdown and had moved out of his home in Regent's Park Road and gone to stay with Tony and Cicely Hancock. He clearly didn't plan on returning home at any time in the near future as his mail was being sent to the Hancocks' address in Queen's Gate Place, west London. Larry spent a few more weeks trying to flush the nightmares out of his mind by gulping down large quantities of rum.

Luckily he still had a little income trickling in as Spike struggled to suddenly produce a script every week rather than on a fortnightly basis, and programme 20 was therefore another rehash of material previously written by the two of them, which meant Larry was due a repeat fee. By programme 24, Spike had sought help from elsewhere as a BBC memo mentions that 'a certain amount of material for this programme was received from a source other than the scriptwriter'.[8] This 'outside source' does not appear to be named anywhere but if it wasn't Larry, another likely candidate is a man called Maurice Wiltshire. When he was interviewed by members of the Goon Show Preservation Society in 1976, Peter Eton stated that he believed Maurice had written one or two shows although Spike's name appeared on them for contractual reasons. But more of Maurice later.

Bleak as things may have seemed to him for a while, Larry still had plenty of support from his friends and from his agent. An advertisement for Kavanagh Productions Ltd appeared in *The Stage* in February and, underneath a graphic naming some of the top radio and television shows, Larry was listed among the writers, with Kavanagh saying they were proud to represent them all.

Eventually Larry began to pull himself together and even completed a script for the *Goon Show* called 'Western Story', which was broadcast as programme 26 on 22 March. Tony Hancock was also helping out;

Brad Ashton remembers Larry later told him that 'he was writing all the solo radio appearances for Tony Hancock and that Hancock gave him his entire £40 broadcast fee each time, keeping nothing for himself'.[9] Friends were finding other projects for him to work on too.

27

Bucket and Spade Oscar

On 15 July 1954, a new musical comedy series called *Happy Holiday* started, the synopsis of which bears some striking similarities to *Vacant Lot* and *Welcome to Welkham*. It was set in a rundown seaside resort called Littleton-on-Sea, where diversions included the likes of ankle competitions, and it starred Dennis Price (as Major Denzil Pierce) and Bill Owen (as Charlie Unkers) with Jean Brampton, Elizabeth Larner, Graham Stark and Dick Emery. Peter Sellers also starred, and played the Mayor of Littleton and all the other characters.

At that time, Brad Ashton was writing for Dick Emery and used to go along to watch the rehearsals of *Happy Holiday* every Sunday. Although the scriptwriting credits were given to Jimmy Grafton and Jimmy Griffiths, Brad recalls that the actors didn't bother to begin rehearsing properly until Larry showed up at the last minute and did a major rewrite, pepping up the comedy.

One of the other *Happy Holiday* actors, Graham Stark, who had become one of Larry's closest friends, also had a project for him to work on. Graham had been asked by Clive Dunn to join him in a summer show in Norfolk, and as it was to be Graham's first ever summer season, he needed an act for it. He asked Larry to write some sketches for him and the result was apparently more esoteric than the general comedy routines of the time. Graham had trained in ballet and had played the part of the Dancing Master in a 1950 production of Molière's *Le Bourgeois Gentilhomme* at the Edinburgh Festival. Graham remembered that 'Larry was fascinated by this. He wrote a very funny sketch about a dancing instructor who was giving a lecture on dance but while wearing big, army boots.'[1] Larry probably also drew inspiration from his own role in the same Molière classic during his schooldays when 'the stony silence of Stephens'[2] was mentioned in his school magazine's review of the production.

Graham's summer show, *Fraser and Dunlop's Take It Easy* at the Summer Theatre in Cromer, was a resounding success. It was a colourful spectacle with attractive dancing girls, talented vocalists and witty comedians. Apart from Clive Dunn and Graham, other notable performers were Michael Darbyshire and a newcomer, Ronald Corbett, who was described in *The Stage* as showing a clear aptitude for comedy. The summer in Cromer was a particular success for Graham though, as he was awarded a 'Concert Party Oscar', or as it was more commonly referred to, a 'Bucket and Spade Oscar', having been judged the best individual act in the UK.

The idea for a Bucket and Spade Oscar had been conceived after an article in a Sunday newspaper declared that seaside summer shows had become passé and the Concert Artistes Association wanted to prove the journalist wrong. The award was sponsored by the South African Outspan orange company as part of their tercentenary celebrations, and Gordon Marsh, chairman of the Concert Artistes Association, went on a six-week tour on the organisation's behalf to find the worthy winners. Graham was presented with his 'Oscar' – a silver trophy in the form of a starfish balancing on an orange and playing a seaside spade like a guitar – in a special ceremony at the Arts Theatre Club in west London at the end of October. Several of Graham's friends, including Peter Sellers and Harry Secombe, attended the celebratory party dressed in Pierrot hats and ruffles and performed a brief chorus in his honour.

A month earlier, series 5 of the *Goon Show* had started its run, the only series during Larry's lifetime that would not include his name as a scriptwriter. The first programme of the new series marked the 100th performance and the BBC provided £10 for a small party. It was originally envisaged that the series would run for six weeks and Spike had been commissioned to write the scripts but, just as the first programme was broadcast, this was extended to thirteen weeks. Spike made it clear that he didn't feel he would be able to write a script every week for so many programmes and so Eric Sykes was commissioned to write the shows for week numbers 7, 9, 11 and 13. Spike had left Kavanagh Productions in July and had formed a new agency called Associated London Scripts (ALS) with Eric Sykes, Ray Galton and Alan Simpson so it was in both their interests that the lucrative contract stayed 'in house'. Even though Spike and Eric had been commissioned to write programmes on alternate weeks, they weren't actually broadcast in a strict rotational order, although they each wrote 50 per cent of the total programmes.

There are hints that Larry was a visitor to the offices above a greengrocer's shop in Shepherd's Bush where ALS were based, and had given Spike a helping hand behind the scenes with some of the early scripts in series 5 before Eric Sykes was brought in. Throughout this series, a synopsis and a list of characters in the order of their appearance was included with the *Goon Show* scripts, and from episode 4 ('The Phantom Head Shaver (of Brighton)'), there is a marked change in the synopsis style as well as the introduction of some distinctive characters.

Among Larry's personal papers is a typed list of names he had created to use in his comedy writing, which was certainly compiled by him before 1954. One of the names, Cretin McDullard, is mentioned in a January 1954 episode of the *Goon Show* called 'The Strange Case of Dr

Jekyll and Mr Crun', and another, Eddie Underblast, is a close match to a role played by Harry Secombe when he made a guest appearance in an episode of *Happy Holiday* in August 1954. Another of Larry's comedy name inventions, Strangler Aagonschmidt, is mentioned in the synopsis of the *Goon Show*'s 'The Canal', credited to Spike and broadcast on 2 November, although the synopsis bears little resemblance to the episode itself. It describes how Ned Seagoon returns to his ancestral home, Seagoon's Folly, after forty-three years at school. When he arrives, he discovers that his father and his four mothers have disappeared, as have the cook, the under-footman and the over-footman. The only people in the house are the butler, Gravely Headstone; a heroin importer; and the valet. Strange noises and knockings are heard coming from the buttery and three strangers begin digging a fifty-foot long grave in the garden, uncovering a secret passage that leads to Seagoon's bedroom. As for Strangler Aagonschmidt, he is discovered trying to set fire to the library.

Shortly after 'The Canal' was broadcast, series 5 was further extended for another thirteen weeks. Spike and Eric were once again commissioned to write programmes for alternate weeks.

Although he had been helping out behind the scenes, Larry had lost his 'official' membership of the Goon gang, as far as the BBC was concerned. But life was finally about to improve for him.

28

The Ladykillers

Trying to put Larry's recent breakdown and his extended absence from home behind them, Larry and Diana decided to make a fresh start and moved into a new flat on the first or second floor of a low-rise block at 154 Adelaide Road in the Hampstead area of London. The living room was decorated in dark autumnal colours, but in spite of this, it was a very light room, with a long row of windows overlooking the street. Big sofas surrounded a coffee table and Larry's white upright piano was close to the entrance leading into the kitchen but was angled so that he wouldn't have his back to the room while he was playing. The galley-style kitchen was divided from the living room with a beaded curtain rather than a door and it gave a rustle and clack every time someone walked through it. The bedroom was minimally furnished, with an enormous bed in the middle of the room.

The couple hosted frequent parties in their new home and there was always plenty to drink but not much in the way of food on offer. Ben Cleminson's stepdaughter, Angela Cole, remembers being the only child at one such party, when she was seven or eight years old, and sitting on Larry's knee while he played the piano. 'He chatted away to me as if I was worth talking to, not a child to be patronised or ignored,'[1] she recalls. 'He treated everyone as an equal – men, women, children. He thought everyone was worthy of his attention.'[2]

Brad Ashton remembers being invited to the Stephens' new home and being surprised at what he saw there. Larry had a huge filing cabinet that contained all of his scripts but also a neat file of gags he had written down after hearing them in American radio shows. A shocked Brad said to him, 'I thought everything you were doing was original?'[3] and Larry confirmed it was and that he was just using them as a basis for switching jokes and ideas.

Brad later found out that Galton and Simpson, Muir and Norden were doing exactly the same thing, and that Jimmy Grafton had a tall aerial on top of Grafton's pub to pick up the American Forces Network on shortwave. So there was a big race between all the scriptwriters to see who could adapt the American gags first.

By the end of 1954, Larry had a regular job for a few weeks, working with an old friend: he and Jimmy Grafton were co-writing scripts for *The Forces Show*, joined at times by Peter Griffiths and John Vyvyan. *The Forces Show* had been a regular programme on the radio since 1952. Previous series writers had included Bob Monkhouse and Denis Goodwin, and the sixty-minute show was a mix of music, novelty acts such as a radio conjurer and Leslie Welch the Memory Man, and plenty of comedy sketches.

The year 1955 was to be an incredibly busy one for Larry, as not only did *The Forces Show* continue its run but he co-wrote the script for a special programme to mark the tenth anniversary of *The British Forces Network* with Jimmy called 'Bring on the Girls', an all-female show with performances from stars such as June Whitfield, Irene Handl and Pat Coombs. Larry also had a diverse range of films, radio and television programmes to write for in 1955 but he still had quite a way to go before he could rebuild his previous form and good reputation.

A lucky break came for him when the Goons' first producer, Dennis Main Wilson, began working on a new series called *Pertwee's Progress*. The star of the show was Jon Pertwee, who is now best remembered for playing the third Doctor Who, but in this new series he played several parts, ranging from a BBC current affairs journalist and an eccentric private detective to a 'nouveau pauvre' who is embarrassed by his vast but empty stately homes and the enormous cars he is unable to drive as he cannot afford the petrol for them.

Towards the end of March, with the first programme of the *Pertwee's Progress* series due to be broadcast on 6 April, there was still a final sketch that needed to be written. In a memo to the Head of Variety, Main Wilson explained what subsequently happened:

You may or may not have known that Larry Stephens (who in the days when I was doing the *Goon Show* was one of the best writers in the business) has been off form owing to his personal troubles for more than a year – and we have had none of his early brilliance for a long, long time. I originally wanted Galton and Simpson to write the last sketch for *Pertwee* – this of course was squashed when it was decided to bring the Hancock show back concurrently with *Pertwee*. I then thought of having the Milligan and Sykes/Galton and Simpson complete team to work on the sketch – but having heard their Frankie Howerd show, decided against it. My other writer, Jimmy Grafton, was stuck in Madeira – and for all I know is still stuck there owing to cancellation of flying because of bad weather. I then decided to have a crack at bringing Stephens back onto his early form. It took us ten days, during the latter four of which neither I or my secretary were able to get more than two or three hours' sleep. It was rather pathetic to see this fine brain trying to struggle back to its original brilliance – however, I am most excited to say we achieved it. The script was finished between the three of us at approximately 3am on the morning of the show. Since after the recording Stephens has become a changed man – and I am very much looking forward to his next script which should be produced with far less effort. I make the foregoing points about script, firstly because it does show that Producers in the Corporation can be humane and do a decent thing for a change – and also by way of an apology for the fact that you did not get a script for Saturday.[4]

One of Larry's friends had also been given something of a big break around this time. Peter Sellers had been cast to appear alongside Alec Guinness in a film being made by Ealing Studios called *The Ladykillers*. Shooting for the film began on 19 April 1955 from a script written by William Rose, after the story came to him in a dream.

Film director Alexander Mackendrick had heard Rose describing his dream in the pub and persuaded him to write the script, even though Rose had vowed never to have any further dealings with Mackendrick after they had worked together on *The Maggie*, another Ealing film from 1954.

The plot of *The Ladykillers* concerns a gang of criminals who rent rooms in the house of a sweet little old lady called Mrs Wilberforce. They tell her that they are an amateur string quartet and need somewhere to meet and practise but in reality they are planning to rob a security van at King's Cross station. When 'Mrs W' discovers what they have really been up to, she tells the gang that she is going to report them to the police and they decide that they are going to have to kill her. In the process of crossing and double-crossing each other, all the criminals end up dead and Mrs Wilberforce gets the proceeds of the heist.

The film's director, Mackendrick, and associate producer, Seth Holt, were both *Goon Show* fans, which is how Peter Sellers came to be cast as Harry Robinson, a thuggish Teddy Boy. His skill as an impersonator also helped him to secure additional roles in the film, as the voices of Mrs Wilberforce's parrots.

Before the first draft of the script had been completed, William Rose and Seth Holt had an argument that led to Rose quitting and swearing never to return. Mackendrick and Holt managed to complete the script using Rose's notes but Larry was asked to write some one-liners to include throughout the film. Although he wasn't named in the credits, Mackendrick told Philip Kemp about Larry's contribution when he interviewed him for his book, *Lethal Innocence – The Cinema of Alexander Mackendrick*: 'After Bill [Rose] did his famous storming off the picture, we did need some ad-lib lines and so we brought in another writer [Larry Stephens] to provide them… he was good at it.'[5]

This wasn't Larry's only *Ladykillers* contribution though. At the wrap party Sellers handed out very special gifts to members of the cast and crew. Based on a script written by Larry, he had made recordings of his own version of the film trailer and had voiced all the different characters. This seven-minute recording still survives and the script for the spoof is as follows:

FEMALE VOICE: 'Ere! I've forgotten me glasses, Bert.
ANNOUNCER: Once again Ealing Studios who gave you such great successes as *The Cruel Sea* starring Mario Lanza; *The Night My Ship Died of Shame*; *Above Us the Joneses*; *Passport to Golders Green*; *The Man in the Right Boots*; now bring you their latest hilarious comedy, *The Ladykillers*. Adapted from *Tomorrow's New Yesterday*, the Wurlitzer Prize-winning novel by Otto Heller, *The Ladykillers* tells of a ruthless gang of criminals headed by Alec Guinness CBE, the man of a thousand faces. Remember Fagin? He plays Professor Marcus, the cool, cunning, calculating

leader. Herbert Lom, direct from his great success as Anna in *The King of Siam*, plays Louis, the suave continental crook whose villainous past combines well with that of Major Courtenay, a masterpiece of underplaying by Cecil Parker of Vista-Vision fame. His partner in death is Peter Sellers of radio's *White Coons*. Next in this scintillating array of stars comes Danny Green as One-Round, the punch-drunk actor-boxer. With him it's brawn, bulk and a hideous sense of humour. And introducing Katie Johnson as Mrs Wilberforce, the lovely little old landlady who in the end captivates the cold hearts of the Ladykillers. Here are but a few scenes from the Sir Ealing Balcon Michael Studios Production.

HARRY: How do we know we can trust her to do it right if she don't even know what she's doing?

LOUIS: I tell you I hate little old ladies. I want it settled here and now.

PROFESSOR: No one is indispensable, Louis. Only the plan, my plan. Do you agree, Major?

MAJOR: Ha! Well, I... I'm with you, Professor. After all, it is twelve thousand pounds all round. One-Round?

ONE-ROUND: I'm staying with <u>Ma</u>. I'm <u>staying</u> with Ma. <u>I'm</u> staying with Ma. What do you say, Louis?

LOUIS: I want it settled here and now.

ANNOUNCER: See them pleading with Mrs Wilberforce in a vain attempt to prevent her going to the bogies, the rozzers, the Peelers, the flatfeet, the police.

PROFESSOR: Mrs Wilberforce, I really should tell you...

MRS WILBERFORCE: Don't you speak to me, Professor Marcus; I'm disgusted to say the least. Huh! I know what I must do, I must ask you to vacate my rooms immediately.

ONE-ROUND: Oh! Now listen lady we went to a whole load...

MRS WILBERFORCE: You be quiet. <u>Your</u> dinner's in the oven.

ONE-ROUND: OK Ma. But I'm staying buttoned up.

ANNOUNCER: All of this plus Frankie Howerd, bringing drama to the screen as the naughty barrow boy.

HOWERD: So eh, ooh, oh, oooh, ah, ah, ooh, oh, oh, ah...

ANNOUNCER: No expense was spared to make this film the pick of the Ealing bunch this year. Here in a candid shot by our newsreel camera is a brief glimpse of the brilliant technique of Alexander Mackendrick, Director, hard at work on the floor.

MACKENDRICK: Tom, er, er, Tom, Tom, um, er, can we go, Tom?

PEVSNER: Yes, Sandy. Lock the doors and let's have it quiet. I said QUIET! OK, Otto?

OTTO HELLER: No, no. Not OK. But who cares?

PEVSNER: We're waiting to shoot, Otto.

OTTO: Hmph. Now he tells me.

PEVSNER: All right. Turn over.

CLAPPER LOADER: Mark it. Scene 5. Take 73.

PEVSNER: Action!

GRAMS: Speeded-up voices.

PEVSNER: Cut! Cut!

MACKENDRICK: Peter, Peter, that's, er, very good. We'll do another.

ANNOUNCER: Yes, folks, don't fail to miss *The Ladykillers*, coming to this cinema <u>soon</u>. <u>Coming</u> to this cinema soon. Coming to <u>this</u> cinema soon. Coming <u>to</u>...

LOUIS: Look! I want it settled here and now.

The Ladykillers wasn't the only film Larry and Sellers worked on during 1955. Along with vast swathes of the population, Michael

Deeley and Harry Booth were obsessed with the *Goon Show* and, as up-and-coming film producers, they devised a plan to transfer the show from radio to television. They raised £4,500 from three different sources to finance the project and as they couldn't afford the services of all three Goons, they hired Peter Sellers to star at a fee of £900, with Spike and Dick Emery in support. They needed someone to write the script though, and Michael Deeley and his colleagues sought suggestions for suitable writers before eventually making a decision to hire Larry. 'The reason we picked Larry to do our script was because of Peter Sellers' recommendation which was certainly good enough for us,'[6] Deeley later commented.

Larry came up with a story entitled *The Case of the Mukkinese Battle-Horn* which concerned 'a look at the world-famous CID at work through the medium of a true real-life case; a factual documentary record straight from the files of Scotland Yard'.[7] Superintendent Quilt (Sellers) and Sergeant Brown (Milligan) are called to investigate the theft of a Mukkinese battle-horn from the Metropolitan Museum and meet an interesting assortment of characters in their quest to discover its whereabouts. Larry's list of comedy character names provided two of these: the assistant commissioner, Sir Jervis Fruit (also played by Sellers) and Sid Crimp the janitor (Emery); but *Goon Show* characters Eccles, Henry Crun and Minnie Bannister also feature.

Filming started at the small Merton Park studios on the Kingston Road in south-west London at the end of October. The film took five days to shoot and members of the press were invited along to watch it in production. A double-page illustrated spread subsequently appeared in *Picturegoer* magazine.

At just under half an hour, the film was considered the ideal length to sell to the American networks, but a preview showing met with a stony silence; it seemed British humour was not appreciated by an American audience. So instead, the *Mukkinese Battle-Horn* was released in the UK as a short to accompany ninety-minute main features and received much better reviews from home audiences. It premiered at the Marble Arch Pavilion in January 1956, and according to the *Daily Film Renter* magazine, it kept the audience laughing throughout. It was now too late to use an alternative and preferred title for the film the team had since come up with: *The Yard has Three Feet*.

Michael Deeley is now better remembered as the Oscar-winning producer of films such as *The Italian Job*, but in his book *Blade Runner, Deer Hunters and Blowing The Bloody Doors Off* he says that *The Case of the Mukkinese Battle-Horn* turned out to be the most profitable film he ever made in relation to cost. To date, it has earned more than ten times its original budget. This was no doubt partly achieved by its being resurrected in 1975 when it was chosen as the supporting film for *Monty Python and the Holy Grail*.

It has been suggested by Goon aficionados that Larry makes a cameo appearance in the film, and there is certainly one scene which offers a possibility for this theory. About half way through we see a couple standing face to face and shrouded in fog:

VOICEOVER: With nightfall the weather took a turn for the worse but even in the darkest, foggiest streets London's indomitable police searched on, stopping late wayfarers and ruthlessly questioning them.

POLICEMAN: Hey! Hey, you two!

MAN: Er, yes?

POLICEMAN: Can you tell me the way back to the Police Station?

MAN: Er, it's just over there.

POLICEMAN: Thank you.[8]

The man in this scene is wearing a hat and has his collar turned up so that only his profile can be seen through the fog. He does, however, have a large and distinctive nose.

Anyone who has watched the original version of the film can't fail to notice the closing credits, which mention characters who did not appear, such as Freda Clench, The Underwater Soprano (own tank) and Lurgi The Wonder Dog, but there is also a name mentioned in the opening credits that has caused much discussion among fans – the film editor, Ferne Muleboot. There have been various suggestions as to who the mysterious Ferne Muleboot may be, since his/her career was limited to this one film. Is the name an anagram? Was Muleboot tragically killed not long afterwards, cutting short a promising career in the motion-picture industry? The answer is neither of these things. The editing was actually done by Harry Booth and Michael Deeley, who were also working together on the *Adventures of Robin Hood* television series at the time. They didn't think it would be a good idea to give themselves another screen credit and so Larry used the fictional Ferne Muleboot instead (whose brother, Yhogort Muleboot, had appeared in a series 2 episode of the *Goon Show*). It wasn't the first time he had used the name. In 1953, he had created one of his spoof adverts for Peter Sellers to place in *The Stage* in which Sellers gave thanks to 'Arnold Fringe, Harold Vest, The Arloo Tour, The Flunge Circuit and Fern Muleboot for their continued guidance in the face of overwhelming odds'.[9]

29
The Tony Hancock Show

Although he still wasn't officially writing for the *Goon Show*, Larry continued to have opportunities to work with the Goons on other projects during 1955. Harry Secombe had been given his own television show called *Secombe Here!* which ran bi-monthly for three episodes between May and September in 1955 with scripts written by Larry, Jimmy Grafton, Spike and Eric Sykes.

An outline development for the first programme is held in the BBC Archives and this appears to have been Larry's copy as one of the blank rear pages has been filled with his hallmark drawings plus notes in what looks like his handwriting, including the phrases 'Sunday Evening' and 'Guess My Story' written over and over again.

Secombe Here! involved comedy sketches and general clowning around as well as song-and-dance routines and conventional entertainment acts. The character of Eccles popped up throughout the programme and one of the *Goon Show*'s favourite guests, Valentine Dyall, appeared in the guise of a hypnotist called The Great Hugo.

A week after this programme aired, the Goons were back in a studio again – or rather, some of them were. Spike's doctor had issued a certificate stating he was too ill to work and he was once again undergoing a period of incarceration. BBC Radio was producing a series of programmes under the title of *Summer is a Comin'* and one of these was to have been a new show written by Spike. Peter Sellers made an announcement to the studio audience before they began the *Summer is a Comin'* programme and a recording of this pre-show extract is available as a bonus item on *The Goon Show Compendium* Volume 2 (Series 5, Part 2), which was released in 2009 by BBC Audiobooks.

Sellers began by telling the audience that Spike was unwell, which meant they would be doing the show without him. He explained that having found out Spike wouldn't be available, they had decided to do a different show instead and their colleague Larry Stephens had started writing the script but then he too had become suddenly rather ill and couldn't continue. So instead, they had decided to perform an old Goon Show: 'The Dreaded Batter Pudding Hurler of Bexhill-on-Sea' – and as Sellers would be playing all Spike's parts as well as his own, he was going to be talking to himself for much of the evening.

Larry must have been taken *very* suddenly ill as the front page of the script giving details of the performers, rehearsal and recording times bears his name as the sole writer. Perhaps something had woken the malaria parasites in his liver and brought on an attack of the disease.

The sixth series of the *Goon Show* proper started in September 1955 and halfway through it was announced that Peter Eton would be leaving the programme to join the Granada Television network. He wanted more comedy programmes to be shown on television and he outlined his plans in an interview with *The Stage*, saying he felt there was a big future for such humour and ad lib comedy and he wanted to see more emphasis on comedians' personalities.

Pat Dixon replaced Peter Eton as the new producer of the *Goon Show* on 14 February 1956 with a very unromantic offering for Valentine's Day called 'The Choking Horror', but what was significant was that it was announced as having been written by Spike Milligan and Larry Stephens. So, two years after he had been deemed to have broken the terms of his contract, Larry was back in the fold and officially writing the *Goon Show* again. Although there is no explicit documentary evidence to show he had been helping Spike before this without being credited, memos in the BBC archives do show that Spike was tired and uptight around this time. At the beginning of the year, he had asked if series 7, which wasn't due to start its run for another eight months, could be delayed and he had another major falling-out with Peter Sellers, resulting in Sellers' agent contacting the Variety Booking Manager, Patrick Newman, to tell him that he didn't want anything to do with the *Goon Show* ever again. Newman didn't take the threat very seriously and commented that Sellers and Spike tended to fall out on a regular basis. But perhaps all the upheaval was why Spike decided he needed Larry's calming influence back in his life on a more permanent basis. Larry's name also appeared as co-writer for the final three episodes in series 6 of the *Goon Show*, including 'The Fear of Wages', which was later named as being Spike's all-time favourite episode.

In the break between the end of series 6 and the start of series 7, Larry worked on two very diverse projects, the first with Jimmy Grafton and the second in collaboration with Eric Sykes.

Jimmy Grafton had devised a spectacular stage show entitled *Summer Stars*, with a cast of sixty, to play at the Coventry Theatre throughout the summer months. Jimmy produced it with Ronnie Boyer for S. H. Newsome, with choreography by Jeanne Ravel. As the main emphasis of the revue would be on comedy, Larry was appointed as the Comedy Director.

Larry and Jimmy worked together to write a number of sketches for the all-star cast, which included Jon Pertwee, Ronnie Corbett, Jimmy Young and Stan Stennett. No scripts are known to have survived and the titles of the sketches are all that remain: 'Hooray for Mars'; 'The

Search for Colonel Fnutt'; 'Trouble at the Palace' (with Jon Pertwee playing His Highness and Ronnie Corbett playing His Lowness); 'Ad Infinauseam'; 'At the Moulin d'Or'; 'Physical Jerks'; and 'The Mystery of Ghastly Grange'. The show's finale was an old-time music-hall performance using a genuine 1899 Star Automobile.

The press review evening took place on 10 April but the show itself didn't open until 20 June. After the gala opening there were performances every weeknight at 7.30 p.m.; matinee and evening shows on Saturdays and bank holidays; and the occasional special Thursday matinee. After seven weeks in Coventry, the production moved to the Palace Theatre in Manchester for a four-week season.

Not long after the press review performance of *Summer Stars*, the second of Larry's projects, which he had worked on with Eric Sykes, made its appearance. Tony Hancock had by now become a household name as star of the radio programme *Hancock's Half Hour*, but two months before the programme made the transition to television, Hancock appeared in a series of six programmes for Associated-Rediffusion Television called *The Tony Hancock Show* and the first two of these were scripted by Larry with Eric. The show was broadcast live and so to fill the gaps while scenes and costumes were changed, there were song or dance routines, sometimes performed by June Whitfield, who was a regular in the series.

There were four sketches in the first episode: an opening party (during which June Whitfield sang and everyone ignored her); a coffee-bar scene; a skit on *A Streetcar Named Desire* (with Hancock as Marlon Brando and Whitfield as Vivien Leigh); and a Spanish dance routine. In the coffee bar, Hancock, dressed in a chef's whites, tries to serve customers while grappling with a 'Depresso' coffee machine and a plant that won't stop growing. At closing time, he is slowly lowered behind the counter in the manner of an old-fashioned cinema organ. For the Spanish dancing finale, Hancock took to the floor with Pamela

Deeming to dance flamenco and finished the episode off by stamping his way through the floor.

The second episode, the only other of the series that Larry worked on, included a sketch set in a library where every book Hancock wanted seemed to be on the top shelf; a take-off of a natural history programme with Hancock and Whitfield pretending to be Armand and Michaela Denis, the TV wildlife presenters; and a Balinese dance routine featuring 'Ram Hancock'.

Hancock was also becoming more involved with the Associated London Scripts agency, or at least he planned to. Following an announcement on 2 August that ALS and Frankie Howerd (Scripts) Ltd were to merge and form a new company to be known as Associated London Scripts Limited (ALS Ltd), the proposed directors were later named as Stanley Dale; Raymond Percy Galton; Anthony John Hancock; Francis Alick Howard; Terence Alan Milligan; Peter Richard Henry Sellers; Alan Francis Simpson and Eric Sykes. Hancock withdrew his official link to ALS Ltd not long after as he didn't feel he really belonged, not being a writer. He continued to be a regular visitor to the ALS Ltd headquarters in Shepherd's Bush though.

To reach the offices you needed to turn right out of the Underground station and walk along Uxbridge Road for 100 yards or so, past various shops and the Wellington Arms pub, until you arrived at the greengrocer's. ALS Ltd's domain was situated through a green door and up three flights of stairs, and the walls of the landing were decorated with various papers, oil paintings and items of memorabilia, including a sketch of someone being dragged from a lake, above which was scrawled, 'Do you come here often?' with the reply, 'Only when I'm drowning.'

Larry was now sharing Spike's office in the building, with its three cream walls and one red wall. The office was crammed with files, reference books, pens, paper, ink and a battered flintlock pistol. Pinned to one of the walls was a large Union Flag with Queen Victoria's portrait in the centre, bearing the legend, 'For Queen and Empire'. Spike's fellow directors at ALS Ltd, Ray Galton and Alan Simpson, remembered that 'Larry was very, very tidy and Spike was chaotic. Larry wouldn't start writing until everything was neat and tidy and he had to have a spotless desk, sharp pencils and everything laid out in straight lines with military precision. This was the routine he followed every day.'[1] While Spike roamed and fidgeted around the office, Larry would sit and type the ideas they came up with.

Series 7 of the *Goon Show* launched on 4 October 1956 and now there was no doubt that Larry was back as a regular co-writer of the show, although not through the BBC's 'legal' eyes.

30

Back in the Goon Gang

With *Goon Show* producer Pat Dixon away and Peter Eton filling in, Larry had taken the opportunity to phone Dixon's secretary, Diane, before the start of the new series to try and work his charm on her. During the conversation he asked if he could be given a credit in the *Radio Times* as he was writing half of the *Goon Show* scripts. Diane asked Larry if it could wait until Dixon returned but Larry insisted it would need to be actioned immediately since the *Radio Times'* credits needed to be inserted quite some time before the actual broadcast. Diane subsequently sent a request for the addition of Larry's name but shortly afterwards members of the Variety Department noticed the memo and discovered that it hadn't been agreed by the Copyright Department. Frantic memos covered in red-inked comments began flying around Broadcasting House. The Assistant Head of Variety put a halt to Larry's name being included in the *Radio Times* as copyright issues needed to be sorted out, especially as there was a fear that Spike and Larry would ask for more money. Spike did in fact manage to sneak Larry's name into the *Radio Times* ahead of programme 1 though; the launch of the new series had warranted a half-page spread with photos of Spike, Sellers and Secombe, listing the characters they played. Spike's entry read: 'alias Eccles, Count Jim Moriarty, Minnie Bannister, Adolphus Spriggs and Larry Stephens'.[1]

The decision eventually reached by the BBC was that before Larry could receive a billing in the *Radio Times*, Spike would need to confirm that any co-writing would be a private arrangement between them. A letter was sent to Spike outlining the corporation's conditions.

Miss Ross of the Copyright Department was asked to get involved and she also sent a letter to Spike, to reiterate that as he had been contracted to be the sole writer of the show, he would need to set out in writing that any arrangement he had with Larry was a private one and that Spike, and not the BBC, would be responsible for any payments to him. Miss Ross concluded that when Spike complied with this, a credit for Larry would be inserted into future editions of the *Radio Times*.

Spike seemed to find the whole thing preposterous and rather than agreeing to Miss Ross's suggestions he wrote back to her saying that in order to keep everyone happy, he had spoken to the Assistant Head of Light Entertainment, Jim Davidson, and suggested that his name be removed from the *Radio Times* too. That way, the BBC would be satisfied and he would be able to make Larry feel happier about the situation. He concluded by wishing her a merry Christmas – this being a letter sent at the beginning of October!

A few more memos were circulated around the various BBC departments with words such as 'childish' being bandied about, but the popularity of the *Goon Show* was such that they needed to find a solution. They considered making a formal contract with Larry but the issue surrounding money again put a stop to this. However, while discussions at the BBC were still going on, Spike conceded and wrote another letter to confirm that he alone would take responsibility for any payments due to Larry, adding that he had already paid him in advance for the entire series anyway.

Spike and Larry's friendship was going through a honeymoon period again. Their time apart, while Larry struggled with his mental health, had highlighted just how much they relied on each other. Their roles in the relationship had been reversed during Larry's dark period from 1953 though, and Spike had now become the dominant one in the partnership, having grown more confident in his ability as a writer and performer. Larry had lost the trust of the BBC and the Corporation had since become accustomed to dealing with Spike, so he was the one they now consulted first and deferred to.

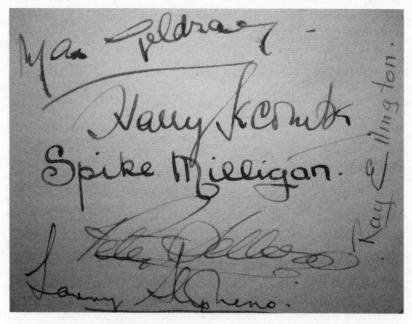

Autographs of Max Geldray; Harry Secombe;
Spike Milligan; Peter Sellers; Larry Stephens; and Ray Ellington.
Held in the Goon Show Preservation Society's archives.

As well as collaborating on the *Goon Show*, Spike and Larry had begun to turn their attention to other areas towards the end of 1956. A musicians' strike earlier in the year had meant Ray Ellington, Max Geldray and the BBC Orchestra weren't available to provide the musical links and consequently the cast had supplied their own. Spike had performed 'I'm Walking Backwards for Christmas', which was subsequently released as a single and proved so popular that a decision was made to produce more Goon records.

Larry and Spike wrote 'A Russian Love Song' and 'Whistle Your Cares Away', which were released by Decca in October 1957. 'A Russian Love Song' was first of all partially censored by the BBC for including an impersonation of Sir Winston Churchill and then completely banned when they realised its lyrics satirised the Cold War.

The first Goon song with evidence of Larry being involved was 'You Gotta Go Oww!' for Parlophone at the end of 1956, where he played the piano accompaniment under the pseudonym Graveley Stephens (Pharmacological Pianist). It is also more than likely he joined in with the coughing and shushing that punctuate the song. The record was produced by Sir George Martin, who would later go on to work with The Beatles.

'Gravel(e)y' was a name that Larry was fond of. Gravely Headstone was mentioned along with Strangler Aagonschmidt in the synopsis for the *Goon Show* episode 'The Canal' in series 5 and among Larry's personal papers is a letterhead he had designed:

Graveley Stephens
Est. 1887 (B.C.)
APOTHECARY
Purveyor of Wondrous Physicks, Nostrums, Remedies, Counter-Poisons, Specifics, Etc., Etc., Etc. Also Sole Agent for MILLIGAN'S SECRET EASTERN PILULES[2]

Articles about 'You Gotta Go Oww!' appeared in the *Daily Mirror* and *Daily Express* but a general feature about the Goons was printed in a more highbrow publication just before Christmas. The *Manchester Guardian* (now simply the *Guardian*) paid a visit to ALS Ltd and described what they found there: 'Over a fruit shop in Shepherd's Bush, up three flights of narrow brown stairs, there is an office containing teapots, typewriters, electronic devices, encyclopaedias and books... and it is here that the extraordinary hallucinations of the *Goon Show* are hammered into script form every week by Spike Milligan and Larry Stephens.'[3]

At the start of 1957, Larry was officially accepted by the BBC as being a writer of the *Goon Show* again. Series 7 needed to be extended by another five programmes and both Spike and Larry were contracted by the Copyright Department to write these at a fee of 100 guineas per script. In addition, Pat Dixon asked Miss Ross in Copyright to ensure that Larry received a credit for co-writing all the programmes in series 7, including the 'specials'. Beryl Vertue at ALS Ltd accepted the terms on behalf of the writers, which indicates that Larry must have left Kavanagh Productions some time previously.

With Beryl now handling contracts and dealing with the day-to-day administration, Larry and Spike were able to concentrate on writing. This had enabled them to get into the habit of producing their scripts a week or so in advance, which reduced last-minute stresses and made them both calmer and less likely to argue. The new regime led to them producing some of their best work, including this glorious exchange from the February 1957 episode, 'The Mysterious Punch-up-the-Conker':

BLUEBOTTLE (BB): What time is it, Eccles?

ECCLES: Just a minute – I got it written down here on a piece of paper... A nice man wrote the time down for me this morning.

BB: Oh! Then why do you carry it around with you, Eccles?

ECCLES: Well, if anybody asks me the time, I can show it to them.

BB: Wait a minute, Eccles, my good man.

ECCLES: What is it, fellow?

BB: It's writted on this bit of paper, what is eight o'clock, is writted.

ECCLES: I know that, my good fellow. That's right. When I asked the fellow to write it down, it was eight o'clock.

BB: Well, then supposing when somebody asks you the time, it isn't eight o'clock?

ECCLES: Oh, then I don't show it to them.[4]

In mid-January, ALS Ltd had been visited by more journalists and several photographers. Some of the photos were used in a *TV Times* article about Eric Sykes and others made their way into the BBC Photo Library. Three of the pictures were of Larry and Spike in their shared office, hamming it up for the camera in a variety of 'serious writer' poses. An ebony Indian elephant ornament with one broken ivory tusk is featured in two of the photographs and has clearly been moved from elsewhere, as fingerprints are visible in the layer of dust covering its plinth. With their jacket collars turned up and wearing matching paisley cravats, Larry and Spike pretend to pore over books and scripts. Although the photos are black and white, compared to Spike, Larry's skin seems to have an unhealthy pallor and he looks almost like a waxwork. It is evident that he has put on quite a lot of weight as a second chin is beginning to establish itself below his dimpled first one. The shelves behind the pair are crammed with an eclectic selection of books such as *Churchill. His Life in Photographs*; Planiscig's *Lorenzo Ghiberti*; *The Dead Sea Scrolls*; *A Thousand Shall Fall*; William Golding's *The Inheritors*; *The Dialogues of Plato*; *The Oxford Dictionary of Quotations* and *Cassell's New English Dictionary*. Volumes two and three of Hooke's *Roman History* have been stacked on the desk for use as a teapot and milk-bottle stand. A two-bar electric fire has blackened the wall above it but this has been partially disguised by a pencil-sketched mantelpiece complete with a mantel clock with its hands pointing to half past ten. ('It's writted on this bit of wall, what is half past ten, is writted.')

In March of 1957, ALS Ltd moved from above the greengrocer's to more salubrious offices at Cumberland House in Kensington High Street. The new offices were directly opposite Kensington Gardens and a short stroll from Fu Tong's Chinese restaurant, which became a favourite lunchtime haunt for them. The writers ate there so regularly that the restaurant gave them each their own personalised set of chopsticks, decorated with their initials. Spike's new office, which he again shared with Larry when they were collaborating on the *Goon Show*, was larger than the one in Shepherd's Bush and so had room for a piano. Ray Galton, Alan Simpson and John Antrobus remembered being able to hear Larry's beautiful playing in between typing bouts. Galton and Simpson admitted that they sometimes found Larry's performances frustrating, even though he was a brilliant modern jazz pianist and played in the style of Oscar Peterson, of whom they were both fans. Alan Simpson remembered that Larry 'would start to play "Blue Moon", for instance, but then he would get bored halfway through and never get to the end of anything'.[5] Sometimes Spike would accompany Larry's piano-playing on his trumpet.

A six-minute recording of Larry playing the piano survives. He can be heard improvising around 'Night and Day' and other popular songs of the era and it is a clear demonstration of his talent as a pianist.

The first *Goon Show* to be broadcast after the move to the new offices in Kensington High Street was 'Ill Met by Goonlight'. This is often credited solely to Spike rather than as a joint effort with Larry, and yet this is one of the episodes that most shows evidence of Larry's influence. An original script does bear Larry's name as co-writer and so his later omission seems odd. The story concerns a 1942 commando mission to Crete to capture the German Commander General Von Gutern (a character who makes another appearance in 'The African Incident' in series 8, purely so that the line 'Von Gutern deserves another'[6] can be used again). The mission is led by Lieutenant Seagoon, who must first undergo training at the Marine Commando Spaghetti Hurling Depot in Rhyl.

The commandos had also been mentioned in 'Operation Christmas Duff', a special Christmas edition of the show that was broadcast on Christmas Eve 1956 to listeners overseas. The plot of this festive episode revolves around the making of a Combined Services Christmas pudding and 45 Commando are sent in under cover of daylight to gather samples of the pudding for the Army Catering Corps to test. It had originally been scripted that the samples would be collected by 5 Commando, the unit Larry served with during the Second World War, but during the final rehearsals the '5' was crossed through and replaced with '45'.

The commandos were obviously at the forefront of Larry's mind again. There had been a reunion for the Army and Royal Marine members of 3 Commando Brigade in 1955 and there was an annual event for all former Army Commandos in London. Five years previously, a memorial had been erected at Spean Bridge, unveiled by the Queen Mother on 27 September 1952. At seventeen feet tall, the Memorial is a cast bronze sculpture of three commandos standing on a stone plinth, looking towards Ben Nevis and out over the landscape where the commandos had been trained. Whether Larry attended the official unveiling is not known but he certainly visited the monument at some point. Perhaps a recent visit is what sparked references to the commandos in the *Goon Show*, or perhaps he was using them as a kind of therapy to help ease PTSD symptoms.

As well as collaborating with Spike on the *Goon Show*, Larry had also started working with a new writing partner called Maurice Wiltshire.

Maurice, a former writer for the *Daily Mail*, had been represented by the Kavanaghs from as early as 1947 before joining ALS Ltd, so even if Larry hadn't met him there he would certainly have heard of him. The first evidence of them working together is a letter sent by Beryl Vertue at ALS Ltd to the BBC on 5 June 1957, giving a rundown on the availability of the agency's writers and listing their current projects. Larry and Maurice are both mentioned as just coming to the end of writing for a Granada Television programme called *My Wife's Sister*.

My Wife's Sister had started life in September 1956 as *Our Dora* with Dora Bryan in the lead role, but after the first episode had aired, Granada announced that Ms Bryan had been taken ill and would be unable to continue in the programme's planned fifty-two-week run. Eleanor Summerfield was drafted in to replace her and the show was rewritten, retitled and had its run reduced. It was originally written by Reuben Ship and it is not clear when or how Larry and Maurice became involved.

The thirty-ninth and final edition of *My Wife's Sister* was aired on 11 June 1957, a few days after Granada had begun advertising a new comedy programme called *The Army Game* that they had in the pipeline. *The Army Game* would become incredibly significant for both Larry and Maurice.

31

CBC and TV

Back in April of 1957, Spike had lunched with Malcolm Frost, the Head of the BBC's Transcription Service, who mentioned that the Canadian Broadcasting Corporation wanted to air some *Goon Shows* and asked Spike if it would be possible to adapt some of the old shows. As Spike was extremely busy at the time he suggested that Larry could do the rewrites, and Larry agreed to this on condition that he was given plenty of advance warning if the shows were required and that terms were agreed beforehand. Nothing more was heard until the end of June when a letter was sent to the ALS Ltd offices with a recording date of less than four weeks away. Having assumed that the Canadian rewrites weren't going to be needed after all, Larry had by now taken on some other assignments, writing for two television shows concurrently. Unbeknown to Larry and Spike, Pat Dixon had sent some old scripts to Transcription Services towards the end of May with a list of suggested amendments. Spike was now panicking that he would somehow be blamed so he sent a letter to the producer, Jacques Brown, with copies to almost everyone at the BBC, outlining the situation (concluding with a 'Merry Christmas' in case he didn't see any of them in the six months before!) and explaining that Larry would be trying to sort things out by telephone.

A transcription of the main points of the conversation Larry had with Jacques is held in the BBC's archives:

LARRY: A rewrite would be necessary because the old shows would have to be brought up to date from the point of view of characters, gimmicks and running gags. (a) The audiences in this country would be familiar (as would the Transcription audience) with the shows and the reaction would not be there.

JACQUES: After so many years?

LARRY: Yes. Running gags and sequences leading up to certain formation of characters, e.g. the Bluebottle routine, may have run through the programmes each week covering a good many programmes. These routines may have been repeated over and over again until they finally 'die' and are gradually dropped from the shows; (b) In the old shows characters weren't developed to the point they are now and they will have to be brought up to date. Transcription have taken the last two series and our listeners here are right up to date. It would therefore be damaging to the show if we went back to the more elementary type of character and show. All the character gimmicks would have to be rewritten because the audience has heard the gradual development of these gimmicks. Consequently, quite a lot of rewrite necessary according to Spike as well, in addition to the minor alterations and the odd things given by Derick Simond of Transcription. The reason I haven't had time is that I wasn't given any warning at all. I was totally unprepared for it after months of hearing nothing.

JACQUES: Pat Dixon had written giving all the facts to Spike.

LARRY: Spike told me at the time but had no confirmation that all this was actually going to happen. They said they couldn't find out whether the artists would be available (trouble with Harry Secombe or something). There was no point in going ahead with something that may not come off. First definite information was four or five days ago by which time it was much too late as I will be tied up with *Bernard Braden Show*, *Dickie Valentine Show* and ITV.

JACQUES: What would be the first date that you could undertake these things?

LARRY: The domestic series scheduled for the end of September. We will want three or four of them completed in shape before the domestic series actually begins.

JACQUES: When do you think you will be in a position to revamp these shows?

LARRY: At the beginning of September when we have actually started work on the domestic shows. This is the time Spike and I have arranged to get together on the domestic programmes.

JACQUES: Could you do both?

LARRY: The domestic series will take nearly all the week but the decision would be up to Spike. It <u>would</u> be possible to do the rewrites and the domestics each week.

JACQUES: Can you undertake to revamp the Transcription shows any time to start running them concurrent with the domestics?

LARRY: Entirely depends on Spike as he is working on them as well. We <u>could</u> both do the rewrites each week but we will have to be three or four weeks in hand with the domestic series.

JACQUES: I have been unable to get hold of Spike. I have rung him several times. Hasn't he the interest in this thing that I have?

LARRY: I'll pass it on to Spike![1]

After speaking to Jacques, Larry filled Spike in on their discussion and it was eventually agreed that the Canadian rewrites would be tackled at the same time as series 8 at the end of September.

For the time being, Larry was busy writing for the two television shows – one for the BBC and one for ITV. The BBC programme was *Early to Braden* and the plans for it had been in progress for some time. Several writers were being asked to contribute and they all met at a script conference on 20 June. Photographs were being taken at every stage with the intention that the resulting images would give a view of a light entertainment programme from start to finish and would appear in television magazines and in the press.

One of the photographs from the script conference shows Larry dressed in a dark jacket and a light cravat, with his arms folded and a wry smile on his face. Ray Galton and Alan Simpson are sitting to his right and Bernard Braden is standing behind him. The desk in front of them is cluttered with papers, an anglepoise lamp, several typewriters and mugs of tea and coffee. Larry, Ray and Alan weren't the only writers at the meeting as *Early to Braden* was taking a new approach by employing lots of scriptwriters and giving them a free rein. Other contributors to the programme were Frank Muir and Denis Norden; Maurice Wiltshire (who partnered with Larry); and Dave Freeman.

The sketches were linked by Bernard Braden sitting at a piano where he tapped out tunes and filled the time by randomly singing brief snatches of popular songs, smoking, drinking from a pint glass of beer and telling entertaining stories. Whenever he wanted to move around or changes of scenery were needed, a film clip of a baby in a rocking chair was shown or Braden would chat to a caged bird in the studio. Presumably this was a one-sided conversation.

The *Daily Mirror* found it pleasant, easy viewing whereas the *Guardian* initially hated it but began to warm to it as the series progressed.

When *Early to Braden* started on 11 July 1957, the other television show Larry had been writing for was already into its third week. Larry collaborated on the scripts with Jimmy Grafton and Maurice Wiltshire and the programme, *Monday Date*, was aired on commercial television. The star of the show was the chart-topping singer Dickie Valentine, joined by Shani Wallis. *The Stage* rated it as 'the brightest, slickest and most likeable show on TV', describing it as 'a smooth-moving show with a very funny script'.[2] Very little information about *Monday Date* seems to have survived but a description of one of the comedy sketches is mentioned in *The Stage* review, which the writer considered to be perfect television comedy: with not a word spoken between them, Kenneth Carter plays a tennis racket like a banjo and a policeman accompanies him by playing some park railings as a harp. Perhaps you had to see it in action to appreciate its humour...

A letter sent to the BBC by ALS Ltd at the beginning of August gave details of Larry's current commitments and future availability. As well as the Bernard Braden and Dickie Valentine TV series, Larry was working on *Goon Shows* for the Canadian Broadcasting Corporation with Spike. He had also begun writing *The Army Game* for Granada Television with Maurice.

32

The Army Game

The Army Game series had started on 19 June 1957 and was being aired on Wednesdays fortnightly across the whole ITV network. Recordings of only around fifty episodes from the programme's run between 1957 and 1961 are known to have survived, partly owing to them having been broadcast live at first with no recordings made. Written records are also scant. It is therefore almost impossible to determine exactly who wrote which episodes, but along with Larry and Maurice, other writers who contributed to the first series were Sid Colin, Lew Schwarz and John Jowett. The first programme is likely to have been written by Sid Colin alone but eventually a team of writers collaborated on each episode. Larry and Maurice had probably started working on *The Army Game* by its fifth episode, which was transmitted on 14 August. The writers would gather for a weekly script conference at Granada's offices in Golden Square, west London and the actors would also rehearse in London, at the Arts Theatre in Great Newport Street, although the programme itself was filmed at Granada's studios in Manchester.

The programme, which was produced by Peter Eton, was very much of its time and concerned a group of National Service conscripts who shared 'Hut 29' at the fictional Nether Hopping Transit Camp and Surplus Ordnance Depot, three miles from the nearest village and ten from the nearest town. The National Service Act of 1948 had made it compulsory for healthy males aged between seventeen and twenty-one to serve in the Armed Forces for a period of eighteen months, later extended to two years. National Service began to be phased out from 1957, just as *The Army Game* began.

To make sure that every last detail was authentic, Granada appointed Major John Foley as their military advisor and the War Office named an official liaison officer for the programme staff to work with. The War Office also granted permission for the scriptwriters to visit any army camp they liked when in search of material.

Initially, the five main characters were Corporal Springer, played by Michael Medwin, a Cockney 'wide boy' who worked the system so he could get away with doing as little as possible; Private Hatchett, nicknamed 'Professor' (Charles Hawtrey), who was a well-read, sensible young man; Private 'Popeye' Popplewell (Bernard Bresslaw), all brawn and not much brain; Private Cook (Norman Rossington) known as cupcake, thanks to the numerous food parcels he received from his doting mother; and Private Bisley (Alfie Bass), who was the only regular soldier among the group, nicknamed 'Bootsie' as he had been 'excused boots' and wore plimsolls instead. In charge of them all was Company Sergeant Major Bullimore (William Hartnell) and Major Upshott-Bagley (Geoffrey Sumner).

The Army Game quickly became very popular, much to the surprise of its stars. Michael Medwin told Simon Hoggart in an interview for *The Spectator* in 2010 that early in the life of the comedy he and Norman Rossington had stopped off for a cup of tea while on their way to Blackpool and noticed that the street outside the café had suddenly become crowded with people. They sat wondering what the big attraction was before eventually realising *they* were the big attraction![1]

The programme is generally believed to have been the main influence behind the making of the first of the *Carry On* films, *Carry On Sergeant*, which was released in 1958. Several of the *Army Game* regulars went on to appear in the *Carry On* series, among them Bernard Bresslaw, Charles Hawtrey and William Hartnell.

The first *Army Game* episode which can definitely be ascribed to Larry is 'The Mad Bull', broadcast on 11 September 1957, as this is one of the recordings to survive with the scriptwriting credits intact. Written in collaboration with Maurice, the plot concerns the inhabitants of Hut 29 learning that there will be a NATO training course in the south of France for the smartest and most knowledgeable conscripts in the camp. Believing that this will be the perfect opportunity for a 'holiday' away from Nether Hopping, Corporal Springer convinces the others that they must do everything within their power to ensure they are the ones selected. This includes memorising the manual for a dummy bomb that is sent to the CO by NATO – a Mark VI High Ferguson mortar bomb that has been developed for use in support of assault landings. Actor Frank Williams took the role of a psychiatrist in this episode and wrote about the experience in his autobiography *Vicar to Dad's Army*:

Upon our arrival at the Granada Television Studios we rehearsed the show with the cameras before doing the final performance as a live transmission. The size of the sets and the lack of space for the studio audience meant that they were seated in the canteen next door watching the episode on monitors. Their laughter was to be fed back to us through loudspeakers in the studio. As the opening titles began and the first scene went into action all seemed to be going well. The studio audience was obviously enjoying the show as there was much laughter coming from next door. My first entrance went down well and all seemed to be going smoothly. Suddenly the laughs stopped. For a moment our hearts stopped as well as we wondered if we had hit a part of the script that was hideously unfunny. We carried on in silence for a time until one of the technicians whispered that the sound system had broken down between the canteen and the studio. It was a relief to know that the audience was still laughing even though we couldn't hear them.[2]

The culmination of the episode is when CSM Bullimore eventually discovers what the group from Hut 29 are up to and informs them that even though they have been chosen to go to France, he will be accompanying them. He then remarks to the camera, 'I'll give them a nice little holiday; I'll give them a commando course!'

Larry's marriage had also become something of a commando course around this time and he and Diana underwent a temporary split. Larry moved out for a while and took refuge in the spare room of *Ladykillers* director Alexander Mackendrick and his wife Hilary. 'Afterwards it ended happily and he went back to his wife,'[3] recalled Mackendrick in an interview with Philip Kemp thirty years later.

Larry and Diana Stephens photographed by Graham Stark.
(Larry Stephens Estate collection)

When they had made up and were back together again, Larry and Diana agreed that they wanted to move forward on a firmer footing. They decided that rather than continue to rent flats, they would buy a house. They began to make enquiries about obtaining a mortgage, and as part of the application process Larry needed to undergo a medical examination. He had put on weight and friends had noticed that his complexion was becoming increasingly florid, but as a former commando who had always been fit, he believed that his medical would just be a formality. Unfortunately, this was far from the truth.

33

A Year to Live

Larry's medical examination had been far from straightforward. He later told his friends what the doctor had said to him: 'You have the highest blood pressure I've ever seen. If you give up drink and cigarettes you might live for a year.'

It is impossible to imagine just what a shock this must have been. Everything in Larry's life had been going so well. He was writing *The Army Game* with Maurice and he had recently started writing another series of the *Goon Show*, the eighth, with Spike. To be given just a year to live seemed ludicrous.

High blood pressure, also called hypertension, is known as a silent killer as most people don't suffer any symptoms. Blood pressure can rise slowly over many years with the body adapting to the increase so Larry probably had no previous indication there was a problem. Whether it was caused by drinking, smoking, stress or a combination of all three, we cannot know for sure what caused his blood pressure to reach such dangerous levels. It may also have been as a result of PTSD as recent studies have concluded there is a correlation between PTSD and an increased risk of hypertension in later life.

As well as recommending he quit smoking and drinking, Larry's doctor had told him to be careful about what he ate and advised he restrict his salt intake and follow a low-fat diet. He also prescribed opium-based tablets to help alleviate stress. But Larry felt sure there was more he could do to beat this death sentence. Like Neddie Seagoon, he was 'the man who smiled in the face of danger and laughed in the face of death'.[1]

He thought back to his commando days when he had learned it was possible to overcome any obstacle or physical discomfort if you put your mind to it and really believed you could. He remembered the first time he had heard the instructors yelling 'it's all in the mind' at him and how he had yelled the same thing at the recruits when he became an instructor himself. That was the answer. As long as he truly believed it, he could prove the doctor wrong.

On 28 October 1957, the phrase 'it's all in the mind, you know' appeared at the end of a *Goon Show* broadcast for the first time. It was as if Larry was sending himself a reminder to keep believing and to keep going. The phrase was only ever included in the show when Larry was involved in writing the script; following this initial mention it wasn't used in any of the eight episodes from series 8 that Spike wrote alone or in collaboration with John Antrobus; only in those that Larry wrote single-handedly or jointly with Spike or Maurice Wiltshire.

A mistrust of doctors and matters of life and death became significant themes in Larry's art. He drew a doctor with medicine jars labelled 'eeny' 'meeny' and 'miny' on a shelf behind him; he drew another writing out a prescription seemingly unaware that his patient had hanged himself from the ceiling. He drew Dickensian-looking undertakers with top hats and mourning veils. He wrote out a prescription for himself, as illustrated.

BENJAMIN STEPHENS
APOTHECARIC LEECH

2nd Day of October 1790

Item 1 tin McNosh & O'Nathan's
            Goitre Salve .... — 2d.

Item 1 Bot. "Wyndfree" Raspberry
            Carminative .... — 4½d.

Item 2d Debility Tablets .... ⅓d.

Item 1 bot. Hannigans Patent
            Head-Restorer .... — 7¼d

Item 4d "Lucky Dip" mixture (Asstd.
       Ear Tablets, Pile Pilules, Gout
            Lumps, Etc., Etc., Etc.) .... 1d.

Item 3 Gal. Chudlthorpe's Brackish Purge ----- 3¾d

                                    1s. 7¼d.
                    Plus Discount   4d
                                    1s. 11d

Remittance Will Oblige.

Larry Stephens' prescription. (Larry Stephens Estate collection)

Larry wasn't alone in suffering health problems as Spike was showing signs of nervous strain again. His wife, June, sent another doctor's note to the BBC on 5 November which certified that Spike was unable to work and explained in an accompanying letter that Larry would be writing that week's show – 'The Red Fort'.

Larry's health may have been deteriorating but his career was definitely on the up. *The Army Game* had proved to be such a hit that it was moved from its fortnightly Wednesday slot and began a weekly run on Fridays at half past eight in the evening from 20 December 1957. Five days prior to this, some very special guests had attended a recording of the *Goon Show* episode 'The Great British Revolution'. A list of names is held in the BBC Archives, dated 6 December, which was probably prepared for the visit. Spike tops the list and is described as Writer/Performer; Larry is second as Co-Writer and Harry Secombe and Peter Sellers are shown below, in that order, as Performers. The guests were the Duchess of Kent, her daughter Princess Alexandra, her sister Princess Olga and her niece Princess Elizabeth of Yugoslavia.

There had been a request from the royal party that their proposed visit be kept a secret but Pat Hillyard, the Head of Light Entertainment, had agreed that Spike, Peter and Harry could be warned a few days before. Unfortunately, due to a misunderstanding, the performers weren't alerted to expect some important additions to the studio audience until the actual day of the recording. Although he perhaps wasn't wearing exactly what he would have chosen to meet royalty, had he known about the visit beforehand, Larry was always immaculately dressed. Spike on the other hand was not and in addition he had made a dinner arrangement for after the recording which he was unable to cancel.

While the BBC's butler served champagne, the Duchess and her relations chatted to the writers, performers and production staff. Spike, however, didn't have long to chat and had to dash away to his prior engagement. Peter Sellers later told *Australian Women's Weekly* magazine that the Duchess had asked him if his colleague was in the habit of leaving parties early. Sellers couldn't think what to reply and so blurted out something about Spike being an Irish rebel who didn't like to get too involved with royalty.

Spike felt betrayed and embarrassed. He reacted to the incident by taking to his bed and staying there with the door locked and the telephone off the hook. His doctor diagnosed excessive stress caused by overwork and recommended total rest.

Spike wrote a letter of apology to the Duchess and her response was included in a letter from her private secretary to Pat Hillyard, saying that she completely understood why Spike had to leave early. This did little to placate him though and he fired off another letter – this one full of animosity – to Hillyard. The fiasco and Spike's subsequent withdrawal probably explains why the first *Goon Show* of 1958, 'The Thing on the Mountain', was written by Larry with Maurice Wiltshire.

The *Goon Show* had undergone several changes of producer across the different series. At the start of series 8, Charles Chilton was producing but from programme number 6, Roy Speer took over. When Larry and Maurice wrote 'The Thing on the Mountain' Roy Speer was away and had been temporarily replaced by Tom Ronald. Larry was far from impressed with the temporary producer and wrote a letter to the Assistant Head of Light Entertainment, Jim Davidson:

> This letter is purely confidential and I trust you treat it as so.
>
> I heard last Monday's *Goon Show* – the first one of mine which had been done by Tom Arnold [*sic*] – and frankly I was horrified.
>
> Several of the cuts seemed to be senseless but worst of all a lot of the ad libs and messing about by the cast etc. were left in. The latter, I may say, is done by the cast under the assumption that it will be cut out.
>
> I wonder if while Roy Speer is away, it is possible for his secretary (Doreen Mills) to do the cutting.
>
> I am sorry to write to you direct like this – but under the circumstances it was the only thing I could think to do.[2]

Jim Davidson replied that he would be looking into Larry's concerns as it was obviously important to the BBC that their major productions continued to be popular.

Listening to the recording of 'The Thing on the Mountain' in conjunction with the original script, Larry's point of view can be understood. There do appear to have been some odd decisions in respect of what has been left in and what has been cut out, although as the writer, Larry was bound to be more sensitive to such things than other listeners.

The story is set in the Welsh village of Llandahoy which lies at the foot of Mount Snowdon. A monster has been terrorising the locals up on the mountain so the mayor offers a reward to anyone who can capture it and Neddie Seagoon (Harry Secombe) accepts the challenge.

Seagoon is catapulted towards the peak of Snowdon but due to 'double-strength braces'[3] he lands at the top of Blackpool Tower instead where he encounters a ticket collector played by Sellers. The scene begins with Sellers reading the parenthetical direction 'Surly North Country' and midway through a ten-second section has been left in that involves Peter Sellers fooling around almost inaudibly in the background while Harry Secombe giggles at him. Not long after, there have been cuts to a scene between Bluebottle (Sellers) and Eccles (Spike), two of the most popular characters. Seagoon catches a train to the top of the mountain and Bluebottle and Eccles are the engine's driver and fireman. The cut segment is as follows:

BLUEBOTTLE (BB): Eccles – stop pulling my whistle. It is my job to pull my whistle.
ECCLES: Aw go on Bottle.
BB: No – you are the firemans.
ECCLES: Aw – come on. Let me pull it just once.
BB: All right – but only once.
ECCLES: OK.
GRAMS: SINGLE BLAST ON TRAIN WHISTLE[4]

Perhaps this was considered too suggestive by the censors, but it seems unlikely since the line 'Thank you, Little Jim. Now get back in the barrel'[5] has been left in. Although this is perhaps not so significant to modern-day audiences, the barrel reference would have been very familiar to the majority of listeners in the 1950s, many of whom were ex-military. It alludes to the punchline of a dirty joke in which servicemen take it in turns to go into a barrel and help their comrades to relieve their sexual frustrations.

The Censorship Department seems to have been a source of frustration for Larry. One of his surviving drawings is a comic strip-style representation of the BBC and the Censorship Department showing a writer standing to attention in front of a panel comprised of different nationalities while his script is scrutinised. The caption reads, 'Don't you realise a line like that may cause racial prejudice?' Larry's depiction of a Training School for Comics shows them being taught maxim no. 1: 'If it gets laughs the script was poor but you gave a good performance. If it doesn't get laughs the script was poor.' Junior producers and stopwatches also feature heavily.

Larry's complaint about Tom Ronald seems to have been taken seriously as he only produced programmes 15 and 16 in series 8 and a single programme in a series of re-recordings known as the *Vintage Goons*.

As series 8 progressed into 1958, Larry and Maurice seem to have been writing scripts every other week in rotation with Spike. This continued until programme 21, when a reworking of 'The Man Who Never Was', which had been written by Larry with Spike for series 6, was broadcast, due to Spike not being well enough to write a new script. From that point on, Larry and Maurice didn't write anything further for series 8 and Spike wrote the final five programmes either alone or in collaboration with John Antrobus.

Larry and Maurice were probably focusing most of their attention on *The Army Game*, which had by now become a major hit. One of the first programmes in July 1957 had achieved a Nielsen Network Rating of 62 per cent, indicating that 62 per cent of families with a choice of television channels watched *The Army Game* for at least six minutes. By February 1958, this had risen to 73 per cent, with the programme reaching audiences of almost four million, and by April it was ranked as the most popular television programme. The Children's Advisory Committee of the Independent Television Authority commissioned a report on the subject of 'What Parents feel about Children and Television', which was later published by Her Majesty's Stationery Office. Research was carried out across April and May of that year and the survey revealed that 21 per cent of respondents' children had stayed up beyond their usual bedtime in order to watch *The Army Game*.

Larry's wartime comrades had been following his career with interest and were aware he was one of the *Army Game*'s writers. A 2004 newsletter, circulated among the veterans, reveals they used to speculate 'as to which of the characters were modelled on the chaps that Larry knew in 5 Commando!'[6]

Larry's attention had been temporarily diverted away from the popularity of *The Army Game* and towards his wife around this period, as on 22 March 1958 Diana was arrested on suspicion of drink driving, following an accident which put John Junkin in hospital.

34

This Is Where the Story Really Starts

Photographs held at the National Archives reveal exactly what led to Diana being arrested: her somewhat rearranged Ford Anglia is blocking one side of Fleet Street just outside the Law Courts branch of the Bank of England and the remains of a police call box and a City rubbish bin are strewn across the pavement.

City of London Police Constable Dennis Durbridge was on duty in Fleet Street when at quarter to two in the morning he heard the crash. He rushed towards the direction of the noise and was first on the scene of the accident, where he found Diana in the driving seat and John Junkin, a scriptwriter who worked with Larry at ALS Ltd, in the passenger seat. PC Durbridge asked Diana what had happened and she replied, 'I didn't know what happened. I didn't see it. I've been to a party at Swiss Cottage. A lorry pulled up in front of me and I pulled into the kerb as I pulled up.'[1]

Noticing that her breath smelt of alcohol, the Constable asked Diana to get out of her car and as he felt she was unsteady on her feet with glazed eyes, he arrested her on suspicion of 'being under the influence of drink when driving a motor vehicle to such an extent as to be incapable of having proper control of it'. To this charge Diana indignantly replied, 'That's very unfair. I've had a few drinks at the party but I'm not drunk.'[2]

She was taken to the police station in Snow Hill and arrived just after two in the morning, while John Junkin was sent to St Bartholomew's Hospital for treatment to an eye injury he had sustained in the accident. Later he arrived at Snow Hill himself to make a statement. Diana seemed drowsy but other than torn stockings and a trickle of blood down one of her legs, at first glance she appeared to be uninjured.

The police doctor arrived at Snow Hill about half an hour later, took a sample of Diana's urine and began his examination of her. She complained of having a sore mouth and the doctor discovered a cut inside her lower lip. She told him that she had been at a cheese and wine party and had been drinking Châteauneuf-du-Pape and that although she couldn't remember exactly how many glasses she had drunk, it was no more than she was used to. The doctor made her undergo several tests to try and determine whether she was drunk or not and his report is included with the papers held at the National Archives:

> I tested her mental ability to do sums taking 7 from a hundred and then 7 from the result. She got 93, 86, 79 correctly but rather slowly. She then forgot the figure she was subtracting. She got confused and had only done the third sum at the end of 90 seconds. I did not go any further. She said she was confused by the noise in the next room... Her rising was unsteady, there was only slight swaying when she stood with her feet together but she swayed so much with her eyes closed she nearly came off balance. I asked her to walk the length of a long corridor about 30 feet long, 6–7 feet wide; she deviated about 18 inches either side of an imaginary centre line... I asked her to lift coins from the table and place them in her hands. She did so without dropping any

and also she picked them from the floor without dropping any. Towards the end of the examination she went to sit on a chair and she missed the chair by about 2 feet and fell on the floor.[3]

She was charged and bailed at five o'clock in the morning and was committed to stand trial at the Old Bailey on 15 April 1958. Diana would enter a plea of 'not guilty' and John Junkin's statement was to be offered up by the defence. There are no details of the trial itself included in the documentation at the National Archives, nor has the verdict been recorded. The case does not appear to have made it into any of the newspapers either.

Over at the BBC, as the final few episodes of series 8 of the *Goon Show* were being broadcast, news was circulating around Broadcasting House that Spike intended to travel to Australia for an extended stay. Jim Davidson was therefore keen to commission series 9 before Spike's departure and asked Miss Ross in the Copyright Department to begin negotiations for the provision of twenty-six scripts from Spike and Larry. Davidson wished Miss Ross 'good luck' in her dealings. The following day she sent a formal request to Stanley Dale at ALS Ltd although this letter didn't mention Larry, only Spike.

Three weeks later and there was still no response. Pat Newman, the Variety Booking Manager, suggested that this may have been down to Spike 'having found the need… to write to the *Daily Express*… another of his now rather tedious "chip on the shoulder" cracks at the BBC'.[4]

It took a month for Spike's lengthy reply to be sent via ALS Ltd's secretary and general manager, Beryl Vertue, a letter full of demands and stipulations that was despatched a day after his departure for Australia. He wanted the producer to be named in advance and ideally this producer to be Peter Eton; he wanted to be given the name of the person who would censor scripts; he wanted the sound effects personnel to be given at least a week to prepare; he wanted the same team of technicians to work across the entire series (he did however concede that they should be allowed time off if unwell); he wanted to be given plenty of warning if special guests were due to attend recordings of the programme (particularly royalty); he wanted the musicians to perform new numbers and he wanted other actors brought into the show (he was particularly keen for Valentine Dyall to take over some of Peter Sellers' characters). Despite all of this, Spike declared that he would be unable to write series 9 on his own as he already had commitments for the three months between his return from Australia and Christmas, so he provided a list of others he felt would be able to write the scripts: Larry (with Maurice Wiltshire), John Antrobus and Dave Freeman. He suggested that they write four episodes each and that he would edit Antrobus and Freeman's efforts before submission to the BBC. Whether he had actually talked this over with them beforehand is anybody's guess.

The letter was discussed at a Home Service departmental meeting and somewhat backfired as far as Spike was concerned: the BBC felt unable to accept the terms he had offered and consequently withdrew their offer. This led to some frantic backtracking, compounded by the fact that the Press had somehow got hold of the story and were reporting that the series had been cancelled due to Spike's unreasonable demands.

Beryl Vertue needed to act quickly but was unable to contact Spike for guidance as he was by now midway through a six-week boat trip to Australia, and so she needed to resolve the situation herself. She telephoned the BBC and desperately tried to get hold of Jim Davidson, without success. She left a message asking for him to call her back as soon as possible and explained that her letter had been misinterpreted – the list of Spike's 'conditions' weren't conditions after all but 'suggestions'. Also, by a remarkable stroke of good luck, Spike wasn't going to be too busy to write the *Goon Show* when he got back from Australia after all.

The 'misunderstanding' now seemed to be resolved to everyone's satisfaction and Spike was asked to write thirteen programmes for series 9 with an option on a further thirteen. However, the problems continued and in mid-July Spike returned the contract to London unsigned. As his other 'suggestions' had been dismissed, he was now suggesting that he should receive more money and was asking for a rise from 115 to 130 guineas per script.

Larry was a long way away from these sulks and power struggles as he and Diana had gone to the French Riviera for their annual holiday. They were photographed strolling along the Promenade du Soleil in Juan les Pins with the iconic Le Provençal hotel in the distance behind them. Larry was looking relaxed and slim, having lost the extra weight that was evident in photographs taken in the previous few years. He was dressed in an open-necked, short-sleeved striped shirt, shorts and canvas deck shoes. His attention was caught by something or someone out at sea.

Diana and Larry Stephens, Juan les Pins, 1958.
(Larry Stephens Estate collection)

Antibes was a favourite location for the rich and famous to spend their holidays and the likes of Audrey Hepburn and Elizabeth Taylor could be spied sipping cocktails in the bars of the resort's luxury hotels. Antibes was also a favourite holiday destination for the Stephenses and their circle of friends, but they would all stay at a cheap guesthouse called Chez François rather than the luxury hotels. Not long after Larry and Diana had checked in to the boarding house, Alan Simpson turned up, much to their surprise, and spent about three days with them. Tony and Cicely Hancock also joined them.

Larry may have been looking fitter than he had for a while but he still wasn't in very good health. Alan remembered that Larry tired easily and that he 'had to be looked after by Diana; she did everything for him. He was having to watch what he was eating and drinking so he was a bit fed up with everything because he enjoyed a drink. He hadn't given it up completely but he wasn't what you would have called a drinker. He was more of a sipper.'5

When the Stephenses returned from their holidays, series 9 of the *Goon Show* was still a long way from being sorted out. With time ticking on and with a series production target date of mid-September, the BBC began to look for suitable alternatives to fill the gap in the schedule. It was decided to rebroadcast six old programmes under the title *Vintage Goons* in advance of the new series. Recordings that had been made for the Transcription Service were selected and it is almost certain that they were the ones Larry and Spike had worked on for the Canadian Broadcasting Corporation.

Larry is not credited as having written any of the scripts for the *Vintage Goons* and yet this series of programmes was based on episodes from the fourth series, several of which he contributed to. They were slightly amended for the re-recordings but if, as suggested, they were produced for the Canadian Broadcasting Corporation, this seems to have been a collaboration between Larry and Spike. In addition, some of the original *Vintage Goons* scripts bear Larry's name and his handwritten notes so he was definitely involved in their production.

As for series 9, Larry didn't have much involvement at all and he only wrote one episode in the series, in collaboration with Maurice Wiltshire, when Spike was too ill to work. 'The Seagoon Memoirs' was broadcast on 15 December 1958 and would be the last thing Larry ever wrote for the show.

Spike was struggling to write the scripts on his own and the newly appointed producer, John Browell, sent a memo to Jim Davidson in mid-January 1959, informing him that Milligan was suffering from anxiety neurosis caused by strain and would be unable to write anything for the programme due to be recorded on 25 January either. Browell had planned to ask Larry to write the script for that week again as he admired Larry's intelligent writing style and later recalled that he, like Eric Sykes, would write clever scripts with a rational storyline and a plausible ending, whereas Spike's scripts tended to be more fanciful with illogical conclusions.

As it turned out, Larry was too heavily involved with his writing commitments for *The Army Game*, which continued to be one of the most popular television programmes in the country, and so an old script from series 5 of the *Goon Show* was slightly reworked instead and given the title 'Dishonoured – Again'.

On the evening of the recording, Larry arranged to go out to a restaurant for dinner. At some point during the meal he collapsed, his head crashing onto the table in a clatter of plates and cutlery.

35

The Man Who Never Was

The recording of the *Goon Show* episode 'Dishonoured – Again' at Camden Studio finished just after nine o'clock on the evening of 25 January. The orchestra closed the programme with 'Old Comrades March' and then Max Geldray played the studio audience out with a rendition of 'Crazy Rhythm'. As everyone began to file outside, Larry left his seat in the theatre and made his way over to the stage to have a quick word with his friends. He waited until the auditorium had emptied before saying goodbye and heading for the exit himself. A few groups of people were still milling around on the pavement outside, chattering excitedly about the evening's entertainment. None of them gave Larry a second glance. He tugged his collar up around his neck and plunged his hands deep into his pockets. The temperature was already below freezing but at least it wasn't raining or snowing. The winds were a *Goon Show* favourite of light to variable. Larry headed off along Camden High Street and went to meet Ben Cleminson. Diana was out working so Larry had arranged to meet his friend for something to eat.

The evening with Ben started off well and the two friends had an agreeable time, enjoying their meal and catching up with each other's news. Without warning, Larry felt a sudden searing pain in his head and his hand flew up to his temple. His vision began to blur and he tried to tell Ben what was happening to him but the words seemed to lodge in his throat and then tumbled out of his mouth in a tangle. He began to feel very dizzy and as the room started to whirl around him, he felt unable to hold himself upright. Confusion creased his brow as he fell forward onto the table.

Larry was still conscious but clearly very poorly so Ben bundled him out of the restaurant and into a taxi to rush him to hospital. On the way there Larry was violently sick, but by now Ben was so worried about his friend that he barely registered the taxi driver's bad-tempered rantings about the mess.

By the time they arrived at the Whittington Hospital, Larry was slipping in and out of consciousness, so he was rushed into the Highgate Wing, where frantic efforts were made to save him; he died at ten past two in the morning on Monday 26 January 1959. He had suffered a cerebral haemorrhage brought on by hypertension. He was just thirty-five years old.

Recent commentators on Larry's death have put his early demise down to him being a chronic alcoholic, seemingly based on the BBC memo that mentioned him drinking more than four bottles of rum a week. He was certainly fond of a drink but there isn't any evidence to suggest he was an alcoholic. Peter Eton believed that Larry had worked his way into an early grave. During his interview at a Goon Show Preservation Society meeting in 1976, he talked about the pressure on writers of the show:

To write this sort of material and keep up a standard, after you've been writing for about ten or twelve weeks, it's an absolute killer, I mean, that's why Larry Stephens died, he worked himself to death. And Larry was a sick man, had high blood pressure... It's an enormous strain actually trying to write funny stuff. It's not the pace, it's a terrific strain... knowing that you've got to go out next Sunday with a half an hour script and you're going to be blamed for it if it's a load of rubbish and trying to get it right when you're doing two other programmes also... It's a terrible strain and for the writer it was even worse because he had to produce thirty-five to forty pages every week.[1]

In an extraordinarily bad piece of timing, Alexander Mackendrick woke up on the morning of 26 January with a feeling that he'd like to see Larry again as it had been a fair while since Larry had availed himself of the Mackendricks' spare room. Later that day, Hilary Mackendrick picked up the phone to issue an invitation and 'was greeted by sobs from his wife, because he had died the night before'.[2]

Obituaries began to appear in the press from the 27th – in the *Mirror*, *Express*, *Guardian* and *Stage*, among others – none of them more than a few lines long. They were mostly headlined something like 'Army Game Writer Dies' and mentioned that Larry was a founder member of the *Goon Show* and had been a commando captain during the war.

His death permeated the corridors of ALS Ltd's offices. John Antrobus remembers that 'opposite the entrance, there was a blackboard and upon it written in chalk were the writers' names and their current assignments, rather as if we were in an ops room of Bomber Command... I came back into the office late afternoon, slightly sozzled. I could see no point in this board, drunk or sober, nor can I still. I picked up a piece of chalk and rubbed out Larry's assignment and wrote, RIP. I thought it was funny then. Now I don't think it's so funny.'[3]

On 30 January, episode 20 of the third series of *The Army Game* was broadcast; it was one of the last scripts Larry had worked on. The following day, a Saturday, his funeral was held at Golders Green Crematorium.

The little crematorium was packed and the mourners included many of the comedians Larry had worked with: Peter Sellers, Tony Hancock, Spike Milligan et al. To Alexander Mackendrick, the sight of so many comedians with melancholic expressions had a real air of black humour about it and he later described it to Philip Kemp as one of his 'choicest memories'.[4]

Barry Cryer relates an anecdote in his book *Butterfly Brain* which suggests the funeral service may not have been as solemn as Mackendrick believed: 'Spike began to moan, putting his head in his hands. People thought that he was consumed with grief. But Spike wasn't crying, he was laughing. He'd just seen a sign to show where the nearest fire extinguisher was. In a crematorium.'[5]

The BBC sent a magnificent wreath but Diana had asked Larry's friends to make donations to the Commandos Benevolent Fund rather than sending floral tributes. The sum of £29 (equivalent to around £1,800 in 2017) was presented to the Fund, which had been established in 1943 to offer assistance to former Army Commandos, their wives, dependants or widows who were in need of financial help.

Additional evidence to suggest Larry believed he would be able to prove his doctor's prognosis wrong was that he had died intestate; had he truly believed he only had a year to live, surely he would have written a will to make things easier for his wife following his death. An announcement appeared in the *London Gazette* on 3 July 1959, asking for any claimants to contact the firm of solicitors Tarlo Lyons by 5 September, but with no one coming forward, Diana inherited Larry's entire estate, which amounted to £1,096 19s 9d (equivalent to around £70,000 in 2017).

Larry had expressed a wish to his wife that his ashes should be scattered in the vicinity of the Commando Memorial at Spean Bridge. Although this is now a common request and an area has since been allocated close to the Memorial specifically for the purpose, at the time of Larry's death it certainly wasn't so usual. Diana made the 500-mile journey to the Highlands and with the help of the Reverend Moore, Minister of Spean Bridge, ensured that Larry's final resting place was close to the peaks of Ben Nevis and Aonach Mòr and the 'country that was his training ground'. The Minister's assistance was acknowledged in the September 1959 edition of the Commando Association newsletter. Not long afterwards, Diana travelled to Russia, where she spent time mourning and getting drunk.

Commando Memorial, Spean Bridge. (© Richard Brown)

When she returned to London, most of Larry's friends helped Diana to put her life back together by offering both emotional and financial support. Harry Secombe, having recognised her talent as a singer, paid for her to have voice training with a renowned teacher and she went on to sing with the London Philharmonic Choir. Graham Stark also helped her out financially and they became very close friends, bonded by grief. Spike, on the other hand, had been spreading rumours while Diana was away about her having made a big play for him at Larry's funeral, later referred to in John Antrobus' book, *Surviving Spike Milligan*:

> Spike went to the funeral. He told me later that he had found a woman to be sexually aroused who was close to Larry...
>
> 'How can they be like that on such an occasion?'
>
> 'Sex and death,' I said. 'Anyway it takes two to tango, doesn't it?'
>
> Spike stared at me. Was I shifting the blame on to him for something he may have done? He could not bear to be in the wrong.
>
> 'They're meant to be the better sex,' he said, as if it were irrefutable.[6]

Peter Sellers was finding it difficult to cope with the fact that his friend had gone. He and Larry had discussed life after death and had made a vow that whichever of them died first would make every effort to cross back to the land of the living and make contact with the other. At the outbreak of the war, Sellers had made friends with a young man in Ilfracombe called Terry who was the son of a famous medium, Estelle Roberts. Shortly after Larry's death, Sellers contacted Terry to see if his mother would be willing to give him an appointment as he had a feeling Larry was trying to get in touch.

Ian Carmichael worked with Sellers on the film *I'm All Right Jack* in 1959 and remembers him being convinced that Larry 'was trying to get in touch with him – he felt *very* strongly about this. Certain things would happen – that's Larry Stephens...'[7]

Peter and his wife Anne travelled to Estelle Roberts' home in Esher and the medium's spirit guide, Red Cloud, was ready with a message to pass on to Peter. He recounted the experience in an interview with the *Sunday Times* in 1962 and with *Photoplay* magazine in 1971. The medium told Peter she knew there was a young man he wanted to contact but as it hadn't been long since he had crossed over to the other side, he was still a little confused. He was apparently clutching his head and struggling to try and communicate. Eventually he said that the codename 'Fred' should help Peter to identify him.

The name 'Fred' was what convinced Peter that Larry had indeed made contact with him from beyond the grave, since it was a name they adored for its comic possibilities. They had used it throughout the *Goon Show* and as the title of television programmes they made together, *A Show called Fred* and *Son of Fred*.

Satisfied with his success at having reached Larry on 'the other side', Sellers' interest in spiritualism and mysticism grew to the point where he was apparently reluctant to make any major decisions without first consulting a clairvoyant.

The *Goon Show* finally came to an end in 1960, just short of a year after Larry's death. A puppet programme called the *Telegoons* was shown on television in 1963, using original scripts that had been adapted by Maurice Wiltshire. Repeats of surviving episodes of the *Goon Show* continue to be broadcast worldwide to the present day, and yet despite this Larry's name has faded into obscurity.

A variety of things have contributed to this. He was a quiet man and unless he was playing the piano, he didn't want to be on the stage performing. It was enough of a thrill for him to sit in the audience and watch his talented, funny friends step into the spotlight, bringing his words to life and making people laugh. Additionally, only a small proportion of the *Goon Show* episodes Larry wrote have survived as recordings. Just a single episode of the 100 programmes from the first four series was retained in the BBC archives as the Corporation was in the habit of reusing their tapes. There are some unofficial recordings from the early years, which were made by fans using home equipment, but these tend to cut off before the closing credits are announced. Four of these amateur recordings from 1954 were digitally remastered and released on a CD[8] in 2010:

1. 'The History of Communications'/'The Siege of Khartoum' (series 4, episode 18)

2. 'The Toothpaste Expedition' (series 4, episode 20)

3. 'Western Story "Drain!"' (series 4, episode 26)

4. 'The Great Bank of England Robbery' (series 4, episode 29)

When you listen to this CD, each of the four episodes includes the closing credit, 'script by Spike Milligan', but two of these four programmes were Spike and Larry collaborations and 'Western Story' was written by Larry single-handedly. So why is Spike mentioned as the sole scriptwriter for all of them, with no mention of Larry's contribution?

The reason is a matter of fate. Few of the original recordings for the CD release included closing credits and so these had to be digitally 'glued' on to the end. It wasn't possible to use credits from later series as the fourth series orchestra had strings and these were dropped from the fifth series onwards. The single episode that the BBC had retained from the first 100 programmes was 'The Greatest Mountain in the World', which was written by Spike alone. The fact that 'Western Story' is incorrectly credited to Spike rather than Larry on the CD sleeve pushes him further into the sidelines of *Goon Show* history.

As well as the release of programme recordings, several books containing *Goon Show* scripts were published between 1972 and 1987 but these generally only included Spike's solo scripts (or scripts where only Spike had been named as the writer). Larry's drawings often made it into these books, sometimes credited but sometimes not. If theatre groups wish to stage performances of the *Goon Show*, although Larry Stephens' Estate is amenable to such requests, the episodes he wrote with Spike are rarely produced as permission is generally only granted for the use of scripts where Spike is credited as the sole writer.

The mantra 'Spike Milligan was the creator and writer of the *Goon Show*' has been repeated so often that it is now accepted as fact. After Larry's death, Spike described him as someone who never came up with any ideas; as someone who wasn't much of a writer; and as an inconsequential hanger-on who only did the typing for him. Spike's other co-writers have commented that he had a tendency to take sole credit for anything that was successful so perhaps this is why he went on record and belittled Larry's contribution to the *Goon Show* in this way in later years. Or maybe the comments he made were intended to be funny. Or could it be that Spike somehow felt that his friend and co-writer had abandoned him by dying and the vitriol stemmed from a need to protect himself from the pain of losing someone he loved and relied on? Whatever the truth of the matter, these remarks became part of the *Goon Show* legend and they stuck. In the late 1990s, when speaking to David Bradbury and Joe McGrath, Spike even claimed that Larry had died in his arms in a restaurant.[9] Ben Cleminson had no memory of Spike having been with them and the doctor who treated Larry at the Whittington Hospital didn't recall Spike being there either. It is almost as if he couldn't bear Larry to have done something flamboyant and dramatic – even dying – without being there himself and playing a starring role.

Sadly, all of Larry's scripts were thrown away a few years after his death so we will probably never know the true extent of his work and his influence. But he was still having an effect on British comedy as late as 1992 when a nod to him popped up in an episode of *'Allo 'Allo* called 'A Winkle in Time'.

Although the sitcom is not known for its historical accuracy, there is a strange quirk in this sixth episode from series 9. Set at the end of the war, with the Allied forces liberating France, Café René receives a visit about halfway through the episode from some officers who will be taking the formal German surrender in there: Major Twiselton-Smythe and Captain Starkington from 5 Commando, British Special Forces. Of course, in reality, 5 Commando were still out in India at the time of victory in Europe but one of the episode's writers, Jeremy Lloyd, had been a regular at Grafton's in the 1950s and had mixed with the Goon gang. There were around thirty different Commando units to choose from, and No. 5, which was one of the more obscure ones, only existed for six years and was nowhere near France in 1945, so it is unlikely to have been picked at random. Larry and his war service had obviously made a lasting impression on Jeremy.

Larry Stephens was a pioneer and achieved a lot in his short life. He was an incredibly talented musician, artist and writer. He put words into the mouths of Alec Guinness, Peter Sellers and Tony Hancock. He was one of the writers credited with creating the 'World's Funniest Joke'. Expressions and words that he and Spike invented have made their way into the *Oxford English Dictionary*. He was an officer and instructor with the elite fighting force that spawned today's Royal Marines Commandos, Paratroopers and SAS. He was involved in writing the television series that led to the *Carry On* sequence of films. And above all, he was one of the originators of the *Goon Show*, a comedy that is cited as having influenced luminaries from Monty Python to the Beatles and the fans of which include members of the royal family, rock stars and Hollywood actors.

He deserves to be remembered.

Appendix One

GOONOPEDIA

For copyright purposes, *Goon Show* writers often received a credit even though they may not have contributed to the script. Using BBC memos, original scripts and interviews with some of the people involved, I have tried to determine who was responsible for actually writing each of the episodes.

Abbreviations
John Antrobus (JA)
Jimmy Grafton (JG)
Spike Milligan (SM)
Larry Stephens (LS)
Eric Sykes (ES)
Maurice Wiltshire (MW)

SERIES 1

EPISODE	PROBABLY WRITTEN BY	TITLE/SKETCHES	RADIO TIMES ENTRY	SCRIPT FRONT	SCRIPTED ANNOUNCEMENT	RECORDED ANNOUNCEMENT	NOTES	RECORDED
1	SM LS JG	1. Herschell & Jones 2. The Story of the BRM 3. Dick Barton, Special Agent 4. The Quest for Tutankhamen 5. Salute to Britain	Material compiled by SM	Material compiled by SM	No reference to scriptwriters	Not available	First use of the word 'lurgi'	27 May 1951
2	SM LS JG	1. Herschell & Jones 2. Ernest Splutmuscle, Rat-Catcher 3. A Hundred Years from Today 4. The East Pole	Material compiled by SM	Material compiled by SM	The script was concocted by SM. Additions to the mixture made by LS	Not available		3 June 1951
3	SM LS JG	1. Herschell & Jones - Jones' Schooldays 2. Russian Sports 3. Sounds Effects 4. The Bluffs 5. History of Flight	Script by SM	Script by SM. Additional material by LS & JG	The script was written in Urdu by SM and LS and translated by JG	Not available		10 June 1951
4	SM LS JG	1. Herschell & Jones - Jones Goes to Prison 2. Slimming 3. Honeymoon Memories 4. Parliament in Session 5. The Conquest of Everest	Script by SM. Additional material by LS & JG	Script by SM. Additional material by LS & JG	The script was mapped out by SM and LS and plotted by JG	Not available		17 June 1951
5	SM LS JG	1. Herschell & Jones - Jones' Adventures in Russia 2. Visit to the Health Clinic 3. Story of the Airliner 4. Holidays 5. Story of the Yukon Gold Rush	Script by SM. Additional material by LS & JG	Script by SM. Additional material by LS & JG	The script cargo was swung aboard by SM and LS and lashed and stowed by JG	Not available	First scripted appearance of Major Bloodnok but the name 'Bloodnok' has been crossed through and replaced with 'O'Shea'	24 June 1951
6	SM LS JG	1. Further Adventures of Herschel 2. The Story of Civilisation 3. Splutmuscle - The Boxer 4. Operations of MI6 5. African Adventures	Script by SM. Additional material by LS & JG	Script: SM, LS & JG	Script equipment and stores including a Bentine bundle were supplied by Messrs SM and LS through selling agent JG	Not available		1 July 1951

SERIES 1 (cont.)

EPISODE	PROBABLY WRITTEN BY	TITLE/SKETCHES	RADIO TIMES ENTRY	SCRIPT FRONT	SCRIPTED ANNOUNCEMENT	RECORDED ANNOUNCEMENT	NOTES	RECORDED
7	SM LS JG	1. Herschel & Jones 2. The History of Communications 3. Adventures of Phillip String 4. Sea Stories 5. The Building of the Merseygoon Tunnel	Script by SM, LS & JG	Script: SM, JG & LS	Script was dug up by SM and LS and refined by JG	Not available	First named appearance of a character called Eccles (although voiced by Sellers)	8 July 1951
8	SM LS JG	1. Herschel & Jones 2. BBC Skit 3. Episode 2 of Phillip String 4. Commentaries from the Funfair 5. The Goonbird	Script by SM. Additional material by LS & JG	Script: SM, LS & JG	SM and LS wrote the log which was then chopped up by JG	Not available	Eccles appears again, voiced by Spike in the now familiar voice	15 July 1951
9	SM LS JG	1. Herschel & Jones 2. Summertime Activities 3. Episode 3 of Phillip String 4. Splutmuscle the Private Investigator 5. Journey into Space	Script by SM, LS & JG	Script: SM, LS & JG	Script was by SM, LS & JG	Not available	Contains what was voted as being the 'World's Funniest Joke' in 2001	22 July 1951
10	SM LS JG	1. Herschel & Jones 2. The Building of the Sydney Harbour Goon Bridge 3. Air Pageant and Widdigoon Country Fair Commentary 4. The Story of Colonel Slocombe	Script by SM, LS & JG	Script by: SM, LS & JG	Regimental orders were scripted by SM and LS and the seal was affixed by JG	Not available		29 July 1951
11	SM LS JG	1. Herschel & Jones 2. Stories of Scotland Yard 3. Mock Sea–Battle Commentary 4. The Quest for the White Queen	Script by SM, LS & JG	Script by: SM, LS & JG	The script was discovered by SM and LS and dusted off by JG	Not available	First actual appearance of Major Bloodnok	5 August 1951
12	SM LS JG	1. Herschel & Jones 2. The Bentine Lurgi–Driven Tank 3. The Quest for Cloot Wilmington	Script by SM, LS & JG	Script by: SM, LS & JG	The script was written in cipher by SM and LS and decoded by JG	Not available		12 August 1951
13	SM LS JG	1. Herschel & Jones 2. Survey of Britain 3. Clushboot-on-Sea 4. The Story of Colonel Slocombe	Script by SM, LS & JG	Script by: SM, LS & JG	The script was designed for me by SM and LS under the watchful eye of my publicity agent JG	Not available		19 August 1951

SERIES 1 (cont.)

EPISODE	PROBABLY WRITTEN BY	TITLE/SKETCHES	RADIO TIMES ENTRY	SCRIPT FRONT	SCRIPTED ANNOUNCEMENT	RECORDED ANNOUNCEMENT	NOTES	RECORDED
14	SM LS JG	1. Herschel & Jones 2. Dick Barton, Special Agent 3. The Boxer Rebellion	Script by SM, LS & JG	Script: SM, LS & JG	The whole thing was deliberately planned by SM and LS and callously approved by JG	Not available		26 August 1951
15	SM LS JG	1. Herschel & Jones 2. The Goonitania 3. The Quest for the Ring-Tailed Yakkabakaka	Script by SM, LS & JG	Script: SM, LS & JG	The funeral notices were written by SM and LS and printed by JG	Not available		2 September 1951
16	SM LS JG	1. Courting Hydia Harbinger 2. The Salvaging of the Goonitania 3. Sound Effects Men on Trial 4. Bloodnok of Burma	Script by SM, LS & JG	Script: SM, LS & JG	History was created by SM and LS and chronicled by JG	Not available		9 September 1951
17	SM LS JG	1. Music Lessons 2. The Brabagoon 3. Holiday Time 4. Bloodnok the Peacemaker	Script by SM, LS & JG	Script: SM, LS & JG	Passes were made out by SM and LS and signed by JG	Not available		16 September 1951
Special	SM LS JG	Cinderella	Script by SM, LS & JG	Script by: SM, LS & JG	No reference to scriptwriters	Not available		16 December 1951

SERIES 2

EPISODE	PROBABLY WRITTEN BY	TITLE/SKETCHES	RADIO TIMES ENTRY	SCRIPT FRONT	SCRIPTED ANNOUNCEMENT	RECORDED ANNOUNCEMENT	NOTES	RECORDED
1	SM LS JG	1. Handsome Harry Secombe (Pursues Lo Hing Ding) 2. Captain Pureheart Builds the Suez Canal 3. Broadcasting in 1999 4. Major Bloodnok's Quest for the Abominable Snowman	Script written by SM and LS. Edited by JG	Script: SM, LS (Edited by) JG	The script was written by SM and LS and edited by JG	The script was written by SM and LS and edited by JG		20 January 1952
2	SM LS JG	1. Handsome Harry Secombe Chases Ho Fu Chang 2. Captain Pureheart Builds the Trans-Siberian Express 3. Education Sketch 4. Bloodnok in the Highlands in 1745	Script written by SM and LS. Edited by JG	Script: SM, LS (Edited by) JG	The script was written by SM and LS and edited by JG	Not available		27 January 1952
3	SM LS JG	1. Handsome Harry Hunts the Lost Drummer 2. Captain Pureheart Builds the Crystal Palace 3. Major Bloodnok Protects the Women from Sonapatti & His Tribesmen 4. Queue Vaddit Sketch	Script written by SM and LS. Edited by JG	Script: SM, LS (Edited by) JG	The script was written by SM and LS and edited by JG	The script was written by SM and LS and edited by JG		3 February 1952
4	SM LS JG	1. Handsome Harry Secombe Chases Andrew Timothy 2. Captain Pureheart Constructs Croydon Airport 3. BBC Programmes Crammed Together 4. Colonel Slocombe Fights the Chippawar Tribe	Script written by SM and LS. Edited by JG	Script: SM, LS (Edited by) JG	The script was written by SM and LS and edited by JG	Not available		17 February 1952
5	SM LS JG	1. Handsome Harry Secombe Guards a Vineyard in France 2. Commentaries on the Monte Carlo Car Rally 1952 3. Captain Pureheart Photographs the World	Script written by SM and LS. Edited by JG	Script: SM, LS (Edited by) JG	The script was written by SM and LS and edited by JG	Not available		24 February 1952

SERIES 2 (cont.)

EPISODE	PROBABLY WRITTEN BY	TITLE/SKETCHES	RADIO TIMES ENTRY	SCRIPT FRONT	SCRIPTED ANNOUNCEMENT	RECORDED ANNOUNCEMENT	NOTES	RECORDED
6	SM LS JG	1. Handsome Harry Secombe Goes Home 2. Major Bloodnok's Quest for the Golden Idol 3. Fred Bogg in the Army 4. Barton & Pureheart's Interplanetary Adventures	Script written by SM and LS. Edited by JG	Script: SM, LS (Edited by) JG	The script was written by SM and LS and edited by JG	Not available		2 March 1952
7	SM LS JG	1. Handsome Harry Investigates a Murder 2. Pureheart lays the Atlantic Cable 3. Swiss Winter Sports Sketch 4. Major Bloodnok Protects the Blarney Stone	Script written by SM and LS. Edited by JG	Script: SM, LS (Edited by) JG	The script was written by SM and LS and edited by JG	Not available	First scripted mention of a Crun	9 March 1952
8	SM LS JG	Her	Script written by SM and LS. Edited by JG	Script: SM, LS (Edited by) JG	You have been listening to a special edition of the Goon Show... a recorded programme featuring Peter Sellers, Harry Secombe, Harry Bentine and SM and LS and edited by JG	Not available	A skit on Rider Haggard's book *She*, this is the first regular episode where a single storyline is used throughout	16 March 1952
9	SM LS JG	1. Handsome Harry the Toreador 2. Pureheart Builds a Jet Fighter, X9 3. Survey of Britain 4. Major Bloodnok (2nd/7th Bombay Biddis at Goonistan) Attacks the Mad Mullah	Script written by SM and LS. Edited by JG	Script: SM, LS (Edited by) JG	The script was written by SM and LS and edited by JG	Not available		23 March 1952
10	SM LS JG	1. Handsome Harry Secombe and the Lost Million 2. Pureheart 3. The Grand National 4. Major von Bloodnok - German Secret Agent	Script written by SM and LS. Edited by JG	Script: SM, LS (Edited by) JG	The script was written by SM and LS and edited by JG	Not available	First scripted mention of a Bannister as aunt to Osric Pureheart	30 March 1952

SERIES 2 (cont.)

EPISODE	PROBABLY WRITTEN BY	TITLE/SKETCHES	RADIO TIMES ENTRY	SCRIPT FRONT	SCRIPTED ANNOUNCEMENT	RECORDED ANNOUNCEMENT	NOTES	RECORDED
11	SM LS JG	1. Handsome Harry is Taken Prisoner in the Army by the British 2. Pureheart's Excavations at Pompeii (Unearths the Roman Villa) 3. Wacklow & Crun Censor a Show 4. Colonel Slocombe in the Southern Army	Script written by SM and LS. Edited by JG	Script: SM, LS (Edited by) JG	The script was written by SM and LS and edited by JG	Not available		6 April 1952
12	SM LS JG	1. Harry Secombe - Secret Agent 2. Bloodnok Fights the Mad Mullah (rehash) 3. Goon Focus on Other Programmes 4. Pureheart Builds a Satellite Town	Script written by SM and LS. Edited by JG	Script: SM, LS (Edited by) JG	Not available	Not available		13 April 1952
13	SM LS JG	1. Handsome Harry - Military Intelligence 2. Filthmuck Gets a Laundry (Pureheart) 3. Presidential Elections 4. Slocombe Goes to the Firing Line	Script written by SM and LS. Edited by JG	Script: SM, LS (Edited by) JG	The script was written by SM and LS and edited by JG	Not available		20 April 1952
14	SM LS JG	1. Handsome Harry & the Ministry of Documentation 2. Captain Pureheart Builds a Time Machine 3. Regent's Park Zoo 4. El Gato, Haroldo Secombe	Script written by SM and LS. Edited by JG	Script: SM, LS (Edited by) JG	The script was written by SM and LS and edited by JG	Not available		27 April 1952
15	SM LS JG	1. Handsome Harry Secombe 2. Pureheart - Mulberry Harbour 3. British Olympic Team in Training 4. Lord Nugent Gascoine	Script written by SM and LS. Edited by JG	Script: SM, LS (Edited by) JG	The script was written by SM and LS and edited by JG	Not available		4 May 1952

SERIES 2 (cont.)

EPISODE	PROBABLY WRITTEN BY	TITLE/SKETCHES	RADIO TIMES ENTRY	SCRIPT FRONT	SCRIPTED ANNOUNCEMENT	RECORDED ANNOUNCEMENT	NOTES	RECORDED
16	SM LS JG	1. Handsome Harry's Dream - On Trial for Singing 2. Pureheart - The Gorilla Hunter 3. Home, Light & Third Programme Gimmick 4. Hi Goon	Script written by SM and LS. Edited by JG	Script: SM, LS (Edited by) JG	The script was written by SM and LS and edited by JG	Not available		11 May 1952
17	SM LS JG	1. Handsome Harry Secombe 2. Sinking of the Goonmark 3. Home, Light & Third Programme Gimmick 4. Welsh Spot	Script written by SM and LS. Edited by JG	Script: SM, LS (Edited by) JG	The script was written by SM and LS and edited by JG	Not available		18 May 1952
18	SM LS JG	1. Handsome Harry Secombe Hunted by a Gang 2. Captain Pureheart Photographs Ghosts 3. Manoeuvres 4. Napoleon's Hours Before Waterloo	Script written by SM and LS. Edited by JG	Script: SM, LS (Edited by) JG	The script was written by SM and LS and edited by JG	Not available	First appearance of Henry Crun & Minnie Bannister as a double act. First use of the word 'deaded'	25 May 1952
19	SM LS JG	1. Handsome Harry Secombe's Clothes 2. Captain Pureheart, Superintendent of Special Branch 3. Giuseppe Saponi's Missing 'Ahhhh' 4. Dr Henry Crun Discovers the Source of the Amazon	Script written by SM and LS. Edited by JG	Script: SM, LS (Edited by) JG	The script was written by SM and LS and edited by JG	Not available		1 June 1952
20	SM LS JG	1. Handsome Harry Secombe's Afternoon Serial 2. Bank Holiday Activities 3. Salute to Commentators 4. The Further Adventures of Dr Henry Crun	Script written by SM and LS. Edited by JG	Script: SM, LS (Edited by) JG	The script was written by SM and LS and edited by JG	Not available		8 June 1952

SERIES 2 (cont.)

EPISODE	PROBABLY WRITTEN BY	TITLE/SKETCHES	RADIO TIMES ENTRY	SCRIPT FRONT	SCRIPTED ANNOUNCEMENT	RECORDED ANNOUNCEMENT	NOTES	RECORDED
21	SM LS JG	1. Handsome Harry Seccombe Looks for TV Sponsors 2. Lost Horizontal – In Search of Shangri-La	Script written by SM and LS and edited by JG	Script: SM, LS (Edited by) JG	The script was written by SM and LS and edited by JG	Not available		15 June 1952
22	SM LS JG	1. Handsome Harry's Circus Act 2. Captain Pureheart's Oil Discoveries in Arabia 3. Sports Commentaries 4. Holiday Survey	Script written by SM and LS. Edited by JG	Script: SM, LS (Edited by) JG	The script was written by SM and LS and edited by JG	Not available		22 June 1952
23	SM LS JG	1. Handsome Harry Seccombe's Audition 2. History of Britain 3. Captain Pureheart Goes in Search of Dhobi Mick 4. Olympic Trials	Script written by SM and LS. Edited by JG	Script: SM, LS (Edited by) JG	The script was written by SM and LS and edited by JG	Not available		29 June 1952
24	SM LS JG	1. Handsome Harry Auditions for a Play 2. Captain Pureheart Discovers the Cure for Lurgi 3. Ivanhoe	Script written by SM and LS. Edited by JG	Script: SM, LS (Edited by) JG	The script was written by SM and LS and edited by JG	Not available	First use of the phrase 'the dreaded lurgi'	29 June 1952
25	SM LS JG	1. Handsome Harry, Private Detective 2. The Green Eye of the Little Yellow God 3. BBC Commentaries 4. Captain Pureheart Finds the Rare African White Carnation	Script written by SM and LS. Edited by JG	Script: SM, LS (Edited by) JG	The script was written by SM and LS and edited by JG	Not available		6 July 1952

SERIES 3

EPISODE	PROBABLY WRITTEN BY	TITLE/SKETCHES	RADIO TIMES ENTRY	SCRIPT FRONT	SCRIPTED ANNOUNCEMENT	RECORDED ANNOUNCEMENT	NOTES	RECORDED
1	SM LS JG	1. It's love, Miss Flangebox! 2. Fred of the Islands 3. Weekend Commentary	Written by SM and LS	Script by LS & SM	Script written by SM and LS - edited by JG	Not available		9 November 1952
2	SM LS JG	1. Handsome Harry Visits a Plastic Surgeon 2. The Egg of the Great Auk	Written by SM and LS	Script by LS & SM. Edited by JG	Script written by SM and LS - edited by JG	Not available	First named appearance of a character called Moriarty	16 November 1952
3	SM LS JG	1. Handsome Harry and the First Cuckoo 2. I Was a Male Fan Dancer 3. Goon with the Wind	Written by SM and LS	Script by SM & LS	Script written by SM and LS. Edited by JG	Not available		23 November 1952
4	SM LS JG	1. Handsome Harry and the Forged Money 2. The Saga of the HMS Aldgate 3. BBC Commentaries	Written by SM and LS	Script by SM & LS. Edited by JG	Script written by SM and LS. Edited by JG	Not available	First appearance of William McGoonagall	30 November 1952
5	SM LS JG	1. Handsome Harry Gets Married 2. The Expedition for Toothpaste 3. Canadian Moose-Hunting Season	Written by SM and LS	Script by SM & LS. Edited by JG	Script written by SM and LS. Edited by JG	Not available		7 December 1952
6	SM LS JG	1. Handsome Harry Smuggles Cigarettes 2. The Archers 3. March of Science	Written by SM and LS	Script by LS & SM. Edited by JG	Script written by SM and LS. Edited by JG	Not available		14 December 1952
7	SM LS JG	Pantomime: Robin Hood	No reference to scriptwriters	Script by Thomas Alcock & William Bull (from the original Alcock and Bull story)	Not available	Not available		21 December 1952

SERIES 3 (cont.)

EPISODE	PROBABLY WRITTEN BY	TITLE/SKETCHES	RADIO TIMES ENTRY	SCRIPT FRONT	SCRIPTED ANNOUNCEMENT	RECORDED ANNOUNCEMENT	NOTES	RECORDED
8	SM LS JG	1. Handsome Harry and the British Museum Heist 2. The Archers 3. Where Does Santa Claus Go in the Summer Time?	Written by SM and LS	Script by SM & LS. Edited by JG	Script written by SM and LS. Edited by JG	Not available		28 December 1952
9	LS JG	1. Handsome Harry Steals a Painting 2. Combined Services Exercise 3. March of Science	Written by SM and LS	Script by SM & LS. Edited by JG	Script written by SM and LS. Edited by JG	Not available		4 January 1953
10	LS JG	1. Handsome Harry Helps Slim Jim Escape 2. March of Science 3. The British Way of Life	Written by SM and LS	Script by LS & SM. Edited by JG	Script by SM and LS. Edited by JG	Not available		11 January 1953
11	LS JG	1. Handsome Harry in Battersea Dogs Home 2. Survey of Britain 3. The Goons Clean up Dead Man's Gulch	Written by SM and LS	Script by LS & SM. Edited by JG	Script by SM and LS. Edited by JG	Not available		18 January 1953
12	LS JG	1. Handsome Harry Dopes a Greyhound 2. Flint of the Flying Squad 3. Pirate Films	Written by SM and LS	Script by LS & SM. Edited by JG	Script by LS. Edited by JG	Not available		25 January 1953
13	LS JG	1. Handsome Harry and the Burglary in a Coffee Factory 2. Seaside Resorts in Winter 3. Two-Gun Crun	Written by SM and LS	Script by LS & SM. Edited by JG	Script by SM and LS. Edited by JG	Not available		1 February 1953
14	LS JG	1. Handsome Harry in the Secret Service 2. The Tragedy of Oxley Towers	Written by SM and LS	Script by LS & SM. Edited by JG	Script by SM and LS. Edited by JG	Not available		8 February 1953

SERIES 3 (cont.)

EPISODE	PROBABLY WRITTEN BY	TITLE/SKETCHES	RADIO TIMES ENTRY	SCRIPT FRONT	SCRIPTED ANNOUNCEMENT	RECORDED ANNOUNCEMENT	NOTES	RECORDED
15	LS JG	1. Handsome Harry Goes to a Ball 2. The Story of Civilisation 3. The Race for the Blue Riband	Written by SM and LS	Script by SM & LS. Edited by JG	Script by LS and SM. Edited by JG	Not available		15 February 1953
16	LS JG	1. Handsome Harry Burgles Sir Whackett Crump's House 2. The Search for the Bearded Vulture	Written by SM and LS	Script by LS & SM. Edited by JG	Script written by LS and SM. Edited by JG	Not available		22 February 1953
17	LS JG	1. The Mystery of the Monkey's Paw 2. The Quest for Colonel Winchmold	Written by SM and LS	Script by LS & SM	The script written by LS and SM. Edited by JG	The script written by LS and SM. Edited by JG		1 March 1953
18	SM LS JG	1. Mystery of the Cow on the Hill 2. The Siege of Khartoum	Written by SM and LS	Script by LS & SM. Edited by JG	Script by LS and SM. Edited by JG	Not available		8 March 1953
19	SM LS JG	1. Handsome Harry the Bullfighter 2. Where Do Socks Come From?	Written by SM and LS	Script by LS & SM. Edited by JG	Script written by LS and SM. Edited by JG	Not available		15 March 1953
20	SM LS JG	1. Handsome Harry the Bodyguard 2. The Man Who Never Was	Written by SM and LS	Script by LS & SM. Edited by JG	Script written by SM and LS. Edited by JG	Not available	First mention of Bluebottle	22 March 1953
21	SM LS JG	1. Handsome Harry's Adventures in a Vineyard 2. The Building of the Suez Canal	Written by SM and LS	Script by LS and SM. Edited by JG	Script written by SM and LS. Edited by JG	Not available		29 March 1953
22	SM LS JG	1. Handsome Harry Insures His House 2. The history of the De Goonley Family	Written by SM and LS	Script by LS and SM. Edited by JG	Script written by LS and SM. Edited by JG	Not available		5 April 1953

SERIES 3 (cont.)

EPISODE	PROBABLY WRITTEN BY	TITLE/SKETCHES	RADIO TIMES ENTRY	SCRIPT FRONT	SCRIPTED ANNOUNCEMENT	RECORDED ANNOUNCEMENT	NOTES	RECORDED
23	SM LS JG	1. Handsome Harry Steals the Crown Jewels 2. Conquest of Space 3. Angus McBloodnok	Written by SM and LS	Script by SM & LS. Edited by JG	Script written by SM and LS. Edited by JG (Changed from 'Script written by LS and SM...')	Not available		19 April 1953
24	SM LS JG	1. Handsome Harry the Investigator 2. The Ascent of Mount Everest	Written by SM and LS	Script by SM & LS. Edited by JG	Script by SM and LS. Edited by JG	Not available		26 April 1953
25	SM LS JG	1. Handsome Harry's Phone Call 2. The Story of Plymouth Hoe & the Armada	Written by SM and LS	Script by SM & LS. Edited by JG	Script by LS and SM. Edited by JG	Not available		3 May 1953
Special	SM LS JG	A Special Coronation Edition	Written by SM and LS	Script written by The Late LS and SM. Edited by Councillor Major J D Grafton (Cons)	Script by SM and LS and edited by JG	Not available		1 June 1953

SERIES 4

EPISODE	PROBABLY WRITTEN BY	TITLE/SKETCHES	RADIO TIMES ENTRY	SCRIPT FRONT	SCRIPTED ANNOUNCEMENT	RECORDED ANNOUNCEMENT	NOTES	RECORDED
1	SM	1. Handsome Harry Robs the Bank of England 2. The Dreaded Piano Clubber	Written by SM and LS	Script written by SM and LS	Script written by SM and LS	Not available		27 September 1953
2	SM	1. Handsome Harry the Lifeguard 2. The Man Who Tried to Destroy London's Monuments	Written by SM and LS	Script by SM and LS	Script by SM and LS	Not available		4 October 1953
3	SM LS	1. The Ghastly Experiments of Dr Hans Eidelburger 2. The Mount Everest Project	Written by SM and LS	Script by SM and LS	Script by SM and LS	Script by SM and LS		11 October 1953
4	LS	The Building of Britain's First Atomic Cannon	Written by SM and LS	Script by SM and LS	Script by SM and LS	Not available	A single storyline is used throughout this episode	18 October 1953
5	SM	1. Fearless Harry the Guinea Pig 2. The Gibraltar Story	Written by SM and LS	Script by SM and LS	Script by SM and LS	Not available		25 October 1953
6	LS	Through the Sound Barrier in an Airing Cupboard	Written by SM and LS	Script by SM and LS	Programme written by SM and LS	Not available		1 November 1953
7	SM	The First Albert Memorial to the Moon	Written by SM and LS	Script by SM and LS	Script written by SM and LS	Not available		8 November 1953
8	LS	1. A Race to the Death 2. The Case of the Missing Bureaucrat	Written by SM and LS	Script by SM and LS	Script written by SM and LS	Not available		15 November 1953
9	SM	Operation Bagpipes	Written by SM and LS	Script by SM and LS	Script written by SM and LS	Not available		22 November 1953
10	LS	1. Fearless Harry Secombe 2. Flying Saucer Mystery	Written by SM and LS	Script by SM and LS	Script by SM and LS	Not available		29 November 1953

SERIES 4 (cont.)

EPISODE	PROBABLY WRITTEN BY	TITLE/SKETCHES	RADIO TIMES ENTRY	SCRIPT FRONT	SCRIPTED ANNOUNCEMENT	RECORDED ANNOUNCEMENT	NOTES	RECORDED
11	SM LS JG	1. Handsome Harry in Battersea Dogs Home 2. The Story of Plymouth Hoe & the Armada	Written by SM and LS	Script by SM and LS	Script by SM and LS	Not available	The first scene is rewritten from Series 3, episode 11. The second scene is rewritten from Series 3, episode 25	6 December 1953
12	LS JG	1. The British Way of Life 2. The Strange Case of Lady Chatterley's Gardener	Written by SM and LS	Script by SM and LS	Script by SM and LS	Not available	The first scene is rewritten from Series 3, episode 10. The remaining two-thirds consists of new material by LS	13 December 1953
13	SM	The Giant Bombardon	Written by SM and LS	Script by SM and LS	Script by SM and LS	Not available		20 December 1953
14	LS	Ten Thousand Fathoms Down in a Wardrobe	Written by SM and LS	Script by SM and LS	Script by SM and LS	Not available		27 December 1953
15	SM	The Missing Prime Minister	Written by SM and LS	Script by SM and LS	Script by SM and LS	Script by SM and LS		3 January 1954
16	LS	The Strange Case of Dr Jekyll & Mr Crun	Written by SM and LS	Script by SM and LS	Script by SM and LS	Not available		10 January 1954
17	SM LS JG	The Mummified Priest	Written by SM and LS	Script by SM and LS	Script by SM and LS	Not available	This episode contains rewritten scenes from Series 2, episode 10 and Series 3, episode 5	17 January 1954
18	SM LS JG	1. The History of Communications 2. The Siege of Khartoum	Written by SM and LS	Script by SM and LS	Script by SM and LS	Script by SM and LS	Remake of sketches from Series 1, episode 7 and Series 3, episode 18. This programme is available on the CD The Goon Show, Series 4, Part 1 (The Golden Age of BBC Radio Comedy) under the title 'The History of Communications/The Siege of Khartoum', but the closing credits are not the originals as they have been cut from episode 23, which was retained in the BBC's archives, and pasted on to the end.	17 January 1954

SERIES 4 (cont.)

EPISODE	PROBABLY WRITTEN BY	TITLE/SKETCHES	RADIO TIMES ENTRY	SCRIPT FRONT	SCRIPTED ANNOUNCEMENT	RECORDED ANNOUNCEMENT	NOTES	RECORDED
19	SM	The Kippered Herring Gang	Written by SM and LS	Script by SM and LS	Script by SM and LS	Not available		31 January 1954
20	SM LS JG	1. Rottingdean 2. The Toothpaste Expedition 3. Canadian Moose Hunting Season	Written by LS	Script by SM and LS	Script by SM and LS	Not available	Remake of sketches from Series 3, episode 5 and Series 2, episode 2. This programme is available on the CD *The Goon Show*, Series 4, Part 1 (*The Golden Age of BBC Radio Comedy*) under the title 'The Toothpaste Expedition' but the closing credits are not the originals as they have been cut from episode 23, which was retained in the BBC's archives, and pasted on to the end.	7 February 1954
21	SM	The Case of the Vanishing Room	Written by SM	Script by SM	Script by SM	Not available		14 February 1954
22	SM	The Great Ink Drought of 1902	Written by SM	Script by SM	Script by SM	Not available		21 February 1954
23	SM	The Greatest Mountain in the World	Written by SM	Script by SM	Script by SM	Script by SM		28 February 1954
24	SM LS	The Collapse of the British Rail Sandwich System	Written by SM	Script by SM	Script by SM	Script by SM		7 March 1954
25	SM	The Silent Bugler	Written by SM	Script by SM	Script by SM	Script by SM		14 March 1954

SERIES 4 (cont.)

EPISODE	PROBABLY WRITTEN BY	TITLE/SKETCHES	RADIO TIMES ENTRY	SCRIPT FRONT	SCRIPTED ANNOUNCEMENT	RECORDED ANNOUNCEMENT	NOTES	RECORDED
26	LS	Drain	Written by SM	Script by LS	Script by LS	Not available	This programme is available on the CD *The Goon Show*, Series 4, Part 1 (*The Golden Age of BBC Radio Comedy*) under the title "Western Story "Drain!" but the closing credits are not the originals as they have been cut from episode 23, which was retained in the BBC's archives, and pasted on to the end.	21 March 1954
27	SM	The Saga of the Internal Mountain	Written by SM	Script by SM	Script by SM	Script by SM		28 March 1954
28	SM	Bulletto	Written by SM	Script by SM	Script by SM	Not available		4 April 1954
29	SM	The Great Bank of England Robbery	Written by SM	Script by SM	Script by SM	Script by SM		11 April 1954
30	SM	The Siege of Fort Knight	Written by SM	Script by SM	Script by SM	Not available		18 April 1954
Special	SM LS	The International Christmas Pudding (insert in Christmas Crackers)	Script by SM & LS	Not available	Not available	Not available		20 December 1953
Special	SM ES	Archie in Goonland	Script by ES & SM	Script by ES & SM	The stuff was written by ES and SM	Not available		16 May 1954
Special	SM LS	The Starlings	Written for radio by SM	Script by SM	By SM	By SM		11 Aug 1954

SERIES 5

EPISODE	PROBABLY WRITTEN BY	TITLE/SKETCHES	RADIO TIMES ENTRY	SCRIPT FRONT	SCRIPTED ANNOUNCEMENT	RECORDED ANNOUNCEMENT	NOTES	RECORDED
1	SM	The Whistling Spy Enigma	Script by SM	Script by SM	Script by SM	Script by SM	First named appearance of Hercules Grytpype-Thynne (spelt as Gritpipe-Thynne in the script)	26 September 1954
2	SM	The Lost Gold Mine (of Charlotte)	Script by SM	Script by SM	Script by SM	Script by SM		3 October 1954
3	SM	The Dreaded Batter Pudding Hurler (of Bexhill-on-Sea)	Script by SM	Script by SM	Script by SM	Script by SM		10 October 1954
4	SM LS	The Phantom Head Shaver (of Brighton)	Script by SM	Script by SM	Script by SM	Script by SM		17 October 1954
5	SM LS	The Affair of the Lone Banana	Script by SM	Script by SM	Script by SM	Script by SM		24 October 1954
6	SM LS	The Canal	Script by SM	Script by SM	Script by SM	Script by SM		31 October 1954
7	ES	Lurgi Strikes Britain	Script by ES & SM	Script by ES & SM	Script by ES & SM	Script by ES & SM		7 November 1954
8	ES	The Mystery of the Marie Celeste (Solved)	Script by SM	Script by ES	Script by ES	Script by ES & SM		14 November 1954
9	ES	The Last Tram (from Clapham)	Script by ES	Script by ES & SM	Script by ES & SM	Script by ES & SM		21 November 1954
10	SM	The Booted Gorilla (Found?)	Script by SM	Script by SM and ES	Script by SM and ES	Script by SM and ES		28 November 1954
11	ES	The Spanish Suitcase	Script by ES & SM	Script by ES & SM	Script by ES & SM	Script by ES & SM		5 December 1954
12	SM	Dishonoured or The Fall of Neddie Seagoon	Script by SM and ES	Script by SM and ES	Script by SM and ES	Script by SM and ES		12 December 1954
13	ES	Forog	Script by ES & SM	Script by ES & SM	Script by ES & SM	Script by ES & SM		19 December 1954

SERIES 5 (cont.)

EPISODE	PROBABLY WRITTEN BY	TITLE/SKETCHES	RADIO TIMES ENTRY	SCRIPT FRONT	SCRIPTED ANNOUNCEMENT	RECORDED ANNOUNCEMENT	NOTES	RECORDED
14	SM	Ye Bandit of Sherwood Forest	Script by SM and ES	Script by SM and ES?	Script by SM and ES	Script by SM and ES		19 December 1954
15	SM	Nineteen Eighty-Five	Script by SM and ES	Script by SM and ES	Script by SM and ES	Script by SM and ES		2 January 1955
16	ES	The Case of the Missing Heir	Script by SM and ES	Script by ES & SM	Script by ES & SM	Script by ES & SM		9 January 1955
17	SM	China Story	Script by ES & SM	Script by SM and ES	Script by SM and ES	Script by SM and ES		16 January 1955
18	ES	Under Two Floorboards	Script by SM and ES	Script by SM and ES	Script by ES & SM	Script by ES & SM		23 January 1955
19	SM	The Missing Scroll	Script by SM and ES	Script by SM and ES	Script by SM and ES	Script by SM and ES		30 January 1955
20	SM	Nineteen Eighty-Five	Script by SM and ES	Script by SM and ES	Script by SM and ES	Script by SM and ES	Remake of Series 5, programme 15	30 January 1955
21	SM	The Sinking of Westminster Pier	Script by ES & SM	Script by SM and ES	Script by SM and ES	Script by SM and ES		13 February 1955
22	SM	The Fireball of Milton Street	Script by SM and ES	Script by SM and ES	Script by SM and ES	Script by SM and ES		20 February 1955
23	ES	The Terrible Blasting of Moreton's Bank/The Six Ingots of Leadenhall Street	Script by SM and ES	Script by ES & SM	Script by ES & SM	Script by SM and ES		27 February 1955

SERIES 5 (cont.)

EPISODE	PROBABLY WRITTEN BY	TITLE/SKETCHES	RADIO TIMES ENTRY	SCRIPT FRONT	SCRIPTED ANNOUNCEMENT	RECORDED ANNOUNCEMENT	NOTES	RECORDED
24	ES	Yehti	Script by ES & SM	Script by ES & SM	Script by ES & SM	Script by ES & SM		6 March 1955
25	SM	The White Box of Great Bardfield	Script by ES & SM	Script by SM and ES	Script by SM and ES	Script by SM and ES		13 March 1955
26	ES	The End	Script by ES & SM	Script by SM and ES	Script by SM and ES	Script by ES & SM		20 March 1955
Special	SM	The Dreaded Batter Pudding Hurler (of Bexhill-on-Sea)	Not available	Script by LS	Not available	Script by SM	This was a remake of episode 3 from Series 5 and was recorded as one of a series of programmes for the BBC under the title of *Summer is a Comin'*. Milligan was taken ill and so all parts were played by Sellers and Secombe	22 May 1955

SERIES 6

EPISODE	PROBABLY WRITTEN BY	TITLE/SKETCHES	RADIO TIMES ENTRY	SCRIPT FRONT	SCRIPTED ANNOUNCEMENT	RECORDED ANNOUNCEMENT	NOTES	RECORDED
1	SM ES	The Man Who Won the War	By SM & ES	By SM & ES	Script by SM and ES	Script by SM and ES	First use of phrase 'needle nardle noo'	18 September 1955
2	SM ES	The Secret Escritoire	Especially written for the wireless by SM & ES	Especially written for the wireless by SM & ES	Script by SM and ES	Script by SM and ES		25 September 1955
3	SM	The Lost Emperor	Script by SM	Script by SM	Script by SM	Script by SM		2 October 1955
4	SM	Napoleon's Piano	By SM with additional material by Overcoat Charlie	Not available	Script by SM	Script by SM		9 October 1955
5	SM	The Case of the Missing CD Plates	Script by SM	Script by SM	Script by SM	Script by SM		16 October 1955
6	SM	Rommel's Treasure	Script by SM	Script by SM	Script by SM	Script by SM		23 October 1955
7	SM	Foiled by President Fred	Script by SM	Script by SM	Script by SM	Script by SM		30 October 1955
8	SM	Shangri-La Again!	Script by SM	Script by SM	Script by SM	Script by SM		6 November 1955
9	SM	The International Christmas Pudding	Script by SM	Script by SM	Script by SM	Script by SM		13 November 1955
10	SM	The Pevensey Bay Disaster	Script by SM	Script by SM	Script by SM	Script by SM		20 November 1955
11	SM	Sale of Manhattan	Script by SM	Script by SM	Script by SM	Script by SM		27 November 1955
12	SM	The Terrible Revenge of Fred Fu Manchu	Script by SM	Script by SM	Script by SM	Script by SM		4 December 1955
13	SM	The Lost Year	Script by SM	Script by SM	Script by SM	Script by SM		11 December 1955
14	SM	The Greenslade Story	Script by SM	Script by SM	Script by SM	Script by SM		18 December 1955
15	SM	The Hastings Flyer	Script by SM	Script by SM	Script by SM	Script by SM	The only difference between this and episode 10, 'The Pevensey Bay Disaster', is the title	18 December 1955
16	SM	The Mighty Wurlitzer	Script by SM	Script by SM	Script by SM	Script by SM		1 January 1956

SERIES 6 (cont.)

EPISODE	PROBABLY WRITTEN BY	TITLE/SKETCHES	RADIO TIMES ENTRY	SCRIPT FRONT	SCRIPTED ANNOUNCEMENT	RECORDED ANNOUNCEMENT	NOTES	RECORDED
17	SM	Attack on the Great International Christmas Pudding	Script by SM	Not available	Script by SM	Script by SM		8 January 1956
18	SM ES	The Tales of Montmartre	Script by SM	Script by SM & ES	Not available	Script by SM and ES		15 January 1956
19	SM	The Jet-Propelled Guided Naafi	Script by SM	Script by SM	Script by SM	Script by SM		22 January 1956
20	SM	The House of Teeth	Script by SM	Script by SM	Script by SM	Script by SM	First reference to a 'Little Jim'	29 January 1956
21	SM	Tales of Old Dartmoor	Script by SM	Script by SM	Script by SM and LS	Script by SM		5 February 1956
22	SM LS	The Choking Horror	No reference to scriptwriters	Not available	Script by SM	Script by SM and LS		12 February 1956
23	SM	The Great Tuscan Salami Scandal	No reference to scriptwriters	Script by SM	Script by SM	...SM, who also wrote the script		19 February 1956
24	SM	The Treasure in the Lake	No reference to scriptwriters	Script by SM	Script by SM	Script by SM		26 February 1956
25	SM LS	The Fear of Wages	Script by SM	Script by SM	Script by SM and LS	Script by SM and LS		4 March 1956
26	SM LS	Scradje	No reference to scriptwriters	Script by SM	Script by SM	Script by SM and LS		11 March 1956
27	SM LS JG	The Man Who Never Was	No reference to scriptwriters	Script by SM	Script by SM	Script by SM and LS	A rewritten version of Series 3, episode 20	18 March 1956
Special	ES	The Missing Christmas Parcel	Script by ES	Script by ES	No reference to scriptwriters	Not available		27 November 1955
Special	SM	The Goons Hit Wales	No reference to scriptwriters	Script by SM	...SM, who also wrote the script	Not available		26 February 1956
Special	SM ES	China Story	Script by SM and ES	Script by SM and ES	Script by SM and ES	Script by SM and ES		24 August 1956

SERIES 7

EPISODE	PROBABLY WRITTEN BY	TITLE/SKETCHES	RADIO TIMES ENTRY	SCRIPT FRONT	SCRIPTED ANNOUNCEMENT	RECORDED ANNOUNCEMENT	NOTES	RECORDED
1	SM LS	The Nasty Affair at the Burami Oasis	Script by SM	Script: SM and LS	Script by SM and LS	Script by SM and LS	First use of the word 'nadger' First use of the word 'spon'	30 September 1956
2	SM LS	Drums Along the Mersey	Script by SM	Script: SM and LS	Script by SM	Script by SM		7 October 1956
3	SM LS	The Nadger Plague	Script by SM	Script: SM and LS	Script by SM and LS	Script by SM and LS		14 October 1956
4	SM LS	The Macreekie Rising of 74	Script by SM and LS	Script: SM and LS	Script by SM and LS	Script by SM and LS		21 October 1956
5	SM LS	The Spectre of Tintagel	Script by SM and LS	Script: SM and LS	Script by SM and LS	Script by SM and LS		28 October 1956
6	SM LS	The Sleeping Prince	Script by SM and LS	Script: SM and LS	Script by SM and LS	Script by SM and LS		4 November 1956
7	SM LS	The Great Bank Robbery	Script by SM and LS	Script: SM and LS	Script by SM and LS	Script by SM and LS		11 November 1956
8	SM LS	Personal Narrative	Script by SM and LS	Script: SM and LS	Script by SM and LS	Script by SM and LS		18 November 1956
9	SM LS	The Mystery of the Fake Neddie Seagoons	Script by SM and LS	Script: SM and LS	Script by SM and LS	Script by SM and LS		25 November 1956
10	SM LS	What's My Line?	Script by SM and LS	Script: SM and LS	Script by SM and LS	Script by SM and LS		2 December 1956
11	SM LS	The Telephone	Script by SM and LS	Script: SM and LS	Script by SM and LS	Script by SM and LS		9 December 1956
12	SM LS	The Flea	Script by SM and LS	Script: SM and LS	Script by SM and LS	Script by SM and LS		16 December 1956
13	SM LS	Six Charlies in Search of an Author	Script by SM and LS	Script: SM and LS	Script by SM and LS	Script by SM and LS		23 December 1956
14	SM LS	Emperor of the Universe	Script by SM and LS	Script: SM and LS	Script by SM and LS	Script by SM and LS		23 December 1956

SERIES 7 (cont.)

EPISODE	PROBABLY WRITTEN BY	TITLE/SKETCHES	RADIO TIMES ENTRY	SCRIPT FRONT	SCRIPTED ANNOUNCEMENT	RECORDED ANNOUNCEMENT	NOTES	RECORDED
15	SM LS	Wings Over Dagenham	Script by SM and LS	Script: SM and LS	Script by SM and LS	Script by SM and LS	First (unscripted) appearance of Little Jim character. He says 'he's fell in the water', which from episode 16 onwards becomes 'he's fallen in the water'.	30 December 1956
16	SM LS	The Rent Collectors	Script by SM and LS	Script: SM and LS	Script by SM and LS	Script by SM and LS	First scripted appearance of Little Jim character using the more familiar catchphrase 'he's fallen in the water'. The name Little Jim is not scripted, just the voice direction 'very dull, young child'.	30 December 1956
17	SM LS	Shifting Sands	Script by SM and LS	Script: SM and LS	Script by SM and LS	Script by SM and LS		20 January 1957
18	SM LS	The Moon Show	Script by SM and LS	Script: SM and LS	Script by SM and LS	Script by SM and LS		27 January 1957
19	SM LS	The Mysterious Punch-Up-The-Conker	Script by SM and LS	Script: SM and LS	Script by SM and LS	Script by SM and LS		3 February 1957
20	SM LS	Round the World in Eighty Days	Script by SM and LS	Script: SM and LS	Script by SM and LS	Script by SM and LS		17 February 1957
21	SM LS	Insurance – the White Man's Burden	Script by SM and LS	Script: SM and LS	Script by SM and LS	Script by SM and LS		24 February 1957
22	SM LS	Africa Ship Canal	Script by SM and LS	Script: SM and LS	Script by SM and LS	Script by SM and LS		3 March 1957
23	SM LS	Ill Met by Goonlight	Script by SM and LS	Script: SM and LS	Script by SM and LS	Script by SM		10 March 1957
24	SM LS	The Missing Boa Constrictor	Script by SM and LS	Script: SM and LS	Script by SM and LS	Script by SM and LS		17 March 1957

SERIES 7 (cont.)

EPISODE	PROBABLY WRITTEN BY	TITLE/SKETCHES	RADIO TIMES ENTRY	SCRIPT FRONT	SCRIPTED ANNOUNCEMENT	RECORDED ANNOUNCEMENT	NOTES	RECORDED
25	SM LS	The Histories of Pliny the Elder	Script by SM and LS	Script: SM and LS	Script by SM and LS	Script by SM and LS		24 March 1957
Special	SM LS	Operation Christmas Duff	(*Radio Times* 1986) All the scripts were written by SM (LS collaborated on Operation Christmas Duff)	Script: SM and LS	Script by SM and LS	Script by SM and LS		9 December 1956
Special	SM LS	Robin Hood	(*Radio Times* 1988) The Christmas Show is part written by LS, who was brought in to help remind Milligan of plots, about which the great man tended to be rather vague. An ex-Commando Captain, Stephens died young in 1958	Script: SM and LS	Script by SM and LS	Script by SM and LS		2 December 1956
Special	SM	The Reason Why	Written for the wireless by SM	By SM	Not available	Script by SM		11 August 1957

SERIES 8

EPISODE	PROBABLY WRITTEN BY	TITLE/SKETCHES	RADIO TIMES ENTRY	SCRIPT FRONT	SCRIPTED ANNOUNCEMENT	RECORDED ANNOUNCEMENT	NOTES	RECORDED
1	SM	Spon	Script by SM and LS	No reference to scriptwriters	Script by SM and LS	Script by SM		29 September 1957
2	SM LS	The Junk Affair	Script by SM and LS	No reference to scriptwriters	Script by SM and LS	Script by SM and LS		6 October 1957
3	SM LS	The Burning Embassy	Script by SM and LS	No reference to scriptwriters	Script by SM and LS	Script by SM and LS		13 October 1957
4	SM LS	The Great Regent's Park Swim	Script by SM and LS	No reference to scriptwriters	Script by SM and LS	Script by SM and LS		20 October 1957
5	SM LS	Treasure in the Tower	Script by SM and LS	No reference to scriptwriters	Script by SM and LS	Script by SM and LS	First appearance of the phrase 'It's all in the mind, you know'	27 October 1957
6	SM LS	The Space Age	Script by SM and LS	No reference to scriptwriters	Script by SM and LS	Script by SM and LS		3 November 1957
7	LS	The Red Fort	Script by SM and LS	No reference to scriptwriters	Script by SM and LS	Script by SM and LS		10 November 1957
8	SM LS	The Missing Battleship	Script by SM and LS	No reference to scriptwriters	Script by SM and LS	Script by SM and LS		17 November 1957
9	LS	The Policy	Script by SM and LS	Script: SM and LS	Script by SM and LS	Script by LS		24 November 1957
10	SM LS	King Solomon's Mines	Script by SM and LS	Script: SM and LS	Script by SM and LS	Script by SM and LS		1 December 1957
11	LS	The Stolen Postman	Script by SM and LS	Script: SM and LS	Script by SM and LS	Script by LS		8 December 1957
12	SM LS	The Great British Revolution	Script by SM and LS	Script: SM and LS	Script by SM and LS	Script by SM and LS		15 December 1957
13	SM LS	The Plasticine Man	Script by SM and LS	Script: SM and LS	Script by SM and LS	Script by SM and LS		22 December 1957
14	SM LS	African Incident	Script by SM and LS	Script: SM and LS	Script by SM and LS	Script by SM and LS		29 December 1957

SERIES 8 (cont.)

EPISODE	PROBABLY WRITTEN BY	TITLE/SKETCHES	RADIO TIMES ENTRY	SCRIPT FRONT	SCRIPTED ANNOUNCEMENT	RECORDED ANNOUNCEMENT	NOTES	RECORDED
15	LS MW	The Thing on the Mountain	Script by SM and LS	Script: LS & MW	Not available	Script by LS and MW		5 January 1958
16	SM	The String Robberies	Script by SM and LS	Script: SM	Script by SM	Script by SM		12 January 1958
17	LS MW	The Moriarty Murder Mystery	Script by SM and LS	Script: LS & MW	Script by LS and MW	Script by LS and MW		19 January 1958
18	SM	The Curse of Frankenstein	Script by SM and LS	Script: SM	Script by SM	Script by SM		19 January 1958
19	LS MW	The White Neddie Trade	Script by SM and LS	Script: LS & MW	Script by LS and MW	Script by LS and MW		2 February 1958
20	SM	Ten Snowballs that Shook the World	Script by SM and LS	Script: SM	Script by SM	Script by SM		9 February 1958
21	SM LS JG	The Man Who Never Was	Script by SM and LS	Script: SM and LS	Script by SM and LS	Script by SM and LS	Remake of Series 6, programme 27	16 February 1958
22	SM	......!	Script by SM and LS	Script: SM	Script by SM	Script by SM		23 February 1958
23	SM JA	The Spon Plague	Script by SM and LS	Script: SM	Script by SM	Script by JA and SM		2 March 1958
24	SM	Tiddlywinks	Script by SM and LS	Script: SM	Script by SM	Script by SM		9 March 1958
25	SM	The Evils of Bushey Spon	Script by SM and LS	Script: SM	Script by SM	Script by SM	The original script is entitled 'The Evils of Bushey Green'	16 March 1958
26	SM JA	The Great Statue Debate	Script by SM and LS	Script: SM	Script by SM	Script by SM, JA & Rabelais		23 March 1958

SERIES 9

EPISODE	PROBABLY WRITTEN BY	TITLE/SKETCHES	RADIO TIMES ENTRY	SCRIPT FRONT	SCRIPTED ANNOUNCEMENT	RECORDED ANNOUNCEMENT	NOTES	RECORDED
1	SM	The Sahara Desert Statue	Script by SM	Script by SM	... SM - who also writes the thing	... SM - who also writes the thing		2 November 1958
2	SM	I Was Monty's Treble	Script by SM	Script by SM	... SM who writes it	... SM, who writes it		9 November 1958
3	SM	The £1,000,000 Penny	Script by SM	Script by SM	... SM who writes it	Not on recording		16 November 1958
4	SM	The Pam's Paper Insurance Policy	Script by SM	Script by SM	No reference to scriptwriters	The script was by SM		23 November 1958
5	SM	The Mountain Eaters	Script by SM	Script by SM	No reference to scriptwriters	Not on recording		30 November 1958
6	SM	The Childe Harolde Rewarde	Script by SM	Script by SM	No reference to scriptwriters	Not on recording		7 December 1958
7	LS MW	The Seagoon Memoirs	Script by SM	Script by LS & MW	Written this week by LS & MW	Not on recording		14 December 1958
8	SM	Queen Anne's Rain	Script by SM	Script by SM	No reference to scriptwriters	Not on recording		21 December 1958
9	SM	The Battle of Spion Kop	Script by SM	Script by SM	Not available	Not on recording		28 December 1958
10	SM	Ned's Atomic Dustbin	Script by SM	Script by SM	No reference to scriptwriters	Not on recording		4 January 1959
11	SM	Who is Pink Oboe	Script by SM	Script by SM	No reference to scriptwriters	Not on recording		11 January 1959
12	SM	The Call of the West	Script by SM	Script by SM	No reference to scriptwriters	Not on recording		18 January 1959
13	SM	Dishonoured - Again	Script by SM	Script by SM	No reference to scriptwriters	Not on recording		25 January 1959
14	SM	The Scarlet Capsule	Script by SM	Script by SM	No reference to scriptwriters	Not on recording		1 February 1959
15	SM	The Tay Bridge	Script by SM	Script by SM	No reference to scriptwriters	Not on recording		8 February 1959
16	SM	The Gold Plate Robbery	Script by SM	Script by SM	No reference to scriptwriters	Not on recording		15 February 1959
17	SM	The £50 Cure	Script by SM	Script by SM	... SM who writes the script	... SM who writes the script		22 February 1959

SERIES 10

EPISODE	PROBABLY WRITTEN BY	TITLE/SKETCHES	RADIO TIMES ENTRY	SCRIPT FRONT	SCRIPTED ANNOUNCEMENT	RECORDED ANNOUNCEMENT	NOTES	RECORDED
1	SM	A Christmas Carol	Script by SM	Script by SM	No reference to scriptwriters	Not on recording		20 December 1959
2	SM	The Tale of Men's Shirts	Script by SM	Script: SM	No reference to scriptwriters	Not on recording		27 December 1959
3	SM	The Chinese Legs	Script by SM	Script: SM	No reference to scriptwriters	Not on recording		3 January 1960
4	SM	Robin's Post	Script by SM	Script by SM	No reference to scriptwriters	Not on recording		10 January 1960
5	SM	The Silver Dubloons	Script by SM	Script by SM	No reference to scriptwriters	Not on recording		17 January 1960
6	SM	The Last Smoking Seagoon	Script by SM	Script by SM	No reference to scriptwriters	Not on recording		24 January 1960

VINTAGE GOONS

EPISODE	PROBABLY REWRITTEN BY	TITLE/SKETCHES	RADIO TIMES ENTRY	SCRIPT FRONT	SCRIPTED ANNOUNCEMENT	RECORDED ANNOUNCEMENT	NOTES	RECORDED
1	SM LS	The Mummified Priest	Script by SM	Script re-written by SM	Script by SM	Script by SM		6 October 1957
2	SM LS	Mount Everest (untitled)	Script by SM	Re-written by SM	Script by SM	Script by SM		20 October 1957
3	SM LS	10 Downing Street Stolen	Not broadcast	Re-written by SM	Script by SM	Script by SM		3 November 1957
4	SM LS	The Giant Bombardon	Script by SM	Re-written by SM	Script by SM	Script by SM		17 November 1957
5	SM LS	The Kippered Herring	Not available	Re-written by SM	Script by SM	Script by SM		1 December 1957
6	SM LS	The Vanishing Room	Script by SM	Re-written by SM	Script by SM	Script by SM		15 December 1957
7	SM LS	The Ink Shortage	Not available	Re-written by SM	Script by SM	Script by SM		29 December 1957
8	SM	The Mustard & Cress Shortage	Not available	Re-written by SM	Script by SM	Script by SM		12 January 1958
9	SM	The Internal Mountain	Not available	Re-written by SM	Script by SM	Script by SM		16 February 1958
10	SM	The Silent Bugler	Not available	Re-written by SM	Script by SM	Script by SM		23 February 1958
11	SM	The Great Bank of England Robbery	Script by SM	Re-written by SM	Script by SM	Script by SM		2 March 1958
12	SM	The Albert Memorial	Script by SM	Re-written by SM	Script by SM	Script by SM		9 March 1958
13	SM	Underwater Gas Stoves for Fort Knight	Not available	Re-written by SM	Script by SM	Script by SM		16 March 1958
14	SM	The Piano Clubber	Not available	Re-written by SM	Script by SM	Script by SM		23 March 1958

MISCELLANEOUS

EPISODE	PROBABLY WRITTEN BY	TITLE/SKETCHES	RADIO TIMES ENTRY	SCRIPT FRONT	SCRIPTED ANNOUNCEMENT	RECORDED ANNOUNCEMENT	NOTES	RECORDED
	SM	The Last Goon Show of All	Written by SM	No reference to scriptwriters	Not available	Script by SM		30 April 1972
	SM LS JG	Goon Again The 50th Anniversary Cardboard Replica Show	No reference to scriptwriters	Not available	Not available	The script was by SM and LS	To celebrate the 50th anniversary of the *Goon Show*, two sketches from Series 3 were recreated (from programmes 15 and 25) with Andrew Secombe, Jon Glover and Jeffrey Holland taking the parts played by Harry Secombe, Spike Milligan and Peter Sellers	23 March 2001

Appendix Two

VACANT LOT SCRIPT

VACANT LOT[1]

Characters in order of their appearance

NARRATOR: An announcer. It is important that this should be someone with a sense of humour.

DR QUINCE: Quiet, cultured, sardonic voice.

AMBROSE TRIPFIELD: In his fifties. A rich, pompous, authoritative voice. Very conscious of his own dignity.

MRS TRIPFIELD: A quiet woman with a quiet sense of humour. Level-headed and conscious of her husband's absurdities. Likes Hancock and is not in the slightest overawed by Tripfield.

GEORGE MADKIN: A rich-voiced, slightly hoarse (I'm thinking of years of shouting 'time' in smoky atmospheres) Yorkshireman. Worked in pubs and hotels all his life. Not very bright, except in his own trade.

FRED CLODLEY: Knows cars like the back of his hand but is otherwise loud-mouthed, blunt, tactless with a childish, stodgy sense of humour. Is known amongst his cronies as a wit, which he is not. Always laughs loudly at his own jokes. Considered a loud-mouthed bore by Hancock, Tripfield et al. and loathed by Quince.

PEMBLE: Sixty-odd. His voice shows his years. Has worked for Hancock and Son all his life. Was originally a very precise, efficient man but is getting old now and forgetful. His voice, if possible, should make him appear a short, thin, shrivelled-up old gentleman.

LEMON: 15/16 years old. Youthful, slightly cockney voice. Usually cheerful and inclined to be cheeky.

MRS SCOWLEY: Full, commanding voice of a woman with a private income from her late husband's investments and accustomed to servants and good service in hotels all over the South of England. The only time her voice softens is when she talks to her dog.

MYRTLE: Mrs Scowley's lady companion. Quiet, timid but cultured voice – the result of years of brow-beating and mock submission to Mrs Scowley. Terrified of the other woman.

HOTEL CLERK: Local man in his twenties. If it is possible, he should sound as if he is trying to speak with a better accent than he really has. This could also be indicated by his dropping into his normal speech when he imitates Mrs Scowley.

BILL GLASS: Cheerful, energetic American. Accent not too exaggerated – after all, people are quite accustomed to the normal, American, localised accent – Texan?

GLADYS COATES: 'Well ai don't know, reely – in mai opinion she's a common girl.'

TWO BOYS OUTSIDE: A couple of urchins, fascinated by and quite serious about cars of all types.

AUNT: In her sixties. Cultured but rambling, vague voice. Quite cheerful and kindly but not quite sure what's going on around her.

ORCHESTRA:	SIG. TUNE (POSS. ANNOUNCEMENTS OVER?) SEGUE INTO WHOLE-TONE SCALE DREAM MUSIC ON STRINGS. FADE UNDER. (DO NOT USE KNOWN NUMBERS OF ANY KIND.)
NARRATOR:	Let us imagine for a moment that we are poised in the air over the South Coast of England. It is just after six o'clock on a winter's evening and already beneath us darkness is shrouding the Sussex Downs and the grey sea-mist is obscuring the outline of the Coast. To the East and

to the West are the big seaside
resorts with their huge hotels,
boarding houses, piers and
amusement parks... But what are
these lights beneath us, shining
through the gloomy dusk? Can
it be...?

ORCHESTRA: SHOCK CHORD ON STRINGS. FADE
              QUICKLY AND ABRUPTLY. OUT.

NARRATOR: Yes — it's Churdley Bay.
              Churdley Bay, of course, is much
              smaller than its neighbours,
              the great holiday towns of the
              South Coast but at least it is
              different... in that whereas they
              are crowded during the summer
              and dull and deserted during the
              winter, Churdley Bay is dull and
              deserted all the year round.
              But let's float gently down and
              take a closer look...

ORCHESTRA: DREAM MUSIC STRINGS DESCENDING.
              OUT.

NARRATOR: There's Churdley Head and the
              ruins of the Martello Tower.

ORCHESTRA: SHOCK STRING CHORD AS BEFORE.

NARRATOR: And let's go down and take
              a look at the Esplanade with
              its bright banners bearing the
              legend: 'Welcome to Britain'.

ORCHESTRA: SHOCK CHORD AGAIN.

FX:	HEAVY RAIN ON STREETS. HOLD, THEN FADE QUICKLY UNDER.
NARRATOR:	Then there are the other famous highways of Churdley Bay… Royal Parade…
FX:	RAIN. UP AND UNDER.
NARRATOR:	Emperor's Walk…
FX:	RAIN. UP AND UNDER.
NARRATOR:	High Street…
FX:	RAIN. UP AND UNDER.
NARRATOR:	… and let us not forget the most important feature of a coastal town — the beach…
FX:	RAIN AND BREAKERS
NARRATOR:	Of course, the citizens of Churdley Bay don't like to boast about their beach but, as an outsider, I can say that it is considered the finest six-foot-wide strip of shingle on the South Coast. Of course, this being a winter's evening it is deserted now but during the summer months you will sometimes find the beach one <u>mass</u> of umbrellas and mackintoshes.
ORCHESTRA:	DREAM MUSIC FLYING
NARRATOR:	But let's fly inland a little way over the shops, the offices and then up the hill into one of the main residential quarters

	of the town. And here on top of the hill is the house of Dr Quince, the local practitioner.
ORCHESTRA:	SHOCK STRING CHORD
DR QUINCE	(QUIET SARDONIC VOICE) There we are, Mrs Hatton — this is the liniment.
FX:	DOOR OPENS
WOMAN:	Thank you, Doctor. Goodnight.
QUINCE:	Goodnight, Mrs Hatton — and don't forget to take a little gentle exercise.
FX:	DOOR CLOSES
QUINCE:	A nice quiet game of football, for instance. (CALLS) Any more, nurse?
NURSE:	No, that's all, Doctor.
QUINCE:	Good. (YAWNS) Well, I hear they're holding the local Council Elections tomorrow.
NURSE:	That's right, Doctor. I've been attending some of the speeches.
QUINCE:	You have? How are they going?
NURSE:	(ENTHUSIASTIC) Well, sir — the Progressive Party are promising social reforms, individual benefits and a higher standard of living.
QUINCE:	How very original of them. And the Reform Party, I suppose, are

	promising a higher standard of living, individual benefits and social reforms. By the way… I hear our esteemed friend — what's his name? — The Auctioneer and Estate Agent fellow…
NURSE:	You mean Mr Hancock.
QUINCE:	Yes — Hancock. I hear he's standing as a candidate.
NURSE:	Yes, Doctor… and he's been telling people that he's thinking of taking up politics seriously.
QUINCE:	Really? (PAUSE) Has Mr Churchill been warned? Incidentally — what party is Hancock standing for?
NURSE:	The Progressives, Dr Quince.
QUINCE:	Oh, yes? I should imagine Mr Tripfield is delighted.
FX:	RAIN UP AND DOWN BEHIND
NARRATOR:	Mr Tripfield is the leader of the Progressive Party. He lives over here… in one of the old houses in Emperor's Walk…
FX:	RAIN UP AND UNDER
MRS TRIPFIELD:	(ALWAYS CALM) Really, Ambrose, dear — I don't see what you're worried about. You're sure to be elected and you know it's your turn for Mayor this year.
TRIPFIELD:	I know, dear. I'm not worried about myself. It's Hancock —

don't you realise he's standing for <u>our</u> party?!

MRS TRIPFIELD: Well, as your party has won the elections for the last forty-seven years, I think he'd be foolish to stand for the other one.

TRIPFIELD: Hmm… at least there's one consolation. He won't stand a chance against old Grimthorpe. That ward has always returned a Reform candidate.

MRS TRIPFIELD: Anyway, Ambrose — I do think you're exaggerating the whole affair. After all — if Mr Hancock does get in… a Councillor's job here is very simple.

TRIPFIELD: Well, in that respect it'll suit him to a T.

MRS TRIPFIELD: — and you must admit he's a respectable character… not like one or two we've had on the Council.

TRIPFIELD: (RELUCTANTLY) Yes — I'll give him that. At least you don't find him in the bar of the Churdley Arms every night.

FX: RAIN UP AND DOWN FOR

ORCHESTRA: DREAM MUSIC UP

NARRATOR: The Churdley Arms, a public house and small hotel, is right in the

	centre of the town. It's owned by George Madkin, who settled here many years ago; and the Saloon Bar is the meeting-place of the so-called 'wits' of Churdley Bay… Fred Clodley, for instance, the proprietor of the local garage and his cronies, and, of course, George Madkin himself…
FX:	RAIN UP AND DOWN BEHIND
MADKIN:	(BROAD, HARD YORKSHIRE) Well, Ah'll tell you, Fred — if Hancock gets in we'll have to watch our Ps and Qs. He might do something drastic!
CLODLEY:	(LOUD-MOUTHED OAF) Ar, George — like buying 'imself a new suit! (LAUGHS LOUDLY AND COARSELY) D'you 'ear that? — Like buying 'imself a new suit…!! (LAUGHS)
OMNES:	(LAUGH)
MADKIN:	(STILL LAUGHING) Ooooh, Fred — you're a right one! You ought to go on the stage, you know! (LAUGHS)
OMNES:	(LAUGH ON FADE)
	<u>X-FADE</u>
NARRATOR:	Come next door to the Saloon Bar — to the Sale Room of the Churdley Arms, where the local Auctioneer and Estate Agent, the

	aforesaid Mr Anthony Hancock, is concluding the day's Auction Sale of the furniture and effects of the late J.G.S. Postlethwaite…
FX:	DOOR OPENS
OMNES:	GENERAL CONVERSATION
TONY:	Come now, gentlemen…
FX:	GAVEL ON DESK
TONY:	Let us proceed. Come, gentlemen… what am I offered for Lot 78 — one handsome oil painting by the late J.G.S. Postlethwaite himself, entitled 'Highland Cattle in Sunset'. Come along gentlemen… do I hear five pounds…? Do I hear four pound ten…? Four pounds from any gentleman…? Surely four pounds is not too much to ask for a masterpiece like th— … Do I hear three pounds…? Thirty shillings…? One pound…? Ten sh— … Lot withdrawn.
VOICE:	(OFF MIKE) I'll give you ten shillings!
TONY:	(QUICKLY) Going-going-gone…
FX:	GAVEL ON DESK
TONY:	… at ten shillings. Lemon! Lemon! Where is that office boy of mine?
LEMON:	'Ere I am, sir!
TONY:	Ah — there you are, Lemon.

	Get that gentleman's name and address, will you...? He's just bought Lot 78 for the handsome price of ten silver shillings or half-a-pound.
LEMON:	Which one was it, Mr Hancock? — The gentleman with the big conk?
TONY:	(SHOCKED) (ASIDE) The gentleman with the—?!... Lemon! — How many times must I tell you not to speak disrespectfully of our clients?!... In any case, that's not the one. It's the gentleman next to the gentleman with the big conk.
LEMON:	Right, sir.
TONY:	Now — the next item is— ... Pemble — hand me the next highly desirable article of household furnishing, will you?
PEMBLE:	(OLD, THIN VOICE) Yes, Mr Hancock — here you are... sir...
TONY:	Thank you. Now gentlemen — next we have this — this beautifully hand-carved and French-polished — er — this well-appointed... this (ASIDE) Pemble — what is it?
PEMBLE:	I'm — er — I'm afraid I don't know, Mr H. I seem to have mislaid my catalogue and—

```
TONY:              (ASIDE) Never mind… (OUT) What am
                   I offered for this exotic item?

INSISTENT VOICE:       (AFTER PAUSE) What is it?

TONY:              What is— (SLIGHT LAUGH) Come,
                   come, my friends — surely that's
                   quite obvious. This is a — a
                   household effect without which
                   no occasional table would be
                   complete. Note, for instance,
                   this little door in the side
                   here… I'll just open it and—

FX:                CLICK. MUSICAL BOX STARTS
                   PLAYING. HOLD UNDER.

TONY:              (SURPRISED) Oh, so that's what it
                   is…! (OUT)… and immediately the
                   themes of the great masters issue
                   forth. This of course stops when
                   we close the door like th— When
                   we close the door … close the—

FX:                MUSIC STOPS

TONY:              Ah — there we are. Now, gentlemen
                   — what am I offered for—

INSISTENT VOICE:    What abaht the door in the
                   other side?

TONY:              Ah — you mean the other little
                   door…? Well, ah — when I open
                   the other lit—

FX:                CONTINUOUS CUCKOO SOUND. AS PER
                   CUCKOO CLOCK. HOLD UNDER

TONY:              (SLIGHT LAUGH) We — er — hear
                   one of the lovely bird calls of
```

the English countryside. I'll
just close this— I'll just close
the… the… Pemble — how do you
stop this?

PEMBLE: I — er — I don't know, Mr H.
Lemon — you do something!

LEMON: Well, <u>I</u> don't know. P'raps if you
open this other—

FX: MUSIC BOX STARTS AGAIN, WITH
CUCKOO CLOCK

TONY: Now look what you've done! For
Goodness sake— (GENERAL ARGUMENT
BETWEEN THE THREE, AS SOUNDS
CONTINUE. ALL STOP TOGETHER ON
DOING! OF SPRING)

TONY: (SLIGHT PAUSE) Lot withdrawn.
Well, gentlemen — I think that's
all for— … Oh, no — one more
item here and a very handsome
piece too. Gentlemen — what am
I offered for this ornate clock
by — er — let me see… Oh, yes
— by Tempus Fugit… complete in
pillared marble case supported on
each side by two carved figures
of… er… of two nudist ladies?
What do I hear? What am I—

VOICE: (OFF) Ten pounds.

TONY: Ten pounds I hear… any advance on
ten pounds?

VOICE: Twelve ten.

VOICE:	(AMERICAN) Fifteen.
TONY:	Fifteen pounds I hear! Any advance on fifteen pounds…? No — Going at fifteen pounds… Going, going, gone!
FX:	GAVEL ON DESK
TONY:	Get the gentleman's name and address, Lemon…
LEMON:	Yes, sir.
TONY:	(OUT) And gentlemen… may I remind you that tomorrow's sale of the remainder of the furniture and effects commences at the usual time, three o'clock… and that the beautiful period house of the Late Mr Postlethwaite is for sale by Private Purchase. Particulars and order-to-view obtainable at my office. Goodnight.
OMNES:	CONFUSED MURMUR OF VOICES GOING OFF AS THE SALE ROOM CLEARS
FX:	DOOR OPENS AND SHUTS OFF SEVERAL TIMES AS VOICES FADE
TONY:	Well, Pemble. Not a bad day's sale eh?
PEMBLE:	No, sir. Shall I clear up now?
TONY:	Yes — we'll check the accounts back at the office.
PEMBLE:	Right, Mr H (GOING OFF). Lemon — have you got those address slips…? (HE AND LEMON TALK

INDISTINCTLY AS MADKIN COMES IN,
THEN FADE AND STOP)

FX: DOOR OPENS

MADKIN: Evening, Mr Hancock.

TONY: Good evening, Mr Madkin. We
               shan't be a moment clearing up.
               And it's arranged that we start
               at the same time tomorrow, eh?

MADKIN: Yes. Ah'll get Charlie to open
               up for you, as I may not be here
               when you start. I've got to go
               to the reading of my Aunt's will,
               up in London, in the morning.

TONY: Your Aunt's died? Oh, I'm sorry
               to hear that.

MADKIN: Oh, nowt to be sorry about. Ah
               never met her but once and that
               were twenty year ago. Right, well
               if you lock up when you… Here.
               (PAUSE AS IF LOOKING AROUND)
               Where's my clock?

TONY: Clock? There was no clock here,
               Mr Madkin, except the one we sold
               in the—

MADKIN: You—! You sold my clock!!

TONY: (HORRIFIED) That was your
               clock?!… The one in the marble
               case?

MADKIN: Yes — it bloomin' well was, and—

TONY: Mr Madkin — I'm terribly sorry… I
               had no idea—

MADKIN:	Never mind about bein' sorry. Hancock — I want that clock back. I only bought it two days ago — specially for this sale room.
TONY:	But — I can't get it back immediately. It will take a little time to find the purchaser…
MADKIN:	Well — get it back by tomorrow… And if you don't, you know what?
TONY:	(MISERABLY) No. What?
MADKIN:	(THREATENING) Can you imagine what it would be like if people found out that the town's auctioneer — a man who's standing for Councillor — who might even be a Councillor by tomorrow — has sold the Sale Room clock… By mistake? Can you imagine that?
TONY:	(MISERABLY) Yes. Unfortunately I can.
MADKIN:	(GOING OFF) Right then. Don't forget. By the time I get back tomorrow.
FX:	DOOR OPENS AND CLOSES
PEMBLE:	(OFF)… and this is the last one. Right, Lemon, you can go now.
LEMON:	(OFF) Thanks, Mr Pemble. (CALLS) Goodnight, Mr Hancock.
FX:	DOOR OPENS AND CLOSES.
PEMBLE:	(APPROACHING) Well — that seems

	to be everything, Mr— What's the matter, Mr Hancock — have you a headache?
TONY:	Pemble — I have the grandfather of all headaches.
PEMBLE:	What do you mean, sir?
TONY:	That clock we sold… the last lot — was Mr Madkin's.
PEMBLE:	Mr Madkin's?
TONY:	Yes. Unless I get it back by tomorrow, he's going to tell everyone and I shall be the laughing stock of the town. (PULLING HIMSELF TOGETHER) Well — I won't do anything by just sitting here. Have you the address there of the man who bought it?
PEMBLE:	Yes, Mr H… Just a moment — Ah, here we are… er… William Glass, 218 Merton Boulevard.
TONY:	Merton Boulevard? Where's that?
PEMBLE:	Los Angeles, California, USA.
TONY:	(GROANS) Ohhh…
PEMBLE:	Oh, wait a minute, sir — there's a note here. He's an American Sergeant from Littlewood Camp but he's on leave at the moment, staying at the Royal Hotel.
TONY:	The Royal? That's at the end of the Esplanade, isn't it? Come on, Pemble… my car's outside.

PEMBLE: But how are you going to get the clock back, sir?

TONY: Oh, I'll spin some story about repairs. I don't care what, as long as I get it back before these elections are over.
Then I'll worry about the rest. Come on — I think it's stopped raining.

ORCHESTRA: MUSIC STARTS

TONY: I don't want to miss him.

ORCHESTRA: LINK

HOTEL CLERK: (YOUTHFUL NERVOUS VOICE) But Madame — the Manager definitely told me — no dogs in the hotel.

MRS SCOWLEY: (IMPERIAL DOWAGER) What!! No dogs?! Stuff and nonsense…! I've been staying at this hotel off and on for years and I've always brought Puffikins with me… (ASIDE) There, there, Puffikins, Mummy is wiv oo… Isn't that so, Myrtle?

MYRTLE: (TIMID, THIN-VOICED LADY'S COMPANION) Yes, Mrs Scowley.

MRS SCOWLEY: Really — the Royal was never like this in Mr Pevensey's day.

CLERK: But, Madam—

MRS SCOWLEY: And another thing — I shall expect the usual service every morning. A cup of senna pod tea

	at seven sharp. The doctor says it's <u>most</u> important for me. Isn't that so, Myrtle?
MYRTLE:	Yes, Mrs Scowley.
CLERK:	(SUBMISSIVELY) Certainly, madam. Shall I get the porter to carry your luggage upstairs?
MRS SCOWLEY:	Certainly not. We can easily manage between us. Myrtle — you take the two suitcases and I'll carry Puffikins. (GOING OFF) You can come back for the trunk later.
MYRTLE:	(EVEN FURTHER OFF) Yes, Mrs Scowley.
CLERK:	(MUTTERING IN IMITATION OF MRS SCOWLEY) Dere, dere Puffikins — Mummy is wiv 'oo… Nyah…!
TONY:	(APPROACHING) (CLEARS THROAT) Excuse me—
CLERK:	(BRIGHTENING) Hello, Mr Hancock. What can I do for you?
TONY:	I understand you have a Mr Glass staying here… Sgt Glass.
CLERK:	Sgt Glass? Oh, yes, sir — he's in the cocktail bar at the moment. Through there…
TONY:	Thank you. (ASIDE) Pemble — wait here, will you? I won't be a minute.
PEMBLE:	Right, Mr Hancock.

FX: GLASS AND	BUTTON DOOR OPENS WITH A CLICK
GLADYS:	(CONVERSATION. GLADYS LAUGHING IN A HIGH-PITCHED COCKNEY VOICE)
TONY:	(COUGHS) Er — excuse me… could you tell me if a Sgt Glass is anywhere about?
GLASS:	(CHEERFUL AMERICAN) Yeah — I'm Bill Glass. What— hey, if it isn't the Auctioneer guy with the little hammer. Bang, bang, going, going, gone! Hey, Gladys? (LAUGHS) Well, glad to see you, Mr—
TONY:	Hancock.
GLASS:	Hancock. Mr Hancock — I want you to meet… well, I guess you'd describe her as a girlfriend of a friend of mine — Miss Gladys Coates.
TONY:	How do you do, Miss Coates?
GLADYS:	(STILTED COCKNEY VOICE) Charmed, I'm sure.
TONY:	Excuse us, Miss Coates but I'd like a word with—
GLADYS:	'Ere — 'aven't I seen you somewhere before?
TONY:	Er — no. I don't think we've met, Madam. Sgt Glass — I wonder if I could—
GLADYS:	'Ere — I remember… my sister's barmaid at the Rose and Crown.

	Aren't you the one who's always pinchin' 'er—
TONY:	(QUICK MIRTHLESS LAUGH, CUTTING HER OFF) No, no, dear lady… You must have the wr—
GLASS:	Oh, come on, Gladys — I'm sure Mr Hancock here couldn't be the person who's always pinching your sister.
TONY:	Of course not. A clear case of mistaken identity. It must have been some <u>other</u> girl. I— I mean some other man. Now, Sgt Glass, I wonder if Miss Coates would mind us having a word in private.
GLASS:	Of course not, Mr Hancock. Let's go over here… Excuse us a moment, dear… (CALLING. PAUSE) Now…
TONY:	Er — it's about that clock you bought, Sgt. The valuers have been on from London and they want it back for a few vital repairs…
GLASS:	Repairs — what's wrong?
TONY:	Oh — er — only a minor thing… just needs a little adjustment, you know…
GLASS:	What sort of adjustment?
TONY:	Well, the — ah — I — the… Well, the fliddle wheel isn't disbursed on the plodden-spring, you see, and the— (CONTINUES AD LIB)

GLASS: Mr Hancock… (TONY CONTINUES) Mr
            Hancock! (TONY STOPS) Mr Hancock
            — do you know what my hobby was
            back in the States?

TONY: No. What?

GLASS: Clock repairing.

TONY: Oh? — Erm — clock repairing. Well
            — what a jolly interesting hob—

GLASS: (INSISTENT) And there is no such
            thing as a fliddle wheel, or, for
            that matter, a plodden spring.

TONY: No such— … Ah, come now — what I
            meant was a … erm… a— … (RESIGNED,
            AFTER PAUSE) Ah, well, you might
            as well know the truth. That
            clock belonged to the owner of the
            hotel. I sold it by mistake.

GLASS: You s— (LAUGHS LOUDLY)

TONY: (BITTERLY) Yes, it's all very
            funny, isn't it?

GLASS: (LAUGH DYING OUT) I'm sorry…
            (SERIOUS) No, I'm really sorry,
            Mr Hancock. It's just that— … but
            anyway — surely it can't be all
            that serious?

TONY: Can't it? Local Auctioneer
            sells Sale Room clock. Imagine
            what a laughing-stock I'd be if
            it came out. And I'm standing
            for Councillor in tomorrow's
            elections as well.

GLASS: Well, I'd like to help you, sir — but I've already given it away, you see.

TONY: Given it away?

GLASS: Yes. — I got engaged to a girl a few days ago and I bought the clock because I thought it would make a nice present for her father. To tell you the truth, I thought it would sweeten him up a bit... he isn't exactly eager to have me as a son-in-law. I took it around straight away. Tripfield's his name... Mr Ambrose Tripfield.

TONY: Oooooh.

GLASS: You know him?

TONY: Know him?!... He's the leader of the party I'm standing for in tomorrow's elections!

GLASS: <u>Oh no</u>... say, that's bad luck. Incidentally — which ward are you standing for?

TONY: How do you know about the wards here?

GLASS: Well — that's why I'm asking. You see — I and a few of the other fellows have volunteered to drive some of the voters to the Polls at the Town Hall... er — for some fellow named Grimthorpe, in the Grimley Street Ward.

337

TONY: Grimthorpe?!… He's my opponent!
GLASS: Say! — You're standing against
          Grimthorpe?!… What a coincidence.
          You know — I'm sorry I said
          I'd help his supporters because
          I like you, Hanky — you're a
          straight-forward guy. I wish
          I could help you in some
          way.
TONY: Well… er… thank you. But I'm
          afraid you can't. You see — I
          haven't a chance. Grimthorpe has
          always won that ward, by a good
          majority. (PAUSE, SIGHS) Ah, well
          — I suppose I'd better go and
          try to get this clock back from
          Mr Tripfield.
GLASS: (SLIGHTLY OFF) Well, goodbye,
          Hanky — and if I can think of
          anything to help tomorrow, I will.
TONY: (NOT VERY CHEERFULLY) Thank you,
          Sergeant. And goodbye.
FX: SAME DOOR AS BEFORE
PEMBLE: (OFF) Well, Mr Hancock? Did you
          get the clock?
TONY: No. He's given it to his
          prospective father-in-law. And
          his prospective father-in-law is
          Mr Tripfield.
PEMBLE: What?!... Oh, but Mr Hancock
          — Mr Tripfield is the head of

	the Progressives here — and he's almost certain to be the next Mayor!
TONY:	I know, Pemble… I know… Well, come on — I can but try. I'll give you a lift back to the office. I'll go and make this speech in the Drill Hall and then I'll call round at Mr Tripfield's later on…
FX:	OUTSIDE DOOR. TRAFFIC NOISES
TONY:	And remind me to get some petrol, will you?... otherwise—
SMALL BOY:	(SLIGHTLY OFF) Nah — the Old Crocks Race goes to Brighton, so it can't be one of them.
2ND SMALL BOY:	Oh. 'Ere — I wonder if it goes by steam? A lot of them very old cars go by steam, you know, 'cause…
TONY:	(SHARPLY) That's enough! Desist! Go away at once, little boys!
BOYS:	(MUTTER AND GIGGLE OFF)
PEMBLE:	(CACKLES)
TONY:	Pemble…! (PEMBLE STOPS)… I see nothing humorous about my car. I've told you before, a good vintage model is far more reliable than these tinpot modern cars. You'd better get in the back with the books.

PEMBLE:	Right, Mr Hancock.
FX:	TWO ANCIENT CAR DOORS OPEN AND SLAM. WHEEZY STARTER. FIRST TIME FAILS. SECOND TIME, ANCIENT ENGINE STARTS UP, BACKFIRES A COUPLE OF TIMES. GEARS CRASH AND CAR CLATTERS AWAY. TWO HONKS OF AN OLD BULB HORN, OVER ENGINE. FADES INTO MUSIC
ORCHESTRA:	LINK
FX:	PHONE RINGS. RECEIVER UP
TRIPFIELD:	Tripfield here… who…? Oh, hello Dawson. What…? His speeches… Yes, I… Yes, I know he's been promising world peace and a new Atlantic Charter… Eh…? No, I didn't know he was going to have a personal chat with Stalin. Hm…? But Dawson, I'm in between the devil and the deep blue sea. — What can I do? If he's not elected we've lost the seat; if he is elected we've got Hancock. Anyway, he won't get in. It'd take more than Hancock to beat Grimthorpe in that ward. Goodbye.
FX:	PHONE DOWN
MRS TRIPFIELD:	Really, Ambrose — I do think you're rather unkind to Mr Hancock. He has such nice eyes.
TRIPFIELD:	(SARCASTICALLY) Such nice eyes… I

suppose you think we'd do better in this country to elect our politicians for their looks?

MRS TRIPFIELD: (QUIETLY) Well, we couldn't do much worse, could we?

TRIPFIELD: Really, Phyllis... sometimes I get the impression that you think you'd make a better Mayor of this town than I would. (LONG PAUSE) Well?

MRS TRIPFIELD: (SMOOTHLY) I think there's someone at the door, dear.

TRIPFIELD: Hm?

FX: DISTANT KNOCKING

TRIPFIELD: Oh, yes.

FX: LIVING ROOM DOOR OPENS. PAUSE. FRONT DOOR OPENS

TRIPFIELD: Yes?

TONY: Ermm... Good evening.

TRIPFIELD: Hancock?!... What the—... Er — come in. Come in!

TONY: Thank you.

FX: FRONT DOOR SHUTS. PAUSE. LIVING ROOM DOOR SHUTS

TRIPFIELD: It's Mr Hancock, dear.

TONY: Good evening, Mrs Tripfield.

MRS TRIPFIELD: Why, Mr Hancock — how are you? You look quite chilly. Would you like a cup of tea or something?

TONY: No, thank you very much... I can only stay a moment.

TRIPFIELD: Well, Hancock…? Something wrong
               about tomorrow? I shall be seeing
               you at the Town Hall, no doubt.

TONY: Oh, no, Mr Tripfield. It's about
               the clock.

TRIPFIELD: The Town Hall clock? What's wrong
               with it?

TONY: No, sir — the clock that Sgt
               Glass bought at the sale this
               afternoon and gave to you.

TRIPFIELD: Oh, that. Well — what about it?

TONY: Well, sir — the — er — the
               valuers rang me from London and
               said there are some important
               repairs to be made before it's
               sold — only they didn't ring
               me until after it was sold so
               as it was already sold the
               repairs couldn't be made before
               it was sold and they said I'd
               have to collect it after it
               was sold and get — I'd — er
               — the repairs… (TRAILS OFF
               INTO SILENCE)

MRS TRIPFIELD: (AFTER SLIGHT PAUSE) Shall
               I get you an aspirin,
               Mr Hancock?

TRIPFIELD: But the clock is working
               perfectly well.

TONY: Well — ah — yes — now… but if
               this adjustment isn't made it

	will — er — break down completely in a few days.
TRIPFIELD:	Sounds most peculiar to me. Did they say what was wrong?
TONY:	Well, yes — you <u>see</u> — the…
TRIPFIELD:	The what?
TONY:	(DESPERATELY) Ah — the burge-wheel is… out of alignment with the… flongle-ratchet… and… and if this isn't adjusted, then… (SUDDEN BURST OF INSPIRATION) then the spancheon-lever will dis-clutch the Parkinson's bloat-balance.
TRIPFIELD:	Sounds Double Dutch to me.
TONY:	It is — I mean you see how serious it is.
TRIPFIELD:	Hm. (PAUSE) What was that first thing again?
TONY:	The fir… (SLIGHT LAUGH)… Oh — erm — the cronge-wheel.
TRIPFIELD:	I thought you said the burge-wheel?
TONY:	Well — that's the Austrian name for it. (BRIGHTLY) I suppose it's all a matter of taste, don't you…? (PAUSE) (NO ONE ANSWERS)… Yes.
TRIPFIELD:	Well, I suppose you'd better take it. It's on the cupboard over there…

TONY:	Thank you, Mr Tripfield. You see, they're calling at my place first thing in the morning so I have to take it now, and—
TRIPFIELD:	Yes, yes — I'll see you off.
FX:	DRAWING ROOM DOOR OPENS
TONY:	Thank you, sir. Goodnight, Mrs Tripfield.
MRS TRIPFIELD:	(OFF) Goodnight, Mr Hancock. And best of luck for tomorrow.
TONY:	Thank you, ma'am.
FX:	FRONT DOOR OPENS. FOOTSTEPS ON STONE STAIRS
TONY:	Well, goodnight, Mr Tripfield. No need to come outside.
TRIPFIELD:	That's alright, Hancock. I … Oh, I see you have your car.
TONY:	Er — yes, yes, I have.
TRIPFIELD:	Well — try to start it quietly, will you… My sister's children are staying with us and I don't want to wake them.
TONY:	I quite understand.
FX:	CAR DOOR OPENS AND SLAMS. WHEEZY STARTER FOR QUITE A TIME, THEN DEAFENING EXPLOSION
TONY:	(EMBARRASSED LAUGH) It — it seems to have broken down.
TRIPFIELD:	(SARCASTICALLY) It does, doesn't it? Hancock — I asked you to be quiet and—

TONY:	(HURRIEDLY) It's quite alright, Mr Tripfield. I'll leave the car here and walk.
TRIPFIELD:	But you can't walk through the streets carrying a clock!
TONY:	Oh, yes, sir — I'll hide it under my coat like this. And there's no one around at this time of night.
TRIPFIELD:	(GOING OFF) Oh, alright… goodnight, Hancock. And — er — (GRUFFLY, RELUCTANTLY) (OFF) Best of luck for tomorrow.
TONY:	Thank you, Mr Tripfield. Goodnight.
ORCHESTRA:	'WALKING' LINK. FADE UNDER AND IN TIME WITH—
FX:	STEADY FOOTSTEPS ON PAVEMENT. HOLLOW, ON SLIGHT ECHO. HOLD UNDER
TONY:	SINGS QUIETLY IN TIME WITH HIS FOOTSTEPS
FX:	ANOTHER SET OF FOOTSTEPS, APPROACHING. THEY SLOW AND STOP
DR QUINCE:	Hello, Hancock.
FX:	TONY'S FOOTSTEPS SLOW AND STOP
TONY:	Oh, good evening, Dr Quince. (GOING OFF) Lovely night. (STARTS SINGING AGAIN)
QUINCE:	Just a second, Hancock. Surely you can spare a moment for a few words with an old friend.

TONY:	(HURRIEDLY) Oh — ah — yes. Lovely night, isn't it? Rather chilly though — probably snow tomorrow — Well — must be off now and—
QUINCE:	(QUIETLY INTERRUPTING) Rather unusual for you to be wandering abroad at this time of night, isn't it?
TONY:	Well — my car broke down you see, and I—
QUINCE:	(INCREDULOUS) That car of yours broke down, Hancock?! I can hardly <u>believe</u> it. Incidentally — I don't want to be curious, but… just what are you carrying under your coat?
TONY:	Under my…? Oh, this…? Oh, just some — some laundry. It's not wrapped, you see and I didn't want to be seen walking along with a pile of shirts, so I put them under my coat and— Well, I must be off, now, bec—
QUINCE:	Your laundry, eh?
TONY:	Yes — (SLIGHT LAUGH) — laundry…
FX:	WHIRRING SOUND THAT A CLOCK MAKES BEFORE IT STRIKES. THEN CLOCK STRIKES TEN, SLOWLY
QUINCE:	Unless I'm very much mistaken, Hancock, your laundry is ten minutes fast.

TONY:	Well, I must be off n—
CLODLEY:	(APPROACHING, LOUD AND BREEZY) 'Allo! 'Allo! 'Allo Doctor Quince — by the way your car's nearly ready. 'Allo…! Who's this…? Not the Prime Minister 'imself — the Right Honourable A.J. 'Ancock, eh? (LAUGHS LOUDLY) Eh? The Right Honourable, eh? (LAUGHS)
TONY:	(DISTANTLY) Good evening, Mr Clodley.
CLODLEY:	Well, well — and what is the great Councillor-to-be doing around at this time, eh?
QUINCE:	He's taking his clock to be washed.
CLODLEY:	Takin' 'is clock to be washed? Well, well — you'd think a Councillor-to-be could wash 'is own clock, wouldn't you? Although it's not a very pretty clock to look at in the mirror, is it, eh? (LAUGHS) Is it, eh? Eh? (LAUGHS)
QUINCE:	I was going to stay and hold a brief discussion with you, Hancock, but I'm afraid a certain person's laugh here is driving me on into the night. (GOING OFF) Good evening.
CLODLEY:	(GOING OFF) Wait a minute, Dr Quince — I'll come with you.

QUINCE:	No, no — Mr Clodley. I can assure you I shall be quite safe on my own.
CLODLEY:	Oh, I don't mind walking with you for a—
QUINCE:	No, but I do— (THEY ARGUE OFF INTO MUSIC)
ORCHESTRA:	LINK
FX:	RATTLE OF KEYS. KEY IN LOCK. FRONT DOOR OPENS AND SHUTS. LIVING ROOM DOOR OPENS. THUD OF TONY PUTTING DOWN CLOCK ON SIDEBOARD.
TONY:	(SLIGHT EFFORT AS HE DOES SO) Phew…
AUNT:	(OFF) Anthony…! Is that you, Anthony?
TONY:	(CALLING) Yes, Aunt Amabel.
AUNT:	(APPROACHING) Ah — there you are. Anthony — you haven't got your scarf on and you're blue with cold—
TONY:	No, I'm alright, Auntie… I— (SNEEZES)
AUNT:	There you are… I told you to watch that cold. Colds can be very dangerous, Anthony… you must keep well wrapped-up when you've got a cold and keep dry and, above all, don't catch cold.

TONY: Yes, yes, Auntie — but isn't it
            time for you to—

AUNT: And then exercises are very
            important. For the bloodstream,
            you know. Dear Titus always used
            to do exercises. I remember him
            saying to me — Amabel, he said —
            he always used to call me Amabel,
            because that's my name, you see.
            Although why I'm telling you that
            I don't know because you know
            already. I must remember to get
            that curry powder. Anyway, Titus
            said: 'Amabel — do exercises
            every morning like I do and
            you'll live for ever.' I remember
            him saying it: 'Do exercises
            every day and you'll live for
            ever.' That was in March 1927. No
            — it was in February 27 because
            we buried him in March.

TONY: Yes, Auntie, but I'm alr—

AUNT: Anthony! You remembered!

TONY: Remembered?

AUNT: Yes — you remembered my birthday!

TONY: Your birthday…? Oh — oh, yes, of
            course… M-many happy returns.

AUNT: Thank you, dear. (DELIGHTED) And
            you've bought me the one thing I
            wanted — a clock!

TONY: Oh, no, Auntie — that's not—

AUNT:	How clever of you to remember me mentioning that I wanted a clock. Especially as only today I remembered that I'd forgotten to mention it.
TONY:	No, Auntie — this… this isn't your present. It's a clock I had to collect for repair.
AUNT:	(ALMOST IN TEARS) It… it isn't my present…?
TONY:	(HURRIEDLY) No, but I've — I've bought you a clock… only… only it wasn't ready today. I have to collect it from the shop tomorrow.
AUNT:	(DELIGHTED) Tomorrow?! … So you <u>have</u> bought me a clock after all! (EXCITEDLY) Is it a nice clock…? As big as this one?
TONY:	Oh, yes — as big as this one.
AUNT:	Oh, how wonderful. And I thought you were going to buy me the usual cheap little thing that people buy, like a box of handkerchiefs.
TONY:	(SEMI-ASIDE) So did I — I mean — yes, it's a nice big clock.
AUNT:	Oh, Anthony — how sweet of you. I'm sure it's going to be dreadfully expensive.
TONY:	I'm sure it is.
AUNT:	I was only thinking today there

isn't a clock in the house, apart from the ones in the bedrooms and the one in the hall and the one in here and the three in the lounge. Well — I must be off to bed now. I have to get to sleep early so that I can get up <u>very</u> early in the morning so I shall be tired enough to get to sleep early tomorrow night. Oh, by the way — this clock you're taking for repair is fast, you know. It's only just ten o'clock. You'll hear the clocks strike in a moment. Goodnight, Anthony.

TONY: Goodnight, Auntie.

FX: DRAWING ROOM DOOR CLOSES. (PAUSE) WHIRRING. ONE CLOCK BEGINS TO STRIKE, IN DISTANCE. THEN ANOTHER. THEN SEVERAL AT ONCE, ALL DIFFERENT TONES

TONY: (RISING TONE OF EXASPERATION, INTO MUSIC) Clocks… clocks…! <u>CLOCKS</u>!!!

ORCHESTRA: LINK. STARTS LOUD. FAIRLY LONG. (LONG, VARIED LINK) TAKES ACTION TO FOLLOWING AFTERNOON

VOICE: (OFF) Eight pound ten!

2ND VOICE: (OFF) A tenner!

TONY: One tenner I hear…! Any advance on ten golden sovereigns for Lot

	65 — one handsome oak bedside table with handy-sized cupboard?
3RD VOICE:	Guineas!
TONY:	Ten guineas that gentleman offers me… Any advance on ten pounds and ten silver shillings…? No… Going then at ten guineas… going, going, gone!
FX:	GAVEL ON DESK
OMNES:	MURMUR OF CONVERSATION STARTS AND FADES UNDER FOLLOWING DIALOGUE
TONY:	Lemon — get that gentleman's address for Lot 65.
LEMON:	Yes, Mr Hancock.
TONY:	Now, Pemble — any more?
PEMBLE:	Only that Lot left over from yesterday, Mr Hancock. (CONFIDENTIALLY) By the way — I see you got the clock back.
TONY:	Yes — but I haven't been able to find Madkin so far. I don't think he's back yet. Still, I'm alright as long as—
LEMON:	(HALF WHISPER) Mr Hancock!
TONY:	Don't interrupt, Lemon. As I was saying — I'm alright as long as Tripfield doesn't come in. Now, Lemon — what is it?
LEMON:	(SAME VOICE) Mr Tripfield's just come in, sir.
TONY:	I knew it. That does it. The

	clock! — Quick, Pemble — give me the clock!
PEMBLE:	Here you are, sir.
TONY:	Now — you keep him in conversation while I slip out of the side door. I may be able to find Madkin if he's back. Try and keep the crowd here.
PEMBLE:	Right, sir.
OMNES:	AS PEMBLE SPEAKS, BRING GENERAL CONVERSATION UP A LITTLE
FX:	DOOR OPENS AND SHUTS
OMNES:	AS DOOR SHUTS, CONVERSATION IS CUT OFF
BARMAN:	(WELL OFF) Maisie — hurry up and get them glasses polished. We're open in five minutes.
MAISIE:	(EVEN FURTHER OFF) Right, Charlie.
TONY:	Ah — Charles. Has Mr Madkin returned yet?
BARMAN:	Yes, Mr Hancock... he's about somewhere. I think he—
MADKIN:	(OFF, LOUDLY, GENIALLY AND PARTLY DRUNK) <u>Hancock</u>!!
TONY:	Ah, Mr Madkin — I've brought your cl—
MADKIN:	Hancock — you must have a drink with me.
TONY:	Well — er — later, Mr Madkin. I haven't finished the sale yet.

MADKIN:	Well, don't forget because I'm celebrating. You mind the Aunt I told you about?
TONY:	Yes.
MADKIN:	Well, she left quite a nice little packet. And d'you know who she left it to…? Me! George Madkin.
TONY:	Oh — congratulations, Mr Madkin. But look — I've brought your clock back.
MADKIN:	My clock? That thing? — 's'not fit for a man of means… Keep it, Hancock. (GOING OFF) Keep it! I was very sharp with you yesterday. So take it…! A present from me… Keep it! (STARTS SINGING OFF INTO DISTANCE)
TONY:	(CALLING) But Mr Madkin— … Mr— (TO HIMSELF)… Well, I suppose he means it…
FX:	DOOR OPENS. CONVERSATION IS HEARD AGAIN. DOOR SHUTS
PEMBLE:	Ah — here's Mr Hancock now, sir.
TRIPFIELD:	Ah — Hancock… I've been looking for you.
TONY:	Good afternoon, Mr Tripfield… I'm sorry I wasn't able to be at the Town Hall during the afternoon but the sale was already

	arranged. And here's your clock, sir — I've had it seen to.
TRIPFIELD:	Thank you, thank you — but that wasn't what I came about. Er — may I take your place on the platform for a moment?
TONY:	Of course, sir.
TRIPFIELD:	Thank you…
FX:	GAVEL ON DESK
TRIPFIELD:	Gentlemen… gentlemen… If I may crave your indulgence for a few moments. I came here with some private news for Mr Hancock but as you're all here I may as well make a public announcement. Apart from — ah — my own re-election today…
OMNES:	MILD APPLAUSE
TRIPFIELD:	…Mr Hancock here was elected Councillor for the Grimley Street ward …
OMNES:	MILD CHEERS
TRIPFIELD:	… by a majority of one vote!
OMNES:	LOUD, RATHER IRONICAL CHEERS
TONY:	Thank you, sir. I'm naturally delighted, Mr Tripfield… but at the same time, I must admit I'm rather — er — rather surprised as well.
TRIPFIELD:	Well, to be quite candid, Hancock — so am I. I don't want to

detract from your victory in any way whatsoever but a strange thing happened today.

TONY: What was that?

TRIPFIELD: Well… as you may know — several of the American officers at the camp very kindly lent their cars for the purpose of driving voters to the Polls and some of their other ranks volunteered to drive these cars. Five of them had arranged to drive some of your opponent… er… Mr Grimthorpe's supporters to the Town Hall — as a matter of fact, a young man who wants to marry my daughter… Sgt Glass — a wild young man of whom I cannot approve — was one of them… and — er — and these voters never recorded their votes.

TONY: Why not, Mr Tripfield?

TRIPFIELD: Well — because they never reached the Town Hall. You see — these American drivers — including this young man Glass — lost their way… Apparently they found themselves up on the Downs… the drivers stopped at a local tavern for directions… the voters followed them in… and…

TONY: (PAUSE) And, sir?

TRIPFIELD: And… er… well… a Mr Biggin, for
               instance, who has been a staunch
               Reform Party supporter for forty
               years was last heard shouting
               'Up the Progressives' and singing
               'Nellie Dean' at the top of his
               voice. However — I don't want to
               interrupt your sale any longer.
               Have the clock taken up to my
               house, will you?

TONY: Yes, Mr Tripfield. Goodbye.

TRIPFIELD: (GOING OFF) Goodbye.

FX: DOOR OPENS AND CLOSES.
               CONVERSATION UP.

TONY: Well, gentlemen… I must apologise
               for that delay. But we shall now
               conclude today's sale by offering
               this final lot which was held
               over by general request from
               yesterday — I mean — this highly
               desirable lot… A beautifully
               carved, hand-finished object
               without which no occasional table
               would be complete. As you will
               see, there are small doors on
               either side. I won't open them at
               the moment but I'll just hold it
               up so that you can—

FX: MUSIC BOX STARTS. HOLD UNDER

TONY: What the—! Pemble — this—

```
FX:              CUCKOO STARTS. HOLD UNDER
TONY:            This thing's started to — Lemon!
                 Do something! Pemble — can't you—
LEMON AND PEMBLE:  START TALKING AT THE SAME
                 TIME WITH TONY'S LAST SPEECH.
                 CONTINUE, WITH MUSIC BOX AND
                 CUCKOO, INTO MUSIC
ORCHESTRA:       UP AND OUT
```

Appendix Three

SYNOPSIS FOR EPISODE 2 OF *VACANT LOT*

VERY BRIEF SYNOPSIS OF SECOND PROGRAMME FOR SUGGESTED TONY HANCOCK SERIES[1]

Tony, now a Councillor, is appointed head of Churdley Bay's Entertainment's Committee. No one else wants the job, as for more years than anyone cares to remember, Councillors have been trying to attract visitors and tourists to this broken-down resort. Tony accepts, partly because he feels it is a position of importance, and secondly because the Mayor and his cronies tempt him with ideas about putting on a concert party, organising a beauty competition, etc.

Tony sets about the job with great enthusiasm, composing an opening chorus for the concert party and insisting on singing it to everyone he meets. He also, in his office that afternoon, composes an advertisement to be inserted in a London newspaper. At the same time, he amuses himself by writing an advert, based on the town as it really is, and reads it out to his clerk and office-boy. It runs on the lines of: '... yes... Churdley Bay, resort of bankrupts and international unknowns... doze lazily in the cool shadows of the Hurpington Road Gasworks... picnic luxuriously on the smooth slopes of the Blatston and Figlow By-Pass slagheaps... or float happily in the cool waters of our famous High Street static water tank. And all this misery for only twice what you would pay anywhere else...' Later in the afternoon, a friend calls and Tony picks up the sheet of paper and starts to read this to him. As he reads, and finds he is reading a perfectly normal advertisement, the awful truth dawns on him, and he realises that the office boy has taken the wrong copy to the office of the agency for the local newspaper. The arrangement is that they will phone it through, and the advert will appear in the following day's paper. Therefore − he cannot cancel it and must find his office boy, who has been given the rest of the day off.

The story of the rest of the programme is his search for the boy, and includes an unfortunate encounter with the office boy's girlfriend, who describes herself as a 'hep chick who is sharp to the cool music'. While questioning her – in a milk-bar – he is discovered by the Mayor's wife. This is a terrible thing for Tony, who is now a Councillor (and keeps reminding people that he is) and has a position of respectability to keep up.

In the end, he fails to find the office-boy until it is too late. The advert appears in a London paper... and to Tony's amazement, the place is swamped with advance bookings for the season. However, he is congratulated by everyone on an astounding and daring idea.

Appendix Four

CHARACTER NAMES

CHARACTER NAMES

This list of character names was created by Larry Stephens for use in his scriptwriting.[1]

D. Khyber Chaddock
Jedwell Mullet
Dawlish Horsefeed
Russell Sponge
Fynmold Hake
Lt. Gen. Julip D. Schmohead
Hamish Pitt McLint
Hobbett Fawning
Gannett Kindle
Paisley Craw
Gurkwell Heartburn
Purgewright Chessitt, Jr.
Cheniscott Finnock
Latherwell Dardo
Madwell Strange
Sid Crimp
Nugent Foot
Langit Harlock
Kirksporran
Pipehaggis
Alvestone Slime
Digby Arabis
Guy Hardrider
Olcott Clung
Basil Nightjar

Sir Philpott Brym
Ozzie Snetchering
Jervis Fruit
Sir Patrick ('Paddy') Ballybullin
    (later Patrick ('Pat')
Ballybullin)
Colonel Mackenzie Purge
Ashley Cavern
Hawkieson Bunt
Timothy Daffil
Martin Pithergo
Dogwort Keyfarthing
'Ginger' Tubscullion
Duncan Rammish
Ulric Ur
Organ McGurke (an idiot studio
    attendant)
Cretin McDullard
    (an executive of the Variety
    Department)
Tollibut Squat
Japhet Dawkie
O. O. Codpeace
Arne van Slackery
Beresford Tench

Titus Hatchie

The Laird Dougal McRabbie
  Robdobbin

Diggory O'nion

Orville Grudgeon

Sir Hartley Straining

Aurelius Pid

Eddie Underblast

The Vicomte de la Pomme

Mrs Amplage

Cuthbert Puddy

'Strangler' Aagonschmidt

Shufflin' Jack

Major Hughie ('Dodo') Spalding

Raspley Blasthard (First
  Thunindusheetist with the
  London Philharmonic)

(Brigadier) Windlas DeFlate

Smelch & Preedy's Medicated

Carminative and Brackish Purge

Doris Gullet

Maisie Thwacker

Mrs Edna Cocoa

Florence Purfinger

Acknowledgements

This book wouldn't have been possible without the help of a great many people and I am incredibly grateful to them all. Far too many are sadly no longer with us.

First of all I would like to thank everyone who pledged and helped to make this a reality – you are all wonderful people.

Those who shared their memories with me included John Antrobus; Brad Ashton; Laura and Richard Brown; Pam Care; Angela Cole; Michael Deeley; Jimmy Dunning; Ray Galton; Helen Gibson; James Grafton; Sir Reginald Harland; Eric and Anne Loffman; Peter Lones; Roy and Jean Lones; Billy Moore; Denis Norden; Alan Simpson; Graham Stark; John Wall; Sally Watson; Peter Watson-Wood; and Rowan Wiltshire.

I visited archives all over the country and was assisted by very knowledgeable people, many of whom went above and beyond the call of duty: Trish Hayes and Louise North at the BBC Written Archives Centre; Birmingham Archives and Heritage Service; British Film Institute; Imperial War Museum; National Army Museum; David Nathan at the National Jazz Archive; David Baynham and Stephanie Bennett at the Royal Regiment of Fusiliers Museum (Royal Warwickshire); and Sandwell Council Community History & Archives Service.

Societies and people who helped to answer my questions were Rod Mackenzie at the Argyll and Sutherland Highlanders; Paul Baylis; Black Country Muse website; Geoffrey Buckingham; the Commando Association (especially Nick Collins, Andy Maines, Pete Rogers and Elaine Southworth-Davies); Laura Edwards; John Fisher; Marian Webb at Golders Green Crematorium; Cliff Goodwin; the Goon Show Preservation Society (in particular Mike Brown, Mark Cousins, John Repsch, Adrian Sherring, Colin Silk and Neil Trickey, whose *Encyclopædia Goonicus* is a masterpiece and a must-have resource for all *Goon Show* fans); GVA's Bob Bould, Annette Ireland, Kevin Marriott and Ian Stringer; Freddie Ross Hancock; The Hong Kong Heritage Project; C. M. Yip at the Hong Kong Jockey Club Archives; Mary Cox and Pete Mann at The International School And Community College; Reina James; Tracey Jennings Harding and Collys Jennings; Philip Kemp; Ted Kendall; Stephen Phillips at Kindred UK; Davie Lamont; Alan and Jackie Lane; Vernon Lawrence; Geoffrey Palmer; Robin Stott; Andrew Beckman at the Studebaker National Museum; the Tony Hancock Appreciation Society (particularly Tristan Brittain-Dissont, Tom Dommett, Tim Elms and Martin Gibbons); Frank Williams and Peter Yeldham.

The following earned my gratitude for their support/patience/advice/general fabulousness: Elliott Beaumont; Guy Bell; Toni Bettis; Simon Blackwell; British Comedy Guide; Angelique Budd; Pandora Busch; Donald Cameron of Lochiel; Anastasia Caramanis; David Davies; John Deering; Alison Dewell and the fellow who sits next to her on the settee; Nick Diamantopoulos; Stephen Donnison; John Dredge; Steve and Jayne Edwards; Mark and Martin Gale; Chris Jardine; Christine Jones; Mark Lancaster; Magpie Latham; Tessa Le Bars; Thomas Leamy; Neil McCowlen; Jon Morter; James Nason; *Newcastle Evening Chronicle*; Steve Newman; Audrey Nicholson; John-Michael O'Sullivan; Neil Pearson; Kevin Pocklington; Quinton Local History Society;

ACKNOWLEDGEMENTS

Kara Rennie; Lee Rulton; Norah Ryan; Peter Shirley; Southend Film Festival; Clemencia, William, Joseph and Peter Stoneman; Paul Tunkin; Unbound Social Club; Stephen Vasconcellos-Sharpe; Wickford Book Club; Elaine Worthington and Ron Youngman. My mum and dad, my cousin Debra and my friends Dreen, Jeweliette and Lisa have listened to me droning on about Larry Stephens for almost ten years – love you all; Dave Freak at the Birmingham Comedy Festival has put on some brilliant performances of *Vacant Lot* with the help of the hugely talented cast and crew of Janice Connolly, Dave Deakin, Mark Earby, Linda Hargreaves, James Hurn, Adam Jaremko, Jimm Rennie, Dave Stokes, Richard Usher and Nick Wiltshire (note to BBC: get them on the radio – they're fab!). Richard Hewitt, guardian of the Larry Stephens archive, was one of the most accommodating people I have ever met and became a dear friend. I miss him very much. Scott Pack will always be in my 'Top Ten of Favourite People'; Mark Bowsher and Maik Kleinschmidt at Rabbit Island Productions produced a wonderful promotional video for me; my former colleagues Vicki Logan, Lizbeth Muschamp, MVGF&EC Steve Reddish, Paul 'Shippers' Shipway, Lisa Spencer, Claire Watson and Craig 'CPW' Wilson ('SPL until I die') contributed to a very generous collection when I was made redundo and enabled me to buy stuff I needed for research purposes; everyone at Unbound has been GREAT but Ella Chappell, Phil Connor and Georgia Odd were particularly patient and helpful.

Finally, I'd like to thank Larry Stephens, who has made it possible for me to have some phenomenal experiences and helped me to find lots of new friends. How lucky I am.

Notes

1. Spike Milligan, personal interview with the Goon Show Preservation Society, 1988.

PART ONE: Glarnies – Quinton and Hinton
CHAPTER 1

1. Conversation between Larry Stephens and Tony Hancock described in *Hancock* by Freddie Hancock and David Nathan, BBC Books, 1986.
2. Hitchmough's *Black Country Pubs*, http://www.longpull.co.uk/.
3. 'District News: West Bromwich Magisterial Proceedings', *Birmingham Daily Post*, 20 May 1872, page 8.

CHAPTER 3

1. Paul Pry, 'Exploration', *The Hammer* (magazine of the CSS (Central Secondary School), Birmingham), Volume XI, No. 9, July 1930, Birmingham Archives.
2. *The Hammer* (magazine of the CSS, Birmingham), Volume XIII, No. 2, July 1939, Birmingham Archives.

PART TWO: Green Berets – Ticks and Mortars
CHAPTER 4

1. *Goon Show*, Series 8, Episode 9, 'The Policy', by Larry Stephens and Spike Milligan, 25 November 1957.
2. 'Naming of Parts' by Henry Reed, reproduced with kind permission of the Royal

Literary Fund.

3.   Brigadier John Gray, *Climbing the Army Ladder*, Xlibris Corporation, 2010.

CHAPTER 5

1.   Speech given by the Queen Mother at the unveiling of the Commando Memorial in 1952.

2.   The National Archives, Kew (TNA), CAB 120/414, Memo written to the Chiefs of Staff, 3 June 1940.

3.   The Reverend Joe Nicholl Manuscript, Documents 78/43/1, Imperial War Museum, with thanks to the Trustees of the Imperial War Museum for allowing access to the collection.

CHAPTER 6

1.   Bill Stoneman Snr, *From Mitcham Road To Mandalay*, diary, http://billstonemansnr.blogspot.com/.

CHAPTER 7

1.   *Third Jungle Book*, No. 9, March 1946, author's collection.

2.   Desmond Edward Crowden, Oral History 22675, 27 March 2002, Imperial War Museum, with thanks to the Trustees of the Imperial War Museum for allowing access to the collection.

CHAPTER 8

1.   Private Papers of Captain L. G. Stephens, Imperial War Museum, Documents 22513, with thanks to the Trustees of the Imperial War Museum for allowing access to the collection.

2.   John Wall, *Bognor Regis to Hong Kong*, unpublished diary.

3.   Private Papers of Captain L. G. Stephens, Imperial War Museum, Documents 22513, with thanks to the Trustees of the Imperial War Museum for allowing access to the collection.

4.   *Third Jungle Book*, No. 1, April 1944, author's collection.

CHAPTER 9

1. TNA, WO 218/67, No. 5 Commando War Diary, March 1944, appendix 1, operation order no. 1, sheet 4.
2. Rudy A. Blatt, *To Live... You Fight – A War Diary*, Collection of the Jewish Historical Museum in Amsterdam.
3. Ibid.

CHAPTER 10

1. Mick Collins, *Memories of 5 Troop, No. 5 Commando*, unpublished memoirs.
2. TNA, DEFE 2/554, Letter from David Shaw, 30 March 1944.

CHAPTER 11

1. Christoph von Fürer-Haimendorf, *The Men Who Hunted Heads – The Nagas of Assam*, film made for the BBC in 1970.
2. 'Living in the Jungle', *Intelligence Bulletin*, Vol. 02, No. 01, September 1943.
3. Desmond Edward Crowden, Imperial War Museum, Oral History 22675, 27 March 2002, with thanks to the Trustees of the Imperial War Museum for allowing access to the collection.
4. *Third Jungle Book*, No. 9, March 1946.
5. Ibid.
6. Peter Harmsen, 'Junglekrig i Burma', *Weekendavisen*, 2 March 2012, page 6.

CHAPTER 12

1. The original quote is: 'let's live our moment, in Bombay cantonment', from the *Goon Show*, series 8, episode 6, 'The Space Age', written by Spike Milligan and Larry Stephens and first broadcast on 4 November 1957.
2. Private Papers of Captain L. G. Stephens, Imperial War Museum, Documents 22513, with thanks to the Trustees of the Imperial War Museum for allowing access to the collection.
3. John Wall, *Bognor Regis to Hong Kong*, unpublished diary.
4. Corporal Robert Hay Shields, RAMC, unpublished *Memoirs*.

CHAPTER 13

1. TNA, WO 203/2940, Movement Control Movement Order No. 236, 3 Special Service Brigade move.
2. *Third Jungle Book*, No. 9, March 1946.
3. Ibid.
4. Private Papers of Captain L. G. Stephens, Imperial War Museum, Documents 22513, with thanks to the Trustees of the Imperial War Museum for allowing access to the collection.
5. Ibid.
6. TNA, WO 218/67, No. 5 Commando War Diary, December 1944, appendix 2, training instruction no. 3, sheet 3.
7. Private Papers of Captain L. G. Stephens, Imperial War Museum, Documents 22513, with thanks to the Trustees of the Imperial War Museum for allowing access to the collection.
8. Ibid.
9. Ibid.
10. John Wall, *Bognor Regis to Hong Kong*, unpublished diary.
11. R. F. Russell, 'Farewell, Soya Link', *Third Jungle Book*, No. 5, August to December 1944, author's collection.
12. *Third Jungle Book*, No. 9, March 1946.

CHAPTER 14

1. Sergeant Dave Richardson, 'Akyab', *Yank Magazine*, China, Burma, India edition, 17 February 1945, http://www.cbi-theater.com/yankcbi/yank_cbi_4.html.
2. John Wall, *Bognor Regis to Hong Kong*, unpublished diary.
3. TNA, ADM 202/94, extract from personal letter from Lieutenant Salt, No. 5 Commando.
4. John Wall, *Bognor Regis to Hong Kong*, unpublished diary.

CHAPTER 15

1. TNA, ADM 202/94, extracts from letters received from Colonel P. Young, DSO, MC, Deputy Commander, 3 Commando Brigade by Brigadier J. F. Durnford Slater, DSO, Deputy Commander, Commando Group.

2. TNA, ADM 202/94, extract from personal letter from Lieutenant Salt, No. 5 Commando.

3. *Third Jungle Book*, No. 9, March 1946.

4. Adapted from 'Three Quarters Of A Century Or Seventy Five Not Out', the personal recollections of Brigadier K. R. S. Trevor, CBE, DSO, https://www.burmastar.org.uk/stories/the-battle-for-hill-170/.

5. TNA, ADM 202/94, extracts from letters received from Colonel P. Young, DSO, MC, Deputy Commander, 3 Commando Brigade by Brigadier J. F. Durnford Slater, DSO, Deputy Commander, Commando Group.

6. Ibid.

7. Bill Stoneman Snr, *From Mitcham Road To Mandalay*, diary, http://billstonemansnr.blogspot.com/.

8. TNA, WO 218/81, 1 Commando War Diary January 1945, Appendix 8: Account of action on Pt 170, 31st January/1st February 1945.

9. Ibid., Appendix 4.

10. TNA, ADM 202/94, extract from personal letter from Lieutenant Salt, No. 5 Commando.

11. Private Papers of Captain L. G. Stephens, Imperial War Museum, Documents 22513, with thanks to the Trustees of the Imperial War Museum for allowing access to the collection.

12. Ibid.

13. Ibid.

14. Ibid.

15. Ibid.

CHAPTER 16

1. *Third Jungle Book*, No. 9, March 1946.

2. Bill Stoneman Snr, *From Mitcham Road To Mandalay*, diary, http://billstonemansnr.blogspot.com/.

3. John Wall, *Bognor Regis to Hong Kong*, unpublished diary.

4. Ibid.

5. Private Papers of Captain L. G. Stephens, Imperial War Museum, Documents 22513, with thanks to the Trustees of the Imperial War Museum for allowing access to the collection.

6. *Third Jungle Book*, No. 9, March 1946.

7. TNA, WO 218/85, No. 5 Commando War Diary, July 1945, appendix 6, move order no 4.

CHAPTER 17

1. TNA, DEFE 2/1686, Release of Royal Marine personnel from 3 Commando Brigade: organisation of Command at Hong Kong: role, composition and future organisation of Royal Marine commandos: minutes of meetings and memoranda, Top Secret Cypher Telegram dated 18 August 1945.

2. Ibid., dated 19 August 1945.

3. *Third Jungle Book*, No. 9, March 1946.

4. '2,000 Commandos Land in Colony', *China Mail*, 13 September 1945, front page, reproduced with kind permission of *South China Morning Post*.

5. TNA, WO 218/81, Prisoners of War, 17 September 1945, Appendix 2 in 5 Commando War Diary September 1945.

6. John Wall, *Bognor Regis to Hong Kong*, unpublished diary.

7. No. 5 Commando Newsletter no. 16, Spring 1995, author's collection.

8. TNA, WO 218/81, Order of the Day by Major General R. E. Laycock, DSO, CCO, 24 October 1945, Appendix in 1 Commando War Diary January 1945–January 1946.

9. 'Fanling Form Guide Is A Chancy Thing', *Hong Kong Sunday Herald*, 25 November 1945, page 2, reproduced with kind permission of *South China*

Morning Post.

10. TNA, DEFE 2/1685, Reinforcements for 3 Commando Brigade Hong Kong: future employment and policy, Top Secret Cypher Telegram, 1 December 1945.

11. 'Thursday Big Day For Commandos' Tiny Proteges', *China Mail*, 6 December 1945, page 2, reproduced with kind permission of *South China Morning Post*.

12. Christmas card held in the personal collection of David Davies.

13. TNA, DEFE 2/41, No. 5 Commando War Diary, December 1945.

14. No. 5 Commando Newsletter no. 24, Spring 1999, author's collection.

15. John Wall, *Bognor Regis to Hong Kong*, unpublished diary.

16. TNA, ADM 202/92, 3 Special Service/Commando Brigade HQ War Diary, A.I. 1/46, 13 March 1946.

17. Ibid.

18. TNA: DEFE 2/1469, Presentation of silver salver to 3 Commando Brigade from the government of Hong Kong, 11 April 1947.

PART THREE: GOONS – HANCOCKS AND MUKKINESE
CHAPTER 18

1. Dennis Main Wilson, personal interview with the Tony Hancock Appreciation Society, 1991.

2. Cliff Goodwin, *When the Wind Changed – The Life and Death of Tony Hancock*, Arrow Books, 2000.

3. Freddie Hancock and David Nathan, *Hancock*, BBC Books, 1986.

4. BBC Written Archives Centre, Kew (BBC WAC), RCONT1, James D. Grafton Scriptwriter's File 1 1949–1962, undated letter.

5. Freddie Hancock and David Nathan, *Hancock*.

CHAPTER 19

1. *Goon Show*, series 7, episode 2, 'Drums Along The Mersey', by Spike Milligan and Larry Stephens, 11 October 1956.

2. TNA, J 77/2622/1495, Husband's petition for divorce, 1929.

3. Ibid.

4. Recorded in *The Gazette* (*London Gazette*), Supplement 35017, Page 7105.

5. Ibid., Supplement 36457, Page 1604.

6. *Goon Show*, series 6, episode 26, 'Scradje', by Spike Milligan and Larry Stephens, 13 March 1956.

7. John Fisher, *Tony Hancock – The Definitive Biography*, HarperCollins, 2008.

8. Ibid.

9. Sir Reginald Harland, personal email, 28 March 2013.

CHAPTER 20

1. Dennis Main Wilson, personal interview with the Tony Hancock Appreciation Society, 1991.

2. James Grafton and Sally Watson, personal interview with the Goon Show Preservation Society, 2009.

3. *Twenty Questions* aired on the BBC from 1947 with a 'mystery voice' (Norman Hackforth) telling listeners which object the panel were attempting to identify. He would give the name of the object twice, the second time slowly and with more emphasis on each syllable.

4. *Radio Times*, listings of 28 May 1951.

5. Advertisement, *The Stage*, 26 April 1951, page 3.

6. BBC WAC, RCONT1, Spike Milligan Scriptwriter File 1, 1951–1962, Dennis Main Wilson to AHVP (Assistant Head of Variety (Productions)), 24 May 1951, BBC copyright content reproduced courtesy of the British Broadcasting Corporation. All rights reserved.

7. *Crazy People*, series 1, episode 1, by Spike Milligan, Larry Stephens and Jimmy Grafton, 28 May 1951.

8. BBC WAC, Variety Programme Planning File 1947–52, R19/1382/2, Peter Eton to Michael. BBC copyright content reproduced courtesy of the British Broadcasting Corporation. All rights reserved.

9. BBC WAC, RCONT1, James D. Grafton Scriptwriter's File 1 1949–1962, undated letter.

10. *Crazy People*, series 1, episode 9, by Spike Milligan, Larry Stephens and Jimmy Grafton, 23 July 1951.

11. Reproduced with kind permission of LaughLab and Gurpal Gosall.

12. *Crazy People*, series 1, episode 4, by Spike Milligan, Larry Stephens and Jimmy Grafton, 18 June 1951.

13. *Crazy People*, series 1, episode 5, by Spike Milligan and Larry Stephens, edited by Jimmy Grafton, 24 June 1951.

14. *Crazy People*, series 1, episode 10, by Spike Milligan and Larry Stephens, edited by Jimmy Grafton, 2 August 1951.

15. *Crazy People*, series 1, episode 16, by Spike Milligan and Larry Stephens, edited by Jimmy Grafton, 13 September 1951.

CHAPTER 21

1. *Crazy People*, series 1, episode 15, by Spike Milligan and Larry Stephens, edited by Jimmy Grafton, 6 September 1951.

2. 'Variety Stage. Peter Sellers', *The Stage*, 11 October 1951, page 3.

3. *Crazy People*, series 1, episode 14, by Spike Milligan and Larry Stephens, edited by Jimmy Grafton, 30 August 1951.

4. BBC WAC, R19/446, Entertainment, 'The Goon Show' File, 1950–1954, Dennis Main Wilson to Deputy Head of Variety (DHV), 8 January 1952, BBC copyright content reproduced courtesy of the British Broadcasting Corporation. All rights reserved.

5. With thanks to the Tony Hancock Archives, http://www.tonyhancockarchives.org.uk/.

6. John Antrobus, *Surviving Spike Milligan*, Robson Books, 2002.

7. BBC WAC, R19/446, Entertainment, 'The Goon Show' File, 1950–1954, Dennis Main Wilson to Head of Variety (HV), 20 March 1952, BBC copyright content reproduced courtesy of the British Broadcasting Corporation. All rights reserved.

8. Ibid.

9. BBC WAC, R19/1382/2, Variety Programme Planning File, 1947–1952, J.C.

Trewin, BBC Variety Department Listener's Report May 1952, BBC copyright content reproduced courtesy of the British Broadcasting Corporation. All rights reserved.

10. Ibid.
11. A *machine à sous billes* is a type of penny arcade bagatelle game.
12. Advertisement, *The Stage*, 29 May 1952, page 5.
13. *Goon Show*, series 4, episode 8, by Spike Milligan and Larry Stephens, 20 November 1953.
14. *Goon Show*, series 2, episode 11, by Spike Milligan and Larry Stephens, edited by Jimmy Grafton, 8 April 1952.

CHAPTER 22

1. Peter Eton, personal interview with the Goon Show Preservation Society, 1976.
2. Ibid.
3. BBC WAC, R19/1370, Light Entertainment, 'Vacant Lot' File 1952, Peter Eton to HV, 8 July 1952, BBC copyright content reproduced courtesy of the British Broadcasting Corporation. All rights reserved.
4. Ray Galton and Alan Simpson, personal interview, 7 February 2011.
5. BBC WAC, RCONT1, Larry Stephens Copyright File, 1952–1962, 5 August 1952.
6. Ibid., 10 August 1952.
7. BBC WAC, R19/1378/6, Entertainments Variety Meeting 1952 File, Notes on Light Programme Variety Meeting on Wednesday 10 September 1952, 11 September 1952, BBC copyright content reproduced courtesy of the British Broadcasting Corporation. All rights reserved.
8. BBC WAC, RCONT1, Larry Stephens Copyright File, 1952–1962, Peter Eton to Mr Walford, 18 September 1953. BBC copyright content reproduced courtesy of the British Broadcasting Corporation. All rights reserved. (NB Although the letter is dated 18 September 1953, it must actually have been written on 18 September 1952.)
9. BBC WAC, R19/1370, Light Entertainment, 'Vacant Lot' File 1952, 16 October 1952.

10. Ibid., Peter Eton to HV, 3 November 1952. BBC copyright content reproduced courtesy of the British Broadcasting Corporation. All rights reserved.

CHAPTER 23

1. By using a name that sounds like 'pommes frites', the French phrase for chips, Larry was perhaps remembering one of No. 5's most popular officers, John Heron, who had been nicknamed 'Chips'.
2. 'Three Men in a Whirl', *Radio Times*, 7 November 1952.
3. John Hamilton, personal interview with the Goon Show Preservation Society, 1995.
4. BBC WAC, R19/446, Entertainment, 'The Goon Show' File, 1950–1954, Michael Standing to Peter Eton, 2 July 1952, BBC copyright content reproduced courtesy of the British Broadcasting Corporation. All rights reserved.

CHAPTER 24

1. Goon Show Preservation Society Newsletter no. 118, January 2007.
2. Peter Eton, personal interview with the Goon Show Preservation Society, 1976.
3. Philip Oakes interview with Spike Milligan, *Books & Art* magazine, December 1957.
4. Ray Galton and Alan Simpson, personal interview, 7 February 2011.
5. BBC WAC, RCONT1, Larry Stephens Copyright File, 1952–1962, 17 September 1952.
6. BBC WAC, R19/1370, Light Entertainment 'Vacant Lot' File 1952, Peter Eton to DHV, 21 November 1952, BBC copyright content reproduced courtesy of the British Broadcasting Corporation. All rights reserved.
7. Spike Milligan, *Spike Milligan, The Family Album*, Virgin Publishing Ltd, 1999.
8. *Goon Show*, series 3, episode 9, by Spike Milligan and Larry Stephens, edited by Jimmy Grafton, 6 January 1953.
9. Spike Milligan, personal interview with Mark Powell for the Goon Show Preservation Society, 6 October 1987.
10. BBC WAC, RCONT1, Larry Stephens Copyright File, 1952–1962, 6 January 1953.

11. Ibid., C. F. Meehan to Larry Stephens, 4 January 1953. BBC copyright content reproduced courtesy of the British Broadcasting Corporation. All rights reserved.

12. Peter Watson-Wood, *Serendipity... a Life*, AuthorHouse, 2012.

13. Peter Watson-Wood, personal email, 8 May 2013.

14. Peter Watson-Wood, *Serendipity... a Life*.

15. BBC WAC, R19/446, Entertainment, 'The Goon Show' File, 1950–1954, Peter Eton to HV, 8 January 1953, BBC copyright content reproduced courtesy of the British Broadcasting Corporation. All rights reserved.

16. Ibid.

17. BBC WAC, RCONT1, Larry Stephens Copyright File, 1952–1962, 3 March 1953.

18. Ibid., 8 April 1953.

19. *Goon Show*, script for series 3, Special Coronation Edition by Spike Milligan and Larry Stephens, edited by Jimmy Grafton, 3 June 1953.

20. Peter Eton, personal interview with the Goon Show Preservation Society, 1976.

CHAPTER 25

1. BBC WAC, R19/1418, Entertainment, *'Welcome to Welkham'* File, 1953, Larry Stephens, *Welcome to Welkham* script.

2. J. C. Trewin, 'Critic on the Hearth, Rockets and Squibs', *Radio Times*, 24 July 1953, page 157.

3. BBC WAC, R19/1418, Entertainment 'Welcome to Welkham' File, 1953, Kenneth Adam to HV, 20 July 1953. BBC copyright content reproduced courtesy of the British Broadcasting Corporation. All rights reserved.

4. Ibid., Listener Research Report, Welcome to Welkham, 5 August 1953. BBC copyright content reproduced courtesy of the British Broadcasting Corporation. All rights reserved.

5. *Radio Times*, listings of 19 July 1953.

6. John Fisher, *Tony Hancock – The Definitive Biography*, HarperCollins, 2008.

7. BBC WAC, R19/1418, Entertainment 'Welcome to Welkham' File, 1953, Larry

Stephens, *Welcome to Welkham* script.

8. BBC WAC, RCONT1, Spike Milligan Scriptwriter File 1, 1951–1962, Peter Eton to Spike Milligan, 10 June 1953, BBC copyright content reproduced courtesy of the British Broadcasting Corporation. All rights reserved.

9. BBC WAC, RCONT1, Kavanagh Productions Ltd Copyright File 17, Jan–Jun 1953, Peter Eton to Miss Ross, 12 June 1953, BBC copyright content reproduced courtesy of the British Broadcasting Corporation. All rights reserved.

10. BBC WAC, R19/446, Entertainment, 'The Goon Show' File, 1950–1954, Listener Research Report, the *Goon Show*, 22 October 1953, BBC copyright content reproduced courtesy of the British Broadcasting Corporation. All rights reserved.

11. Ibid.

12. Peter Eton, personal interview with the Goon Show Preservation Society, 1976.

13. Orchestra direction from *Goon Show* script, series 4, episode 4, 23 October 1953.

14. BBC WAC, R19/446, Entertainment, 'The Goon Show' File, 1950–1954, Peter Eton to HV, 6 November 1953. BBC copyright content reproduced courtesy of the British Broadcasting Corporation. All rights reserved.

15. Goon Show Preservation Society Newsletter no. 99, January 2000.

16. Larry Stephens, private collection, with thanks to the Larry Stephens Estate.

17. *Goon Show*, series 4, episode 9, by Spike Milligan and Larry Stephens, 27 November 1953.

CHAPTER 26

1. *Goon Show*, series 4, episode 10, by Spike Milligan and Larry Stephens, 4 December 1953.

2. BBC WAC, R19/1379/3, Entertainment Variety Memos File 1950–1954, Secretary to Controller, Entertainment (Sound) to HV, 11 December 1953, BBC copyright content reproduced courtesy of the British Broadcasting Corporation. All rights reserved.

3. *Goon Show*, series 4, episode 14, by Spike Milligan and Larry Stephens, 27

December 1953.

4. Graham Stark, personal interview, 21 March 2011.

5. John Antrobus, personal email, 3 November 2015.

6. BBC WAC, RCONT1, Kavanagh Productions Ltd Copyright File 19, Jan–Jun 1954, D. L. Ross to Kevin Kavanagh, 29 January 1954. BBC copyright content reproduced courtesy of the British Broadcasting Corporation. All rights reserved.

7. Brad Ashton, personal email, 30 March 2011.

8. BBC WAC, RCONT1, Kavanagh Productions Ltd Copyright File 19 Jan–Jun 1954, D. L. Ross to Kevin Kavanagh, 18 March 1954. BBC copyright content reproduced courtesy of the British Broadcasting Corporation. All rights reserved.

9. Brad Ashton, personal email, 30 March 2011.

CHAPTER 27

1. Graham Stark, personal interview, 21 March 2011.

2. *The Hammer* (magazine of the CSS, Birmingham), Volume XIII, No. 2, July 1939, Birmingham Archives.

CHAPTER 28

1. Angela Cole, personal letter, 2 January 2018.

2. Angela Cole, personal interview, 26 April 2018.

3. Brad Ashton, personal interview with the Goon Show Preservation Society, 26 November 2011.

4. BBC WAC, R19/900, Entertainment, 'Jon Pertwee Programmes' File, 1949–1955, Dennis Main Wilson to HV, 28 March 1955, BBC copyright content reproduced courtesy of the British Broadcasting Corporation. All rights reserved.

5. Alexander Mackendrick, personal interview with Philip Kemp, October 1986.

6. Michael Deeley, personal email, 14 March 2011.

7. *The Case of the Mukkinese Battle-Horn*, Marlborough Pictures, UK, 1956.

8. Ibid.

9. Advertisement, *The Stage*, 1 January 1953, page 3.

CHAPTER 29

1. Ray Galton and Alan Simpson, personal interview, 7 February 2011.

CHAPTER 30

1. 'WANTED! – The Goons', *Radio Times*, photo caption of Spike Milligan, 28 September 1956, page 9.

2. Larry Stephens, private collection, with thanks to the Larry Stephens Estate.

3. 'Profile – The Goons', *Observer*, 23 December 1956, page 8, courtesy of Guardian News & Media Ltd.

4. *Goon Show*, series 7, episode 19, 'The Mysterious Punch-up-the-Conker', by Spike Milligan and Larry Stephens, 7 February 1957.

5. Ray Galton and Alan Simpson, personal interview, 7 February 2011.

6. *Goon Show*, series 7, episode 23, 'Ill Met by Goonlight', by Spike Milligan and Larry Stephens, 14 March 1957.

CHAPTER 31

1. BBC WAC, R19/2488/1, Goon Show (The) Corres. 1957–8 File, Telephone conversation with Larry Stephens 27/6/57 (main points), 27 June 1957, BBC copyright content reproduced courtesy of the British Broadcasting Corporation. All rights reserved.

2. 'Tele Views. Monday Date', *The Stage*, 18 July 1957, page 6.

CHAPTER 32

1. Simon Hoggart, 'Past perfect', *The Spectator*, 10 February 2010.

2. Frank Williams with Chris Gidney, *Vicar to Dad's Army: The Frank Williams Story*, Canterbury Press, 2003.

3. Alexander Mackendrick, personal interview with Philip Kemp, October 1986.

CHAPTER 33

1. *Goon Show*, series 8, episode 19, 'The White Neddie Trade', by Larry Stephens and Maurice Wiltshire, 3 February 1958.

2. BBC WAC, Associated London Scripts Scriptwriter file 1, 1955–1965, 8 January 1958.

3. *Goon Show*, series 8, episode 15, 'The Thing on the Mountain', by Larry Stephens and Maurice Wiltshire, 6 January 1958.

4. Ibid.

5. Ibid.

6. No. 5 Commando Newsletter no. 34, Spring 2004, author's collection.

CHAPTER 34

1. TNA, CRIM 1/2926, Driving motor vehicle while under the influence of drink or drugs, 15 April 1958.

2. Ibid.

3. Ibid.

4. BBC WAC, RCONT1, Spike Milligan File 2, 1957–1962, Patrick Newman to Assistant Head of Light Entertainment (Sound) (AHLE (S)), 28 March 1958, BBC copyright content reproduced courtesy of the British Broadcasting Corporation. All rights reserved.

5. Ray Galton and Alan Simpson, personal interview, 7 February 2011.

CHAPTER 35

1. Peter Eton, personal interview with the Goon Show Preservation Society, 1976.

2. Alexander Mackendrick, personal interview with Philip Kemp, October 1986.

3. John Antrobus, *Surviving Spike Milligan*, Robson Books, 2002.

4. Alexander Mackendrick, personal interview with Philip Kemp, October 1986.

5. Barry Cryer, *Butterfly Brain*, Orion, 2010.

6. John Antrobus, *Surviving Spike Milligan*.

7. Roger Lewis, *The Life and Death of Peter Sellers*, Century, 1994.

8. Spike Milligan and Larry Stephens, *Goon Show*, series 4, part 1, *The Golden Age of BBC Radio Comedy*, BBC Physical Audio, 2010.

9. David Bradbury and Joe McGrath, *Now That's Funny! Writers on Writing Comedy*, Methuen, 1998.

APPENDIX TWO

VACANT LOT SCRIPT

1. BBC WAC, R19/1370, Light Entertainment, 'Vacant Lot' File 1952, Copyright © Larry Stephens Estate.

APPENDIX THREE

SYNOPSIS FOR EPISODE 2 OF *VACANT LOT*

1. BBC WAC, R19/1370, Light Entertainment, 'Vacant Lot' File 1952, Copyright © Larry Stephens Estate.

APPENDIX FOUR

Character Names

1. Larry Stephens, private collection, with thanks to the Larry Stephens Estate.

INDEX

INDEX

Green, Anthony, 201
Green, Danny, 227
Green, Hughie, 187
Greenaway, Sergeant, 39
Greenslade, Wallace ('Bill'), 10
Griffiths, Jimmy, 218
Griffiths, Peter, 223
Grose, Nick, 129
Guide to Britain, 200
Guinness, Alec, 225–6, 281
Gurkhas, 72, 102

Hale, Sonnie, 200
Hall, C. P., 16
Hamilton, Fusilier, 113
Hamilton, John, 188
Hancock, Cicely, 147–8, 216, 270
Hancock, Tony, 150, 152, 164, 168,
    177–8, 180, 202, 216–17, 224,
    236, 270, 275, 281
    Calling All Forces, 167–8
    Hancock's Half Hour, 186, 193,
    235
    Larry meets, 140–3
    marriage, 147–8
    Royal Variety Performance and
    naval routine, 184–6
    The Tony Hancock Show, 235–6
    Vacant Lot, 178–9, 181–4, 192–3
Handl, Irene, 223
Happy Holiday, 218, 221
Harding, Bill, 179–80
Hardy, Brigadier Campbell, 93, 96,
    106, 125
Hardy, Ron, 136
Harland, Doreen, 148
Harland, Sir Reginald, 147
Hartley, RQMS Sam, 56
Hartnell, William, 253–4
Hawtrey, Charles, 184, 253–4
Hayes, Anne, 204
Hepburn, Audrey, 270
Hill, Benny, 151
Hillyard, Pat, 260–1
Hinton, Dennis R., 17–18, 78,
    135–6, 148
Hirohito, Emperor, 119
HMAS *Napier*, 93–4
HMIS *Jumna*, 96–7
HMIS *Llanstephan Castle*, 121
HMS *Anson*, 122
HMS *Glengyle*, 120–1
HMS *Keren*, 54–5
HMT *Dunera*, 113
HMT *Ranchi*, 44, 46–7
HMT *Reina Del Pacifico*, 42–8, 50
HMT *Rohna*, 44, 46
Hoggart, Simon, 253

Holmes, Major Denis, 60
Holt, Seth, 225–6
Hong Kong, 120–35, 144–5
Housden, Captain Norman, 42,
    76, 83–4
Howard, Fusilier, 99
Howerd, Frankie, 224, 236
Howes, Sally Ann, 179
Hoyle, Freddie, 85
Hubbard, Private, 107
Hulbert, Claude, 200
Hurota, Major, 123

I'm All Right Jack, 277
International Artistes, 140
ITMA, 208

James, Jimmy, 179, 188
Japanese POWs, 123–4
Jessop, TSM, 39
Johnson, Katie, 227
Jowett, John, 252
Joyce, James, 88
Junior Crazy Gang, 153–4
Junkin, John, 264–7
Just Fancy, 172

Kangaw, 102–4, 109, 113, 210
Karen people, 72–3
Kasipur Tea Gardens, 66, 71, 76
Kavanagh Productions Ltd, 202,
    208, 215–16, 220, 242, 246
Kedgaon Camp, 50–4
Kemp, Philip, 226, 255
Kent, Duchess of, 260–1
Kerr, Captain, 64
Kharakvasla Camp, 117–20
King, Captain David, 113, 129
Knox, Ronald, 212
K-rations, 57–8
Kubrick, Stanley, 215

Ladykillers, The, 225–8
Lanza, Mario, 226
Larner, Elizabeth, 218
Laycock, Major General Robert,
    90, 126
Lee, Lieutenant, 117
leeches, 68
Leigh, Vivien, 235
Lewin, David, 153–4
Ling, Peter, 164
Lloyd, Jeremy, 281
Lom, Herbert, 227
London Entertains, 158
London Philharmonic Choir, 277
Lyon-Shaw, Bill, 179

Mabel and William, 15
McGrath, Joe, 280
McKechnie, Alan, 10
McKechnie, Donald junior, 10, 15
McKechnie, Donald, 10, 22
McKechnie, Doris, *see* Stephens,
    Doris
McKechnie, Michael, 122
Mackendrick, Alexander, 225–6,
    255, 274–5
Maggie, The, 225
Maguire, Eddie, 180
Maidment, Lieutenant, 39
Malaria Forward Treatment Units
    (MFTUs), 75–6
Manchukuo, 119
Margaret, Princess, 185
Marks, Alfred, 142, 151
Marsh, Gordon, 219
Martin, George, 241
Mason, H. A., 18
Medwin, Michael, 253
Melody Maker, 17, 136
Milligan, Spike, 147, 150, 154–6,
    158–72, 175–8, 184, 187–8, 209,
    213, 224, 233–4
    and ALS, 236–7, 242–4
    Australian trip, 267–8
    and Canadian rewrites, 247–9,
    251, 270
    friendship with Larry, 169–70,
    238–40
    and Goon Show later series,
    257–63, 267–71
    and Goon Show records, 241
    and Goon Show royal
    performance, 260–1
    and Goon Show scripts, 279–80
    health problems, 193–5, 232–3,
    259–60, 271
    Larry meets, 142–3
    and Larry's death, 275, 277, 280
    and The Mukkinese Battle-Horn,
    229–30
    and 'Operation Bagpipe', 210–11
    rift with Larry, 175–6, 190–1,
    193, 196–7, 204
    and Star Bill, 202–3
    working without Larry, 204–6,
    216, 220–1
    and writers' fees, 180–1, 191–2,
    194–8, 202, 203–4, 207–8,
    238–9
Mills, Doreen, 261
Milne, Lieutenant Iain, 209
Miyazaki, General, 105
Molière, 219
Monday Date, 251

Unbound is the world's first crowdfunding publisher, established in 2011.

We believe that wonderful things can happen when you clear a path for people who share a passion. That's why we've built a platform that brings together readers and authors to crowdfund books they believe in – and give fresh ideas that don't fit the traditional mould the chance they deserve.

This book is in your hands because readers made it possible. Everyone who pledged their support is listed below. Join them by visiting unbound.com and supporting a book today.

Kelly Adey
Rosemary Alder
Martin Allsop
Evonne Ashley
Adrian Baker
Phil Baker
Barry Cameron Barnes
Basildon History
Richard Beadle
Derek Beamish
Andrew Beaty
Elliot Beaumont
Andy Bell
Martin Bell
Alan Bennett
David Benny
Julian Benton
Toni Bettis
Andrew Biggs
Steve Blackwell
Matthew Bladen

Paul Bloomfield
David Bonney
Amanda Booth
Chris Booty
David Bower
Peter Breeden
Darren Brett
Janine Brewer
Thomas Brink
Tristan Brittain-Dissont
Carol Bromley
David Brown
Evelyne Brown
Laura Brown
Richard Brown
Phil Bruce-Moore
Quentin Bryar
Angelique Budd
Daryl Burchell
Sue Burnett
Pandora Busch

Samantha Bush
Donald Cameron
Laura Camuti
Davey Candlish
Owen Care
Pamela Care
Peter Care
Richard Care
Mollie Carlyle
Val Carnaby
Gareth Cartman
Lorraine Cater
Dennis Cattell
Edward Caush
Rodney Challis
Adam Chamberlain
KC Chamberlain
Jim Chapple
Jason Clark
Simon Clark
Sue Clark
Robert Clements
David Coaker
Nick Collins
Jeff Cook
Glenn Cooper
Mark Cousins
Mat Coward
Alan Cowland
Andrew Crowther
Bryan Cutts
Brett Danalake
Anne Dangerfield
Baker Danny
David Davies
Simon Davies
Mick Davison
deadmanjones
JF Derry
John Dexter
Nick Diamantopoulos
Steve Dimmer

Thomas Dommett
Stephen Donlan
Stephen Donnison
Alex Drysdale
Sue Durkin
Mark Earby
Paul East
Barnaby Eaton-Jones
Kyle Ebert
Steve Edge
Stephen Edwards
Jerry Elsmore
Peter Embling
Hunt Emerson
Phil Enright
Ramsey Ess
Carolyn Evans
Edward Evans
Glyndwr Evans
Ian Evans
Leigh Everret Smith
Anthony Fairclough
Michael Ferrier
Jackie Fillary
Terence Flanagan
Matthew Fontaine
Anne Forecast
Andy Fraser
Dave Freak
John French
Allan Frewin
Robert Friedman
Bill Froog (Phil Lee)
Sean Gaffney
Ter Gallagher
Paco B. Garcia
Rita Gayford
GBOF's
Anne George
Martin Gibbons
Helen and John Gibson
Jeremy Gibson

Simon Gibson

Tom Gibson

Christopher Golightly

Christopher Gordon

Kathryn Goulding

James Grafton

Richard P Grant

Mark Gray

Eamonn Griffin

Griff Griffith

Dan Grubb

Sally Hall

Sarah-Jane Hamilton

David Hannah

Linda Hargreaves

Shona Harper

Simon Harper

Eileen Harris

Janet Harriss

Peter Harvey

Peter Hasted

Chris (@barlaventoexp) Hawkins

Julian Hazeldine

Nanny Helen

Graham Hellewell

John Henty

Max Heron

David Higginson

Michael Hill

Robert Hills

David Hoare

Helen Hobkinson

Sue Holden

Juliette Holmes

Neil Holmes

Graham Homer

Steve Hooker

Margaret Hooper

Tim Hooper

Stephen Hoppe

Lisa Hudson

Alan Humphries

Elizabeth 'Betty' Humphries

Michael Humphries

James Hurn

Carole Hynes

Gary James

Chris Jardine

Christopher Jardine

Tracy Jary

Cheryl Jeans

Rob Jenkins

Tracey Jennings Harding

Jonathan Jessop

Bryan Johnstone

Helen Jones

Mark Jones

Helen Keightley

Lesley Kenyon

Trish Kidd

Dan Kieran

Rita Kyrou

Kate Laity

Michael Lang

Roger Langridge

Magpie Latham

Ewan Lawrie

W Tom Lawrie

John Leeming

Phil Lenthall

Allan Lewis

Eric Loffman

Vicki Logan

Con Logue

Stephen Longhurst

Seonaid Mackenzie

Dirk Maggs

Kenneth Mann

Kay Maria

David Marks

Sean Marsh

Faith Martin

John Matthews

Hugh McCallion

Clair McCowlen
Neil McCowlen
Josanne McDonnell
Aidan McQuade
Robert Mead
Estelle Mickelborough
Julie Middleton
Harry Mills
John Mitchinson
Frances Monk
Richard Montagu
Simon Montgomery
Sharon Mottram Innes
George Mullen
Steve Mullins
Multistory
Mike Murphy
Ewen Murray
Liz Muschamp
Carlo Navato
Chris Neale
Jim Nicholson
Lasse Nielsen
Tony Northall
Mark Nutter
John-Michael O'Sullivan
Karen O'Sullivan
Vincent Oberheim
John Orr
Scott Pack
Alan Page
Richard Palmer
Victoria Palmer
David Robert Parker
Lance Corporal Steve Parker
Derek Parry
Dorothy Parry
Ian Patterson
Stephen Penny
Anthony Perry
Elodie Piat
Nigel Planer

Chris Polan
Justin Pollard
Attilio Polo
Sharron Preston
Keith Pugh
Brent Quigley
Helen Rafferty
Sean Raffey
Hugh Rainey
Angela Rayson
Steve Reddish
Nick Reeve
Mike Reinstein
Jimm Rennie
John Repsch
Adrian Reuben
Paul Rigby
Jem Roberts
Andrew Robertson
Peter Rogers
Robert Ross
Lee Rulton
Alistair Rush
Benjamin Russell
Chris Sadler
Stephen Sadler
Karan Sage
David Saltmer
Nancy Sandoval
Alicia Santamaria
Adam Sear
Paul Shacksmyth
Gary Shaw
Allison Shepherd
Tim Shepherd
Paul Shipway
Peter Shirley
Andrew Sholl
Colin Silk
Mike Simmonds
Gillian Skeggs-Gooch
John Smithson

SUPPORTERS

Lisa Spencer
Matt Spiers
Jeeeem Spriggs
Janice Staines
Alan Stammers
Barbara Stammers
Donald Stammers
Lucy Stavrou
Dave Stebbings
Melanie Stephens
Roger Stevenson
Andy Straw
Jonathan Street
Patrick Stroudley
Antonia Suarez
Laurence Sumeray
Andrew Summerhayes
Jodi Swan
Jennifer Swift-Kramer
Steve Taylore-Knowles
Karl Tiedemann
Alexander Tindall
Mark Tinkler
Toast
Neil Trickey
Helen Tucker
Amandeep Uppal
Richard Usher
Gaurav Vaidya
Mandy Vallance
Mark Vent
Sarah Vernon
Dean Wade
Vince Wakerley
Ian Walker
Nick Walpole
Mike Warden
Richard Warner
Debra Warren
Edna Warren
Roy Warren
Sylvia Warren

Andrew Weaver
Shane Wharnsby
Neil Wheelwright
Joan White
Stephen White
David Whitehead
Mark Whitehead
Scott Wilkinson
Derek Wilson
Ian Wilson
Norman Wilson
Stephen Wilson
Rowan Wiltshire
Martin Witty
Stuart Woodcock
Elaine Worthington
Dan Wright
Doreen Young